D1709073

GOVERNMENT ISSUE

U.S. ARMY
EUROPEAN THEATER
OF OPERATIONS COLLECTOR GUIDE

Henri-Paul ENJAMES

Text and photographs by the author, except when otherwise mentioned

Translated from the French by Philippe Charbonnier

Histoire & Collections

CONTENTS

PREFACE   3

INTRODUCTION: THE UNITED STATES ARMY   4

1. INSIGNIA AND DECORATIONS   6

2. UNIFORMS   22

3. INDIVIDUAL EQUIPMENT   68

4. SMALL ARMS AND CREW-SERVED LIGHT WEAPONS   88

5. TENTAGE, SLEEPING AND BIVOUAC EQUIPMENT   110

6. ARMORED TROOPS   126

7. AIRBORNE TROOPS   136

8. MOUNTAIN TROOPS   150

9. FEMALE PERSONNEL   158

10. MILITARY POLICE   166

11. ARMY RATIONS   172

12. THE CORPS OF ENGINEERS   184

13. THE SIGNAL CORPS   192

14. CHEMICAL WARFARE   216

15. THE MEDICAL DEPARTMENT   222

16. ARMY CHAPLAINS   234

17. ARMY PUBLICATIONS AND OTHER PRINTED MATERIAL   236

18. SPORTS AND RECREATION   252

19. PERSONAL ITEMS   254

20. TROPHIES AND SOUVENIRS   264

ABBREVIATIONS   266

INDEX   266

BIBLIOGRAPHY   271

ACKNOWLEDGMENTS   272

Foreword

If retaining the format of the 1943 QMC Supply catalog has appeared both a convenient and pleasant way to show the author's extensive collection, we should also point out that a multitude of items illustrated here were not issued by the Quartermaster Corps, such as weapons and signals equipment for instance, and that these were referred to in specific catalogs of different sizes. Please note that most items are not reproduced to scale.

All period photographs, except when otherwise mentioned, are from the U.S. National Archives.

SUPREME HEADQUARTERS
ALLIED EXPEDITIONARY FORCE

Soldiers, Sailors and Airmen of the Allied Expeditionary Force!

You are about to embark upon the Great Crusade, toward which we have striven these many months. The eyes of the world are upon you. The hopes and prayers of liberty-loving people everywhere march with you. In company with our brave Allies and brothers-in-arms on other Fronts, you will bring about the destruction of the German war machine, the elimination of Nazi tyranny over the oppressed peoples of Europe, and security for ourselves in a free world.

Your task will not be an easy one. Your enemy is well trained, well equipped and battle-hardened. He will fight savagely.

But this is the year 1944! Much has happened since the Nazi triumphs of 1940-41. The United Nations have inflicted upon the Germans great defeats, in open battle, man-to-man. Our air offensive has seriously reduced their strength in the air and their capacity to wage war on the ground. Our Home Fronts have given us an overwhelming superiority in weapons and munitions of war, and placed at our disposal great reserves of trained fighting men. The tide has turned! The free men of the world are marching together to Victory!

I have full confidence in your courage, devotion to duty and skill in battle. We will accept nothing less than full Victory!

Good Luck! And let us all beseech the blessing of Almighty God upon this great and noble undertaking.

Dwight D Eisenhower

Leaflet handed in June 1944 to every member of the American invasion forces bound for Normandy, written and signed by General Eisenhower.

"Ever since my younger years, I have been interested in my country's historic past, especially in the Second World War and the United States Army. I was fascinated by the tremendous power it brought to bear to overcome the enemy. This army not only supplied its soldiers with the most modern equipment and uniforms, suitable for any combat situation, but went as far as treating them with their favorite drinks or candy bars.

I started collecting in the early eighties and I always strove to acquire items in the best possible condition, as their markings, when still readable, provide a wealth of information about manufacture dates and models. My only source then was a photocopy of the 1943 Quartermaster Corps Supply Catalog 3-1, but many books and articles on the subject have been published since.

I have aimed in this book to gather as much information as possible on the uniforms and equipment of the American soldier in Europe during the 1943-1945 period. All the while, I cannot boast that all will be told here, as it is most likely that future research will uncover more material.

The purpose of this book is also to assist the enthusiast in his quest for authentic items while the militaria market is nowadays 'infected' with numerous repros, notwithstanding the leftovers from the wardrobes of recent American war movies and TV serials.

I hope that young collectors reading this book will be attracted to American WW2 militaria, so that the sacrifice of those who fought for the liberation of Europe is not forgotten."

Henri-Paul Enjames

INTRODUCTION

The United States Army, 1941-45

1. Organization

The wartime U.S. Army included three major components: the Regular Army, the National Guard and the Reserves. Regular and Guard units were brought up to war strength mainly by recalling Reserve officers, by voluntary enlistments and the draft ('Selective service'). Length of service for draftees was defined as "for the duration" plus six months.

2. Personnel

The following tables show the approximate allocation of personnel within the main military organizations, as well as the rank of their commanding officers.

TACTICAL UNIT	APPROX. NO. OF MEN	COMMANDER
Squad	12	Corporal
Platoon	50	Lieutenant
Company	200	Captain
Battalion (Inf.)	900	Major
Regiment (Inf.)	3,200	Colonel
Division	15,000	Major General
Corps	75,000	Lt. General
Army	300,000	General

3. High Command

The President of the United States was the commander-in-chief of the Armed Forces. He commanded the military through his Secretary of War and the Chief of Staff he had appointed.

The Chief of Staff directed the Army's three major commands:
– The Army Ground Forces (infantry, artillery, etc.)
– The Army Air Forces
– The Army Service Forces (quartermasters, engineers, etc.).

ORGANIZATION OF ARMY

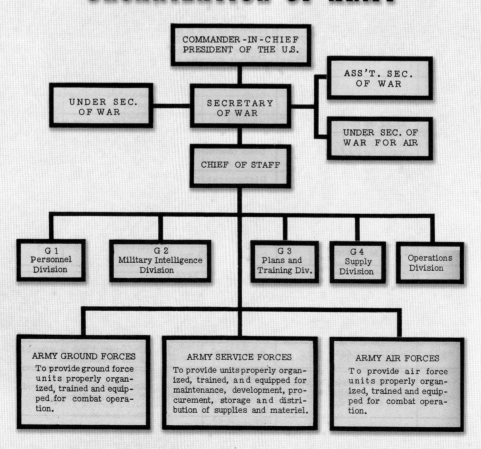

4. The Infantry Division

The Division was the basic organization for sustained action in the field. It was the smallest unit able to pursue strategic aims with its organic means. Depending on the assignment, the division could be supported by the Airforce and Army or Corps level units, such as tank destroyer and tank battalions, as well as engineer and other combat support assets.

The standard "triangular" division had three infantry regiments supported by four field artillery battalions. Among the other components was a mechanized reconnaissance troop.

(see table of organization below)

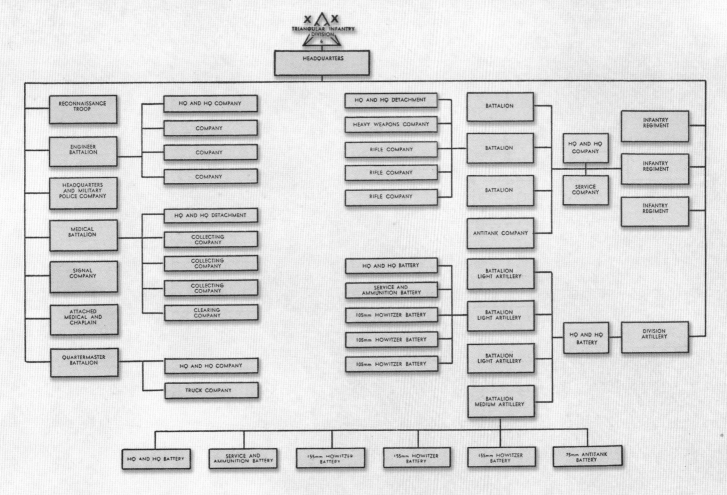

5. A typical infantry division in the European Theater of Operations (ETO): the 1st Infantry Division, 1944-1945

1. 16th Infantry Regiment
2. 18th Infantry Regiment
3. 26th Infantry Regiment

Division Artillery
HQ and HQ Battery
4. 5th Field Artillery Battalion
5. 7th Field Artillery Battalion
6. 32nd Field Artillery Battalion
7. 33rd Field Artillery Battalion

8. 1st Reconnaissance Troop. Mecz
9. 1st Engineer Combat Battalion
10. 1st Medical Battalion

11. 1st Counter Intelligence Corps Detachment
12. Headquarters Special Troops
13. Hq Company, 1st Infantry Division
Military Police Platoon
14. 701st Ordnance Light Maintenance Company
15. 1st Quartermaster Company
16. 1st Signal Company

Attached units:
745th Tank Battalion (attached 6 June 1944-8 May 1945)
634th Tank Destroyer Battalion
(attached 1 August 1944-6 May 1945)
635th Tank Destroyer Battalion
(attached 7 June 1944-30 September 1944)
703rd Tank Destroyer Battalion
(attached 18 December 1944-31 December 1944)
103rd AAA Auto-Wpns Battalion
(attached 16 June 1944-7 February 1945,
24 February 1945-8 May 1945)

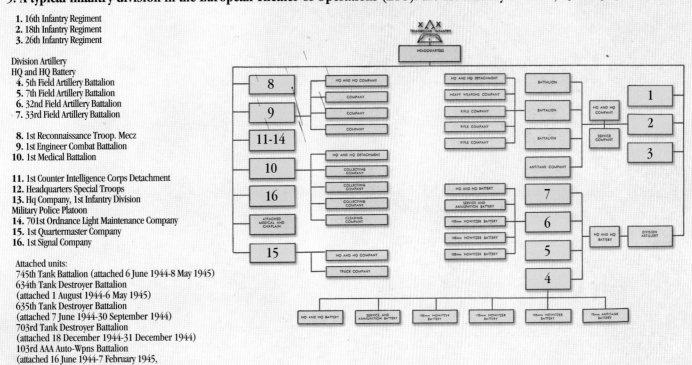

REGULATION BRASSARDS, 1941-1945

GSC

General Staff Corps officers assigned to the HQ of a field army

GSC

General Staff Corps officers assigned to the HQ of an army corps

GSC

General Staff Corps officers assigned to the HQ of a division

TC

Transportation Corps officers (ships, trains…)

TO

Technical Observers and service specialists: civilian technicians and advisers

GAS

Gas Personnel

RECRUITING SERVICE

Recruiting service

FIRE

Engineer fire and truck companies

C

Journalists, Feature writers and Radio commentators

P

Photographers (Press photographers)

US

Emblem, sleeve, combatant and non combatant: worn by Army civilian employees, and civilian personnel of military missions overseas or in the theaters of operations.

✚

Geneva Convention neutrality brassard worn in the field by certain non-combatant personnel of the Medical Department and the Corps of Chaplains

✚

Veterinary service

MP

Military Police

Brassards denoting temporary rank bestowed on enlisted men during basic training,

or within Service schools and the Army Specialized Training Program.

1. Brassards

A brassard is a distinguishing mark worn on the arm to denote a special function or assignment, permanent or temporary.

Regulation-sized brassards were about 4 by 18 inches, worn on the left arm, usually half-way between the shoulder and elbow. Brassards were not issued with any fastening device, they were therefore held on the sleeve most often by a safety pin.

2. Shoulder sleeve insignia

The first cloth unit insignia originated at the end of World War One, they were authorized in 1920. From 1930 to 1966, most unit patches were machine embroidered in color threads on a tan cotton backing ('flat edge' patches). After 1966, regulation unit insignia were manufactured with a thick border to prevent unraveling (the 'merrow edge'). During WW2, the Army ordered most of its cloth insignia from civilian companies, but it also produced some of its own. These patches can be told apart by their distinctive olive drab border, an olive drab thread being also visible in the weave on the back of the insignia.

Many patches were also procured locally in Europe and they offer a great variety of materials, colors and designs.

Shoulder sleeve insignia were worn at the top the left sleeve, 1/2 inch below the shoulder seam (➡ page 12).

These unit patches were sewn on the wool service coat or Ike jacket, the wool or cotton shirt (when worn on its own), the wool overcoat and various field jack-

Brassard worn during training by acting sergeants.

ets. Insignia was not worn on the fatigue uniform. As of 1944, a veteran being assigned to a different unit could continue to wear the patch of its former combat unit (the 'Combat patch') on the right sleeve.

The plates on the following pages illustrate the shoulder insignia for most of the units fielded on the European front, and the captions indicate their official campaigns.

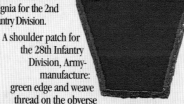

Left.

Back view of the regulation shoulder insignia for the 2nd Infantry Division.

A shoulder patch for the 28th Infantry Division, Army-manufacture: green edge and weave thread on the obverse

A. Army Groups, Armies and Army Corps

1. 1st Army Group. (➜ page 11) Deception HQ activated together with several 'Phantom Divisions'. Became the actual HQ 12th Army Group on 14 July 1944.
2. 6th Army Group — Southern France landings, France, Germany
3. 12th Army Group — France, Belgium, Germany
4. 15th Army Group — Sicily, Italy, occupation of Austria
5. 1st Army — D-Day, Normandy, Battle of the Bulge, Rhineland, Germany
6. 3rd Army — Normandy, Brittany, Eastern France, Battle of the Bulge, Germany, Czechoslovakia
7. 5th Army — Italy landings and campaign
8. 7th Army — Sicily, Southern France landings, Vosges, Alsace, Saar, Germany
9. 9th Army — Brittany, Belgium, Luxembourg, Germany

10. 15th Army — Atlantic ports pockets, Germany
11. 2nd Army Corps — North African landings, Tunisia, Sicily, Italy
12. 3rd Army Corps — France, Battle of the Bulge, Germany
13. 4th Army Corps — Italy
14. 5th Army Corps — D-Day (Omaha Beach), Normandy, Eastern France, Battle of the Bulge, Germany
15. 6th Army Corps — Italy, Southern France landings, France, Germany, Austria
16. 7th Army Corps — D-Day (Utah Beach), Normandy, North-Eastern France, Belgium, Germany
17. 8th Army Corps — Normandy, Brittany, Belgium, Luxembourg, Battle of the Bulge, Germany
18. 12th Army Corps — Eastern France, Battle of the Bulge, Germany

19. 13th Army Corps — Holland, Germany
20. 15th Army corps — Normandy, Eastern France, Siegfried Line, Germany
21. 16th Army Corps — Normandy, Holland, Germany
22. 18th Army Corps — Operation 'Market-Garden,' Battle of the Bulge, Germany
23. 19th Army Corps — Normandy, Belgium, Germany
24. 20th Army Corps — Normandy, Loire region, Eastern France, Germany, Austria
25. 21st Army Corps — Eastern France, Germany, Austria
26. 22nd Army Corps — Germany
27. 23rd Army Corps — provided the 15th Army HQ in 1945

B. Infantry Divisions

MOUNTAIN

AIRBORNE

AIRBORNE

1. 1st Infantry Division — North African Landings, Tunisia, Sicily landings and campaign, D-Day (Omaha beach), Normandy, Battle of the Bulge, Germany, Czechoslovakia

2. 2nd Infantry Division — D +1 at Omaha, Normandy, Germany, Czechoslovakia

3. 3rd Infantry Division — Tunisia, Sicily landings and campaign, Southern France landings (Saint-Tropez), Vosges, Battle of the Bulge, Germany, Austria

4. 4th Infantry Division — D-Day (Utah beach), Normandy, liberation of Paris, Belgium, Battle of the Bulge, Germany

5. 5th Infantry Division — France, Germany, Czechoslovakia

6. 8th Infantry Division — Normandy, Brittany, Luxemburg, Battle of the Bulge, Germany

7. 9th Infantry Division — North African Landings, Tunisia and Sicily, Normandy, Belgium, Germany

8. 10th Mountain Division — Italy

9. 13th Airborne Division — (517th PIR) Southern France, Rhineland, Battle of the Bulge, Alsace, Germany

10. 17th Airborne Division — Battle of the Bulge, Germany (operation 'Varsity')

11. 26th Infantry Division — Eastern France, Saar, Luxemburg, Battle of the Bulge, Germany, Austria, Czechoslovakia

12. 28th Infantry Division — Eastern France, Luxemburg, Battle of the Bulge, Germany

13. 29th Infantry Division — D-Day (Omaha beach), Normandy, Brittany, Germany

14. 30th Infantry Division — Normandy, Northern France, Belgium, Germany

15. 34th Infantry Division — North African landings, Tunisia and Italy

16. 35th Infantry Division — Normandy, Northern France, Rhineland, Ardennes-Alsace, Central Europe

17. 36th Infantry Division — Salerno, Italy, Southern France, Rhineland, Ardennes-Alsace, Central Europe

18. 42nd Infantry Division — France, Germany, Austria

19. 44th Infantry Division — France, Germany, Austria

20. 45th Infantry Division — Sicily, Salerno, Anzio, Southern France, Eastern France, Germany

21. 63rd Infantry Division — France, Germany

22. 65th Infantry Division — France, Germany, Austria

23. 66th Infantry Division — Atlantic ports pockets, Germany

24. 69th Infantry Division — Belgium, Germany

25. 70th Infantry Division — France, Germany.

26. 71st Infantry Division — France, Germany, Austria
27. 75th Infantry Division — France, Germany
28. 76th Infantry Division — Luxemburg, Germany, Czechoslovakia
29. 78th Infantry Division — France, Belgium, Germany
30. 79th Infantry Division — Normandy, Eastern France, Germany
31. 80th Infantry Division — Normandy, Eastern France, Luxemburg, Germany, Austria
32. 82nd Airborne Division — North Africa, Sicily, Italy, Normandy, Holland, Germany,
33. 83rd Infantry Division — Normandy, Brittany, Eastern France, Germany
34. 84th Infantry Division — Belgium, Holland, Battle of the Bulge, Germany
35. 85th Infantry Division — Italy
36. 86th Infantry Division — France, Germany
37. 87th Infantry Division — France, Germany

38. 88th Infantry Division — Italy
39. 89th Infantry Division — France, Germany
40. 90th Infantry Division — D-Day (Utah beach), Eastern France, Germany, Czechoslovakia
41. 91st Infantry Division — Italy
42. 92nd Infantry Division — Italy
43. 94th Infantry Division — Brittany, Eastern France, Luxemburg, Germany
44. 95th Infantry Division — France, Holland, Germany
45. 97th Infantry Division — Germany, Czechoslovakia
46. 99th Infantry Division — Belgium, Germany
47. 100th Infantry Division — France, Germany
48. 101st Airborne Division — Normandy, Holland, Battle of the Bulge, Germany (Berchtesgaden)
49. 102nd Infantry Division — Germany
50. 103rd Infantry Division — France, Germany, Austria
51. 104th Infantry Division — France, Belgium, Germany

52. 106th Infantry Division — Battle of the Bulge, Belgium, Germany.

(Note. Armored Divisions patches are shown on page 126, and Airborne units patches on page 137)

C. Non-divisional units

1. SHAEF (Supreme Heaquarters Allied Expeditionary Force)
2. Allied Forces Headquarters (N. Africa, Italy)
3. North African Theater
4. ETO (European Theater of Operations)
5. ETO Advanced base
6. European Headquarters
7. Persian Gulf Command
8. European Civil Affairs
9. 1st Special Service Force
10. 474th RCT
11. 2nd Cavalry Division
12. 442nd Regimental Combat Team
13. Engineer Special Brigades
14. 36th Engineer Battalion
15. Task Force V (USA)
16. Airborne Command
17. Ports of Embarkation
18. Ranger qualification Badge
19. 2nd Ranger Battalion
20. 5th Ranger Battalion
21. Advance Section (Com Z)
22. Army Service Forces (Com Z)
23. London Base command
24. Red Ball Express Badge

D. Phantom units

Normandy was finally selected on 18 June 1943 as the target for the cross-Channel invasion. A far-ranging deception plan (code-named 'Fortitude') was then initiated. Fortitude was two-fold: firstly, it intended to fool German intelligence into believing the landings would occur in Norway or Denmark ('Skye'). The second intent of the operation ('Quicksilver') was to make the enemy think an alternative would be an amphibious assault on the Pas-de-Calais in Northern France.

The fictitious 1st U.S. Army Group (FUSAG, ➡ page 7) was then activated under Lieutenant General George Patton in East Kent. FUSAG simulated the assembly of a field army, complete with dummy wooden or inflated rubber tanks, etc. Moreover, shoulder insignia were manufactured for two army corps and 19 'Phantom' divisions. Not more than 1,000-2,000 patches were however made for this purpose.

1. 14th Army
2. 31st Corps
3. 33rd Corps
4. 6th Airborne Division
5. 9th Airborne Division
6. 11th Infantry Division
7. 14th Infantry Division
8. 17th Infantry Division

9. 18th Airborne Division
10. 21st Airborne Division
11. 22nd Infantry Division
12. 46th Infantry Division
13. 48th Infantry Division
14. 50th Infantry Division
15. 55th Infantry Division
16. 59th Infantry Division

17. 108th Infantry Division
18. 119th Infantry Division
19. 130th Infantry Division
20. 135th Airborne Division
21. 141st Infantry Division
22. 157th Infantry Division

3. Distinctive insignia

Distinctive insignia (DIs) are small enameled metal insignia, chosen and worn by most regiment or battalion-sized units. More than 2,000 different designs had been authorized between 1923 and 1943. However, on 2 January 1943, owing to more than a thousand designs pending approval and the general shortage of strategic metals such as brass, the War Department suspended all further orders for distinctive insignia. But more insignia were unofficially designed afterwards and privately purchased by individual soldiers.

According to regulations and during the 1944-45 time frame:
– Enlisted men wore distinctive insignia on the left front of the gar-rison cap, and on each lapel of the woolen service coat or Ike jacket ;
– Officers wore distinctive insignia on the shoulder loops of the service coat. It was also pinned on the left side of the officer's garrison cap until August 1942, when it was replaced by rank insignia.

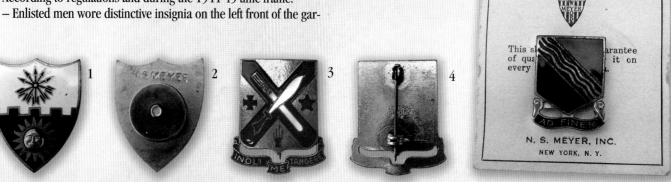

1-2. Distinctive insignia of the 22nd Infantry Regiment (4th Infantry Division), screwback.
3-4. Distinctive insignia of the 2nd Infantry Regiment (5th Infantry Division), pinback.
5. Distinctive insignia of the 379th Infantry Regiment (95th Infantry Division), still on its NS Meyer Inc. card.

4. The clutch fastener

Until 1942, most metal insignia (DIs, collar disks, and officer's rank and arm or service insignia…) were fastened to the uniform with a 'post and round nut' or brooch pin. The first types of clutches, which held the insignia by locking on a vertical pin, had been patented in the twenties, but were seldom used because of their cost.

In 1942, Frederick Ballou and Melvin Moore invented a new type of clutch, cheaply stamped from sheet brass. Two patents were registered in January 1943 under Nos 2308412 and 2308424. The clutch then became the principal fastening device for metallic military insignia.

1. First-type clutch, patented in the 1920s and sometimes seen on early military insignia (officers' insignia of arm and service).
2-3. 1942-type clutch (Patent pending)
4. 1943-1947 clutch. After 1947 the design was improved: eight 'pimples' were embossed on the clutch to prevent it from turning on the pin and therefore slipping (5).

WEARING REGULATION CLOTH INSIGNIA ON THE ENLISTED MEN'S SERVICE UNIFORM
(Overcoat, Service coat, Ike Jacket, wool or cotton shirt)

Shoulder sleeve insignia *(former combat unit)*

Shoulder sleeve insignia *(1/2" from shoulder)*

Chevrons of grade *(half-way between shoulder and elbow)*

Elbow

Overseas bars

Service Stripes

Meritorious unit Badge

4 inches RIGHT — LEFT 4 inches

1. SERVICE STRIPES
Enlisted men were authorized to wear a service stripe for each 3-year period of service. This was positioned on the left sleeve of the service coat or Ike jacket (sometimes on the shirt), the lower edge being 4 inches from the bottom of the sleeve.

2. MERITORIOUS SERVICE UNIT BADGE

The Meritorious Service Unit Plaque was established in August 1944 to reward the efficiency of Army Service Forces units. Their personnel was allowed to wear the Meritorious Service Unit Badge on the lower right sleeve of the service coat or Ike jacket, or the shirt when worn as an outer garment.

3. OVERSEAS SERVICE BARS

One bar for each period of 6 months overseas, worn on the lower left sleeve of the service uniform.

5. Rank insignia

Insignia of grade for officers were pinned on the shoulder loops of the service coat, wool overcoat, cotton field overcoat and field jackets, and on the left front of the garrison cap. The rank badge was also affixed to the shirt's right collar when it was worn by itself (prior to Aug. 1942, rank insignia were pinned on the shirt's shoulder loops).

The rank chevrons for enlisted men (EM) were sewn on each sleeve of the following, half-way between the shoulder and elbow: wool overcoat, wool service coat and Ike jacket, shirts and field jackets. Rank insignia were officially not worn on fatigue (HBT) uniforms (➡ page 40-41).

1-General of the Army
2-General
3-Lieutenant General
4-Major General
5-Brigadier General
6-Colonel
7-Lieutenant-Colonel
8-Major
9-Captain
10-First Lieutenant
11-Second Lieutenant
12-Chief Warrant Officer
13-Warrant Officer, Junior Grade
14-Flight Officer

OFFICER'S RANK INSIGNIA

ENLISTED MEN'S SLEEVE CHEVRONS

Master Sergeant (M/Sgt)
First Sergeant (1st Sgt)
Technical Sergeant (T/Sgt)
Staff Sergeant (S/Sgt)
Technician 3rd Grade (T/3-Tech 3)

Sergeant (Sgt)
Technician 4th Grade (T/4-Tech 4)
Corporal (Cpl)
Technician 5th Grade (T/5-Tech 5)
Private First Class (PFC)

1. Model 1921 wool chevrons for Technicians 5th Grade, made from cut-out pieces of olive drab felt on a dark blue backing. Insignia for wool garments (service coat, shirt, overcoat).
2. Model 1942 chevrons for corporals, embroidered in rayon on a dark blue wool backing. Insignia for woolen uniforms.
3. Model 1942 chevrons for Technicians 5th Grade, embroidered in rayon on a dark blue cotton backing. Insignia for wool or cotton uniforms.

EXAMPLES OF OFFICERS' RANK INSIGNIA

1. 2nd Lieutenant
2. 1st Lieutenant, 'Sterling' hallmarked, pinback
3. Captain, 'Sterling' hallmarked, pinback
4. Major, pinback
5. Lieutenant-Colonel.

6. Officers' insignia of arm and service

Collar insignia

Adjutant General's Department

Aide to General

Aide to Lieutenant General

Aide to Major General

Aide to Brigadier General

Air Force

Cavalry

Coast Artillery Corps

Field Artillery

Infantry

Corps of Engineers

Chemical Warfare Service

Finance Department

General Staff Corps

Chaplains (Christian)

Chaplains (Jewish)

Inspector General's Department

Judge Advocate General's Department

Military Intelligence Division

Ordnance Department

Military Police

National Guard Bureau

Quartermaster Corps

Signal Corps

Officer not member of Arm or Service

Warrant Officer

US Military Academy

Armored Force

Transportation Corps

Tank Destroyer Force

6. Officers' insignia of arm and service

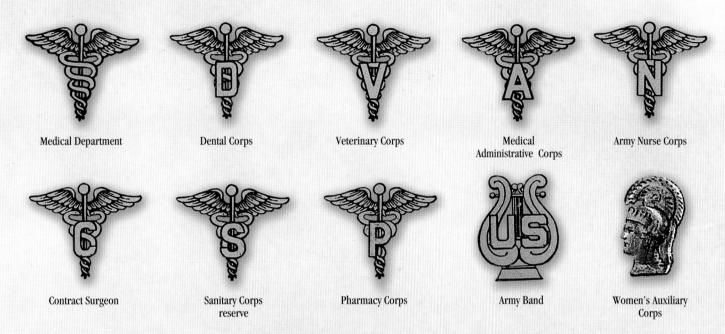

Medical Department	Dental Corps	Veterinary Corps	Medical Administrative Corps	Army Nurse Corps
Contract Surgeon	Sanitary Corps reserve	Pharmacy Corps	Army Band	Women's Auxiliary Corps

Army officers' insignia of arm and service were pinned on the lapels of the service coat, the collar itself bore the U.S. monogram. On the shirt collar – when worn as an outer garment – the rank insignia was placed on the right side and the branch device on the left side. Prior to August 1942, the U.S. monogram had been worn on the right collar, and the rank insignia on the shoulder loops.

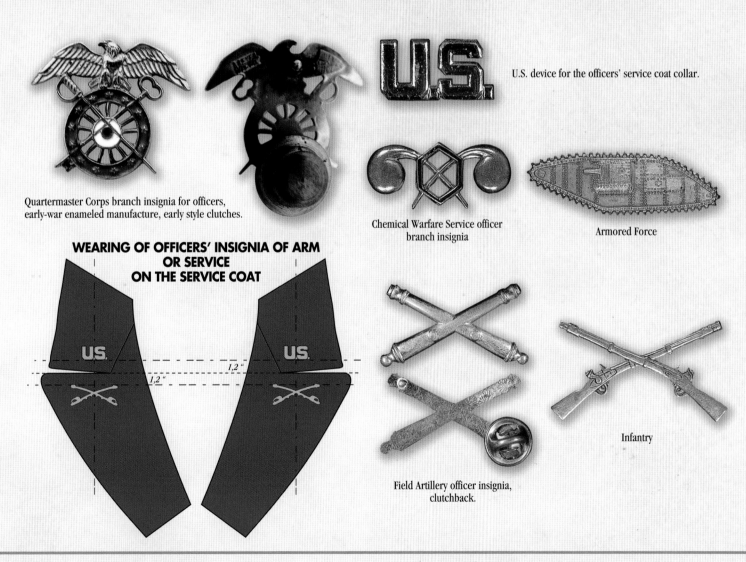

U.S. device for the officers' service coat collar.

Quartermaster Corps branch insignia for officers, early-war enameled manufacture, early style clutches.

Chemical Warfare Service officer branch insignia

Armored Force

WEARING OF OFFICERS' INSIGNIA OF ARM OR SERVICE ON THE SERVICE COAT

U.S.   U.S.

1.2 "
1.2 "

Field Artillery officer insignia, clutchback.

Infantry

7. Enlisted Men's insignia of arm and service

(Photo Militaria Magazine)

| U.S. Monogram | With unit number | US Army Air Forces | Armored Force | Cavalry | Chemical Warfare Service |

| Coast Artillery | Engineers | Field Artillery | Finance Department. | Infantry | Medical Department |

| Military Police | National Guard Bureau | Ordnance Department | Quartermaster Corps | Signal Corps | Tank Destroyers |

| Special Service Force | Transportation Corps | Detached Enlisted Men | Reserve Officers Training Corps | Women's Army Corps |

THE DIFFERENT TYPES OF WW2 COLLAR DISKS
(as classified by collectors)

Coast Artillery, with battery letter.
Type IIIA disk (1937-43), screwback.

Type IIIA U.S. disk.
Screwback, round-shaped nut removed to show detail.

Armored Force.
Type V disk (1943-1971), pinback.

Women's Army Corps.
1943-45 manufacture by the Tinnerman Co., pinback.

WEARING OF METALLIC COLLAR INSIGNIA ON THE SERVICE COAT AND IKE JACKET OF ENLISTED MEN

Enlisted men wore the U.S. collar disk on the right side of the Service coat or Ike jacket, and the arm or service disk on the left collar. The coat lapels and garrison cap bore the unit distinctive insignia, here for the 116th Infantry (29th Division).

8. Medals and decorations

Two categories of medals were awarded to American service personnel:
– Decorations rewarded exceptional bravery or outstanding service
– Service medals were for honorable service or for participation in campaigns ;

**Order of precedence
for wearing United States
military decorations**

Medal of Honor
Distinguished Service Cross
Distinguished Service Medal
Silver Star
Legion of Merit
Soldier's Medal
Bronze Star
Purple Heart

A. Army decorations

1. ARMY MEDAL OF HONOR
Created on 12 December 1861, the 4th pattern (1944)
is illustrated here. The highest American decoration is
conferred for exceptional bravery, at the risk of one's
life, facing the enemy, above and beyond the call of duty.

2. DISTINGUISHED SERVICE CROSS
Authorized 9 July 1918, awarded to Army personnel for
acts of heroism which do not warrant the Medal of
Honor.

3. DISTINGUISHED SERVICE MEDAL
Authorized 9 July 1918, awarded for exceptionally
meritorious service in a position of great responsibility.

4. SILVER STAR MEDAL
The 1918 Citation Star evolved into the Silver Star on
8 August 1932. It is bestowed on Army personnel for
gallantry in action while serving in any capacity, not
warranting the award of the Medal of Honor or
Distinguished Service Cross.

5. LEGION OF MERIT
Created on 20 July 1942, it is the first American
decoration which exists in three degrees (officer,
commander, chief commander) and may be also
awarded to military personnel of friendly foreign
nations, for exceptionally meritorious conduct in the
performance of outstanding services.

6. SOLDIER'S MEDAL
Created on 2 July 1926, awarded to any person within
the Army who distinguished himself by heroism not
involving actual conflict with an enemy.

7. BRONZE STAR
Authorized 4 February 1944, awarded to personnel who
distinguished themselves by heroic or meritorious
service in connection with military operations (except
aerial flights) against an enemy on or after 7 December
1941.

8. PURPLE HEART
Established by General George Washington in 1782,
reinstated in February 1932. It is awarded to military
personnel who receive wounds as a result of enemy
action, and posthumously to soldiers who are killed in
action or die of their wounds.

B. The Army Good Conduct Medal (enlisted men only)

Created on 28 June 1941, this medal is for one year of honorable federal military service during the war, or for 3 continuous years. Additional awards are symbolized by a loop ("hitch") on a bronze clasp to the ribbon.

C. The Distinguished Unit Citation (DUC)

Established 26 February 1942. Award given to American or Allied units for extraordinary heroism against an armed enemy, since 7 December 1941. Renamed Presidential Unit Citation in 1957, it is a ribbon-only decoration worn above the right-hand pocket, and has no corresponding medal.

D. Ribbon bars

Ribbons bars were pinned above the left-hand pocket of the service coat, Ike jacket, and shirt, but not on the field or fatigue uniforms.

Ribbons are usually mounted on a thin metal bar, affixed to the uniform by a brooch pin or by clutches. Ribbon bars can also be found directly embroidered on a piece of cloth in the uniform's color.

Decorations and medals are worn in the following order of precedence:

1/ Decorations
2/ Service Medals
3/ Foreign decorations

The Good Conduct Medal. The obverse was sometimes engraved with the soldier's name.

Below.
Ribbon bar for the American Campaign Medal and the European-African-Middle Eastern Campaign Medal. Pinback fastener.

The Distinguished Unit Citation (DUC)

Right.
Bronze stars and arrowheads were added to campaign medal ribbons for participation in a campaign, and in an airborne or amphibious operation.

UNITED STATES ARMY SERVICE RIBBONS, 1941-1945

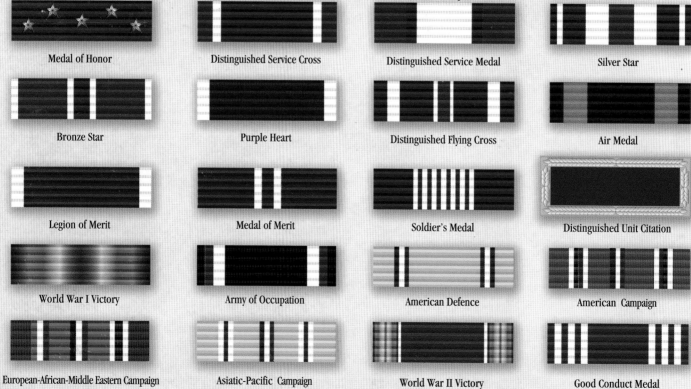

Medal of Honor — Distinguished Service Cross — Distinguished Service Medal — Silver Star

Bronze Star — Purple Heart — Distinguished Flying Cross — Air Medal

Legion of Merit — Medal of Merit — Soldier's Medal — Distinguished Unit Citation

World War I Victory — Army of Occupation — American Defence — American Campaign

European-African-Middle Eastern Campaign — Asiatic-Pacific Campaign — World War II Victory — Good Conduct Medal

E. Campaign Medals

1. MEXICAN SERVICE MEDAL
Established 1917 for service on the Mexican border between April 1911 and February 1917.

2. MEXICAN BORDER SERVICE MEDAL
Created on 9 July 1918. Awarded to personnel of the National Guard for service on the Mexican border between 9 May 1916 and 24 March 1917 ; and to Regular Army personnel for similar service between 1 January 1916 and 6 April 1916 on the provision they were not recipients of the Mexican Service Medal.

3. WORLD WAR ONE VICTORY MEDAL
Established 1919, awarded to officers and enlisted men for at least three months honorable service in Europe, Russia and Siberia in 1917-1920. Sector or battle clasps could be added to the suspension ribbon. *(J. Gawne Collection)*

4. WORLD WAR ONE ARMY OF OCCUPATION MEDAL
Established in 1941 for personnel of the armed forces who served in Germany or Austria-Hungary between 12 November 1918 and 11 July 1923.

5. AMERICAN DEFENSE SERVICE MEDAL
Established 28 June 1941. Issued to military personnel on active federal service for one year or more between 8 September 1939 and 7 December 1941 (i.e. before the declaration of war).

6. AMERICAN CAMPAIGN MEDAL
Established 6 November 1942. Awarded for service within the American Theater between 7 December 1941 and 2 March 1946.

7. EUROPEAN-AFRICAN-MIDDLE EASTERN CAMPAIGN MEDAL
Established 6 November 1942, for service within the theater between 7 December 1941 and 8 November 1945. A bronze star device was pinned on the ribbon for each battle or campaign, and a bronze arrowhead for each airborne or amphibious assault.

8. WOMEN'S ARMY CORPS (WAC) MEDAL
Instituted in 1943 for service both in the Women's Auxiliary Army Corps (WAAC) between 20 July 1942 and 31 August 1943, and the WAC between 1 September 1943 and 2 September 1945 (➡ page 162).

9. Badges

Towards the end of 1943, in order to recognize the service and hardships of the infantry and to promote enlistments in this arm, the War Department established two special badges:
– The Combat Infantryman Badge (CIB), on 11 November 1943;
– The Expert Infantryman Badge (EIB), on 15 November 1943.
These were worn above the left-hand pocket, above the service ribbons.

The CIB brought a $10 monthly pay bonus, and the EIB a $5 bonus.

The EIB was given to officers and enlisted men of infantry regiments or separate battalions who had satisfactorily completed specific proficiency tests in shooting, marching, hand-to-hand fighting, patrolling, first aid, field hygiene and sanitation, discipline, etc.

The CIB was awarded to infantrymen (exclusive of medical personnel and chaplains) who, after 6 December 1941, had engaged in ground combat as members of an infantry unit of regimental or smaller size. Awards were made by commanders of infantry divisions, regiments, and separate battalions.

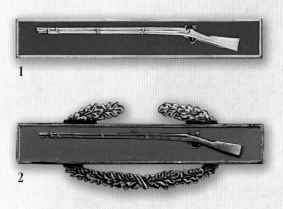

1

2

1. THE EXPERT INFANTRYMAN BADGE (EIB)

2. THE COMBAT INFANTRYMAN BADGE (CIB)

3. MEDICAL BADGE
'Sterling' hallmarked, pinback.
(Coleman collection)

4. BADGE, PARACHUTIST'S
Paratrooper wings, authorized in 1941. This was awarded by commanding officers to soldiers who had completed the prescribed proficiency tests, or who had taken part in at least one combat airborne operation.

5. BADGE, GLIDER
Wings for glider-borne troops, awarded under the same conditions as the paratrooper's badge.

3

4

5

The Medical Badge

Even if it was often exposed to the same hazards as infantrymen, Medical Detachment personnel in infantry units were not rewarded by a special badge similar to the CIB until January 1945. The War Department then created the Medical Badge for such personnel who, after 6 December 1941, had satisfactorily performed medical duties while assigned to the medical detachment of an infantry unit of regiment or smaller size, during any period it was engaged in ground combat. The Medical Badge entailed a $10 pay bonus for enlisted men only. It was worn above the left-hand pocket, above the ribbons bars.

Badge, Driver and Mechanic award

Created on 28 July 1942. Awarded to drivers and mechanics for efficiency and aptitude, it was pinned on the left-hand pocket flap, under the ribbon bars.

Four bars could be suspended from the basic badge:
– Driver-W (Wheeled vehicles)
– Driver-T (Tracked or half tracked vehicles)
– Driver-M (Motorcycle)
– Mechanic.

1

2

3

BADGE, DRIVER AND MECHANIC AWARD
1-2. 'Sterling' hallmarked, pinback.
3. Qualification bars.

10. Badges, arms qualification

The U.S. Army created its first musketry proficiency badges circa 1880 to reward marksmen. According to the system enacted in 1921, three basic badges indicated the degree of proficiency, and additional bars specific weapons or courses.

The three badges were:
– Marksman, Second-class Gunner: minimum score of 60/77% of points, depending on the weapon or qualification course ;
– Sharpshooter, First-class Gunner: 78/87%
– Expert: 85/91%.

The arms qualification badges were placed on the left-hand pocket flap, under the ribbon bars.

Authorized bars for shooting badges	
Rifle	Small bore pistol
Pistol- D (Dismounted)	Submachine gun
Pistol - M. (Mounted)	Small bore MG
Auto-Rifle	Carbine
Machine gun	Antitank
Coast Arty	81-mm mortar
Mines	60-mm mortar
Field Arty	TD 37-mm
Bayonet	TD 75-mm
Tank Weapons	TD 57-mm
CWS weapons	TD 3-inch (90 mm)
Machine Rifle	Antiaircraft weapons
Grenade	Inf. Howitzer
Small bore rifle	

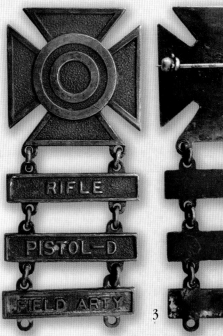

1. Marksman badge. 'Sterling' hallmarked, pinback. Bar for dismounted pistol shooting.

2-3. Sharpshooter badge. 'Sterling' hallmarked, pinback. Bars for qualification with the rifle, pistol and gunnery (field artillery).

WEARING OF METALLIC INSIGNIA AND SERVICE RIBBONS ON THE SERVICE COAT AND IKE JACKET OF ENLISTED MEN

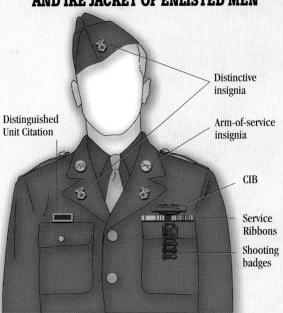

Distinctive insignia

Distinguished Unit Citation

Arm-of-service insignia

CIB

Service Ribbons

Shooting badges

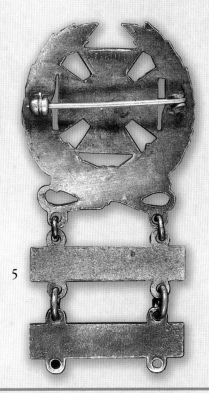

4-5. Expert badge. 'Sterling' hallmarked, pinback. Bar for proficiency with the pistol.

1. Introduction

Quartermaster Corps
officer collar insignia

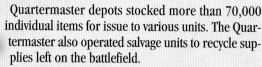

A. The Quartermaster Corps

The Quartermaster Corps' functions were multiple, its main task being however to provide the soldier with most of what he needed to fight. The QMC looked after the soldier, fed him, clothed him, housed him, cared for his laundry, provided coal and gasoline and, if he should die at war, ensured his proper burial and the care-taking of his grave.

Quartermaster depots stocked more than 70,000 individual items for issue to various units. The Quartermaster also operated salvage units to recycle supplies left on the battlefield.

Officers were supposed to provide for their uniforms. The most affluent had them custom-made by tailors. However, the War Department granted newly appointed officers an allowance for this purpose. The QMC also ordered service uniforms from the ready-to-wear clothing industry and sold them almost at cost to officers in special post stores.

Tag for an officer's jacket made in England by a civilian tailor in Yeovil (Somerset).

Regulation tag for officers' service coats and coats ordered by the QMC and retailed at low cost in post stores.

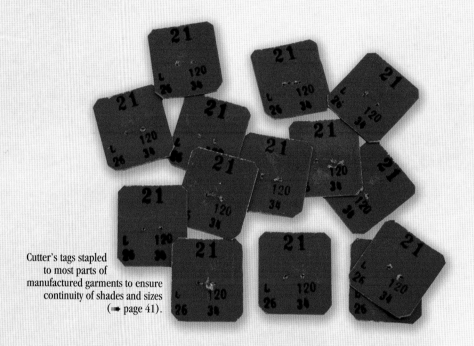

Cutter's tags stapled to most parts of manufactured garments to ensure continuity of shades and sizes (➡ page 41).

B. Standardization

Most articles stocked by the QMC were classified into three categories:

– Standard articles were the current adopted type and had to be procured and issued in preference to any other;

– Substitute standard type articles were not as satisfactory as the standard article but were a usable substitute and therefore could be procured and issued to supplement its supply;

– Limited standard type articles were items either in use or available for issue as substitutes for the standard articles. New orders were not be placed for them, however, and stocks were to be issued until exhausted.

C. Classification according to condition

The QMC issued both new and refurbished uniforms and equipment. Recovered items were sorted out according to their condition:

– Class A: new items, never used
– Class B: used item, but looks as new
– Class C: used item that should be reissued without repairs
– Class CS (Combat Serviceable): used and repaired item, ready for reissue. Such articles were ink marked (or bore a small stapled tag) with the initials

CS where the mark was not visible when article was worn;

– Class X: used item that is beyond repair, marked in ink with a large initial X.

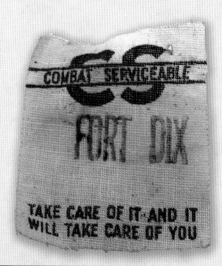

'Combat Serviceable' tag stapled on a piece of clothing or equipment by a quartermaster unit at the Fort Dix (New Jersey) induction center.

D. Size tariffs

Soldiers had to be outfitted with garments that best fit them, most items of uniform were therefore available in adequate sizes.

The size of headgear was indicated by a numeral followed by a fraction, or more simply by the initials S(mall), M(edium) and L(arge). The numeral corresponded with the head size, i. e a size 7 1/4 was for a head measurement of 23 inches.

The size of service coats, field jackets, wool field jackets and wool overcoats was indicated by a number followed by a letter or letters.

The number was for the chest measurement and the letter stood for the individual's height. For instance, R(egular) correspond-

ed to a height between 5'8 and 5'11. S was for Small, R for Regular, L for Long and XL for Extra Long.

Shirt sizes were indicated by two numbers, the first for the neck measurement, and the other for the sleeve length (for instance: 15 x 34).

A shoe size was mentioned by a figure (5 to 18: length of the foot) and a letter (AA to EEE, for the width)

Overshoes and Shoe pacs were supplied in 3 widths only:
N: narrow
M: medium
W: wide.

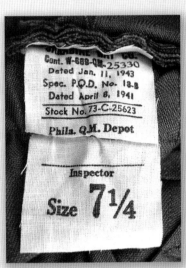

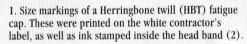
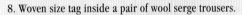

1. Size markings of a Herringbone twill (HBT) fatigue cap. These were printed on the white contractor's label, as well as ink stamped inside the head band (2).

3. Size tag inside a M-1941 Wool knit cap.

4. Printed size tag for a (1941) Field Jacket, sewn inside the back on the flannel lining.

5. Woven size label for a 1943-type HBT fatigue jacket, sewn below the collar.

6. Ink stamped size marking on the lining of an EM's wool overcoat.

7. Size markings inside the waistband of a pair of early khaki cotton trousers.

8. Woven size tag inside a pair of wool serge trousers.

9. Woven size tag in an OD wool shirt. The first number was for the neck measurement and the second for the sleeve length.

10. Size (9 for the foot length) and width (B) markings for a service shoe. These were embossed in the leather at the inside top of the uppers. FV must have been the army inspectors' initials. The size and width were also stamped outside on the instep, and inside on the inner sole.

11. Size markings in paint on the sole of a pair of 'Shoe pacs, high.'

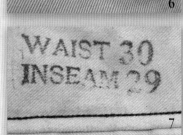

E. The Contractor's label

Most of the garments procured by the Quartermaster corps featured this type of contractor's label. It was located where it would not be visible when the garment was worn, for instance inside one of the lower pockets in the case of the EM's service coat.

The contractor's label was made of thin white linen. The text was most often printed in black, although blue or red letters are also found. The contractor's label does not stand up well to repeated washing of clothing and indications fade very fast.

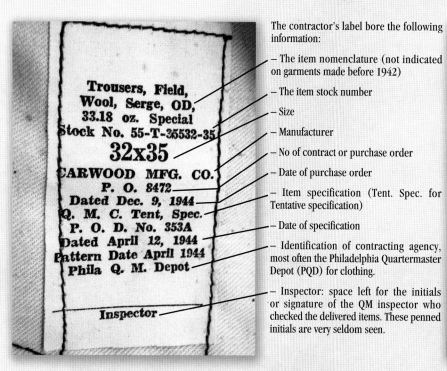

The contractor's label bore the following information:

– The item nomenclature (not indicated on garments made before 1942)

– The item stock number

– Size

– Manufacturer

– No of contract or purchase order

– Date of purchase order

– Item specification (Tent. Spec. for Tentative specification)

– Date of specification

– Identification of contracting agency, most often the Philadelphia Quartermaster Depot (PQD) for clothing.

– Inspector: space left for the initials or signature of the QM inspector who checked the delivered items. These penned initials are very seldom seen.

Contractor's tag for a batch of 10 wool knit caps made in 1943. The cap itself only bears a size label.

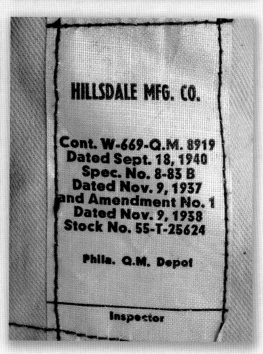

Contractor's label for a pair of wool trousers made in 1940. The item's name is absent.

F. Individual markings

Each item of clothing and equipment from the soldier's initial issue had to bear an identifying mark in ink. It was usually the initial of individual's last name and the last four digits of his Army Serial Number (ASN), separated by a dash. For instance: B-4380.

Some items, such as the barracks or duffle bag, had the full name of the soldier and his complete serial number.

Officer's clothing and equipment had the same type of marks, officers' serial numbers started with the initial O for *Officer*.

Opposite page.
Instructional poster for the marking of equipment and clothing, published by the Western Defence Command (San Francisco).

MARKING
of Equipment

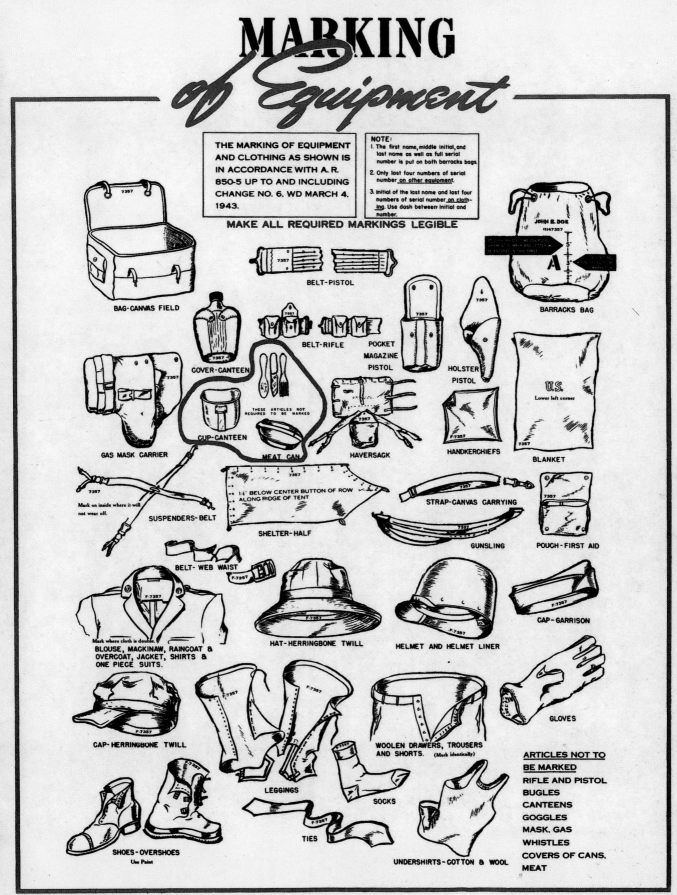

THE MARKING OF EQUIPMENT AND CLOTHING AS SHOWN IS IN ACCORDANCE WITH A. R. 850-5 UP TO AND INCLUDING CHANGE NO. 6, WD MARCH 4, 1943.

NOTE:
1. The first name, middle initial, and last name as well as full serial number is put on both barracks bags.
2. Only last four numbers of serial number on other equipment.
3. Initial of the last name and last four numbers of serial number on clothing. Use dash between initial and number.

MAKE ALL REQUIRED MARKINGS LEGIBLE

BAG-CANVAS FIELD

BELT-PISTOL

BARRACKS BAG

JOHN B. DOE

COVER-CANTEEN

BELT-RIFLE

POCKET MAGAZINE PISTOL

HOLSTER PISTOL

U.S. Lower left corner

CUP-CANTEEN

THESE ARTICLES NOT REQUIRED TO BE MARKED

MEAT CAN

HAVERSACK

HANDKERCHIEFS

BLANKET

GAS MASK CARRIER

Mark on inside where it will not wear off.

SUSPENDERS-BELT

1-1" BELOW CENTER BUTTON OF ROW ALONG RIDGE OF TENT

SHELTER-HALF

STRAP-CANVAS CARRYING

GUNSLING

POUCH-FIRST AID

BELT-WEB WAIST

Mark where cloth is double.

BLOUSE, MACKINAW, RAINCOAT & OVERCOAT, JACKET, SHIRTS & ONE PIECE SUITS.

HAT-HERRINGBONE TWILL

HELMET AND HELMET LINER

CAP-GARRISON

CAP-HERRINGBONE TWILL

LEGGINGS

WOOLEN DRAWERS, TROUSERS AND SHORTS. (Mask identically)

SOCKS

GLOVES

SHOES-OVERSHOES
Use Paint

TIES

UNDERSHIRTS-COTTON & WOOL

ARTICLES NOT TO BE MARKED
RIFLE AND PISTOL
BUGLES
CANTEENS
GOGGLES
MASK, GAS
WHISTLES
COVERS OF CANS,
MEAT

PREPARED BY HEADQUARTERS, NORTHERN CALIFORNIA SECTOR, WESTERN DEFENSE COMMAND, PRESIDIO OF SAN FRANCISCO.

2. Officers' dress uniforms

On 17 August 1938, the US Army adopted two new dress uniforms for officers:
– The Blue dress Uniform
– The Formal White uniform for summer and tropical duty.
In June 1940, the War Department decreed that the possession of the dress uniform would not be mandatory. Its wear became optional as of 1 April 1943 for the war's duration. These uniforms are illustrated here for the sake of information as they were not worn in Europe in 1943-45.

Dress coat shoulder straps, in gilt bullion on artillery red backing, the eagle rank insignia being embroidered in silver bullion.

CAP, BLUE DRESS

Dress cap for a colonel in the artillery. The dark blue top has a band in the distinctive color (here red for artillery). The black leather peak is covered in dark blue cloth, embroidered with gold bullion oak leaves.

The tailor's label, sewn in the dress coat, on the inside pocket.

COAT, BLUE DRESS

Dress coat belonging to the same officer. Made of dark blue wool gaberdine cloth, the coat has four pockets and an open collar. The rectangular shoulder straps, in the arm's color, bear the rank insignia. The officers' braid at the bottom of the sleeves is gilt piped in red. The U.S. and crossed cannons are pinned at the appropriate location on the collar and lapels.

TROUSERS, BLUE DRESS

Dress trousers in wool gaberdine material, the shade being slightly lighter than the coat's. The leg braiding is also in the branch color.

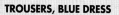

BELT, BLUE DRESS

Leather and brocade belt, done up in gold and red.

A black tie was worn, together with a white shirt, with both dress uniforms.

FORMAL WHITE TROUSERS

Made of the same material as the coat, and worn with low quarter white leather shoes.

FORMAL WHITE COAT

In white cotton, here for a Second Lieutenant in the Quartermaster Corps.

Low quarter shoes in black leather, recommended with the dress uniform.

3. The Enlisted Men's service uniform

CAP, SERVICE, ENLISTED MAN'S

Olive drab wool peaked cap, worn with the service uniform until 1941. It was then officially replaced by the Garrison cap (Overseas Cap) but was often retained or privately purchased for passes and furloughs. The russet leather chinstrap is held by two small gilt uniform buttons. The United States coat of arms, superimposed on a disk, was the cap device for enlisted men.

NECKTIE, COTTON, MOHAIR, KHAKI (STOCK NO 73-N-120)

Necktie in a cotton/wool blend, approved on 24 February 1942 to replace the M-1940 necktie in black mohair and the tan cotton tie introduced in 1939 for the summer/tropical uniform. When the shirt was worn by itself, the loose ends of the necktie were tucked between the first and second apparent shirt buttons.

COAT, WOOL, SERGE, OD, 18 OZ. (STOCK NO 55-C-69299/55-C-69510)

The US Army introduced a service coat with open collar and peaked lapels in 1926. It was also part of the field uniform until 1941 when the new cotton Field jacket was adopted (➡ page 36). The first pattern, approved in 1939 and standardized in 1940 had a partial lining, a pleated back for ease of arm movement, a half-belt and belt hooks. The hooks were eliminated in March 1941, together with the russet leather Garrison belt. The latter was however often retained for off-duty dress. The Service Coat not being part of the field uniform any more, the back pleats were deleted in June 1942 (Revised Service Coat M-1942). During the fall of 1944, the Service coat was classified as Limited Standard, but it was not actually replaced by the Ike jacket before the very end of the war. The coat shown here is the 1939-type, badged up for a sergeant in the 80th Division.

(Militaria Magazine)

JACKET, FIELD, WOOL, OD M-1944 (STOCK NO 55-J-384 510/ 55-J-384 940)

Insignia are for a Technician 4th Grade in the 42d Infantry Division.
This garment, together with two patterns of wool field jackets locally procured in Great Britain (➡ page 37), had been chosen in April 1944 by General Eisenhower (thence it became the 'Ike' Jacket). Manufacture was to start in the US the following month. It was meant to be a field garment like the British Battledress blouse it copied. In the ETO, the new wool field jacket came in as an unwelcome competitor to the M-1943 Field Jacket (➡ page 39) and, as a compromise, was to become a winter liner for the latter. In the end, the Ike jacket would prove an excellent replacement for the Service coat even if it was not available in sufficient numbers before VE-day.

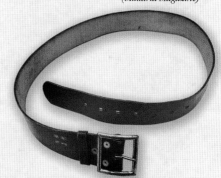

BELT, LEATHER, ENLISTED MAN'S (GARRISON BELT)

Belt in russet leather, worn with the Service Coat until March 1941, and sometimes retained afterwards for off-duty wear.

The Garrison cap (Overseas cap)

In 1939, a new field cap (in the World War One 'Overseas cap' shape) was adopted for barrack and field use. It proved inappropriate for field wear and was then standardized on 19 February 1941 as the 'Cap, Garrison,' to replace the peaked Service cap (previous page). The Garrison cap for Enlisted Men was piped in the arm or service colors around the 'curtain' and adorned with the unit's distinctive insignia on the left front.

The cap was made in Olive drab serge for the winter uniform and in tan cotton for summer/tropical wear. Its cut was slightly altered in June 1942.

CAP, GARRISON, KHAKI (STOCK NO 73-C-17996/ 73-C-18026)

Overseas cap in tan cotton, worn with the cotton shirt and trousers ➡ page 34 (inset, the contractor's label).

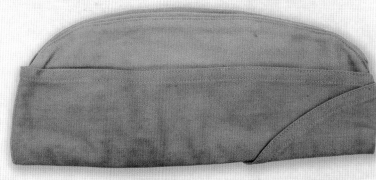

CAP, GARRISON, OD (STOCK NO 73-C-18168/ 73-C-18196)

Cap in Olive drab wool serge, piped here in artillery red. Pattern standardized on 19 February 1941.

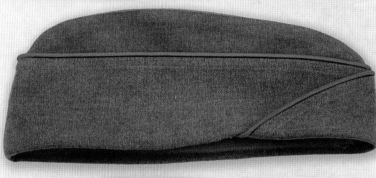

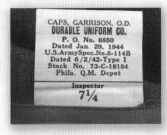

CAP, GARRISON, OD

Cap made according to the 2 June 1942 pattern, piped in light blue for the Infantry.

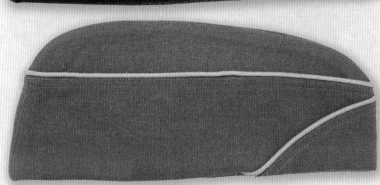

ENLISTED MEN'S GARRISON CAP ARM OF SERVICE PIPING

Infantry	Signal Corps	Finance department
Armored Force	Ordnance Department	Adjutant General's Department
Field Artillery Coast Artillery	Quartermaster Corps	Detached Enlisted men's list
Cavalry	Chemical Warfare Service	National Guard Bureau
Tank Destroyers	Military Police	US Army Air Forces
Engineers	Transportation Corps	1st Special Service Force
Medical Department	Women's Army Corps	

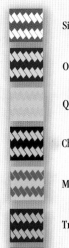

PIPING FOR OFFICERS' GARRISON CAPS

General Officers *(gold)*

Officers *(gold and black)*

Warrant Officers *(silver and black)*

4. Officers' service uniforms

CAP, SERVICE, OFFICER'S (AND WARRANT OFFICER'S)

Officer's cap in Olive drab No 51 'dark shade' wool. The markings inked inside the leather sweatband identify an item procured by the QMC and sold to officers at Post stores. The cap device for officers was the US coat of arms in gilt metal.

COAT, SERVICE, OFFICER'S, OD, DARK ELASTIQUE

Wool coat for a Medical Department Major serving with a service unit in the ETO. The open-collared coat, authorized in 1940, was modified in 1942 by the addition of a cloth self-belt which replaced the leather Sam Browne belt. Towards the end of the war, the coat was sometimes replaced by a M-1944 type field jacket made in the dark shade officers' material.

SAM BROWNE BELT

M-1921 russet leather belt. Mandatory until 1942 with the Service coat.

OFFICER'S BAG

Travel bag in stout canvas reinforced with leather, for carrying the officer's clothing and personal belongings. Unfolded and suspended, it became a sort of wardrobe with hangers and a partition for footwear.

CAP, GARRISON, OFFICER'S, OD, DARK ELASTIQUE

In December 1940, three new types of garrison cap ornamentation were authorized for officers: gold braid for general officers, gold and black for other officers, and silver and black for warrant officers (➡ page 29). The left side of the cap bore the unit Distinctive insignia (➡ page 12) until 25 August 1942, when it was replaced by the rank insignia.

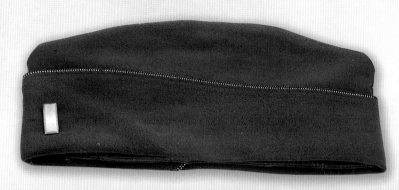

SHIRT, WOOL ELASTIQUE, DRAB, OFFICER'S

Officer shirt in 'Drab 54, light shade' wool gaberdine cloth, otherwise known as 'pink.' Shirts for officers have shoulder loops sewn at the arm and buttoned near the collar. When the shirt was worn as an outer garment, rank insignia were pinned on the shoulder loops until August 1942.

Standard label for officers' ready-to-wear uniform trousers procured by the Quartermaster Corps and retailed at low cost by the Army at Post stores.

TROUSERS, SERVICE, OFFICER'S, OD, DARK ELASTIQUE

Officers' trousers in 'Olive drab 51, dark shade' wool Elastique cloth, matching the service coat. They had two side and hip pockets and a watch pocket. These 1942-type pants are a variant of the original 1938 garment introduced with the Olive drab service uniform.

SHOES, LOW QUARTER, RUSSET LEATHER, OFFICER'S

The shoes illustrated here have been made by Johnson & Johnson.

2-UNIFORMS

4. Officers' service uniforms

CAP SERVICE, OFFICER'S
Bancroft made quality cap, in
dark olive drab fur felt.

Top: the cap badge
for officers.

Bottom: cap badge
for Warrant Officers
(their collar insignia
was identical).

WAR DEPARTMENT GENERAL STAFF IDENTIFICATION BADGE

This badge, created in 1943, was worn on the upper right pocket
of the service coat of officers of the Army who, since June 4 1920,
had served for at least one year on the WD General Staff. It was 2
inches in diameter for all officers except for the chief of staff or
former chiefs of staff, being 3 inches in this case.

**TAILOR MADE SHORT
OFFICER'S JACKET**
Officer's jacket in the style of the Ike jacket,
locally made by Parsons Bros. of Yeovil
(Somerset) for Engineer Captain RC Kane.

JACKET, FIELD, WOOL, OFFICER'S
Regulation pattern officer's Ike jacket for an infantry
1st Lieutenant of the 3rd Infantry Division. The
material is identical in texture and color to the
November 1944 EM pattern (➡ page 28),
but the lining is of rayon.

CAP, GARRISON, WOOL, ELASTIQUE, OFFICER'S

Officer's cap made in 'pink' wool elastique material.

SHIRT, OFFICER'S, WOOL

Tailored in Olive drab 51 dark shade wool cloth.
Inset: the manufacturer's tag for this shirt.

TROUSERS, WOOL, ELASTIQUE, DRAB, OFFICER'S

Officer's pants in 'pink' shade wool. Cut according to the same pattern as the dark olive drab trousers, these were optional for wear with the Olive drab 51 service coat. The trousers illustrated here have been locally procured in Britain.

TROUSERS, Officers, Light
U.S.A., E.T.O.,
SPECFN. No. U/1212F
Size 33 S
Waist — 33 ins.
Leg — 33½ ins.
TODD & CO. LTD.
1944
U.K. CON/292/16/N.1835/14

ARMY OFFICER'S SHIRT
100% WOOL
Form Fitted
LONDON SHRUNK
TAILORED BY
JACKSON RAYMOND CO. INC.

TROUSERS, WOOL, ELASTIQUE, DRAB, OFFICERS'
CODE No. 1850
Dated Feb. 19, 1944
Spec. No. P.Q.D. 49B
P. O. No. 7396
Stock No. 55-T-66263
Phila. Q.M. Depot
Waist 30
Length SHORT
INSPECTOR

Contractor's label for a pair of US-made officer's 'pink' trousers.

SHOES, LOW QUARTER, RUSSET LEATHER, OFFICER'S

One of the many patterns worn by officers with the Service uniform.

5. The summer Service uniform

The US Army authorized in 1938 a summer/tropical service uniform with tan cotton trousers and shirt (otherwise known as the 'chino' shirt and trousers). In 1941-42, this cotton uniform also provided the basis of field dress in the summer or in tropical regions.

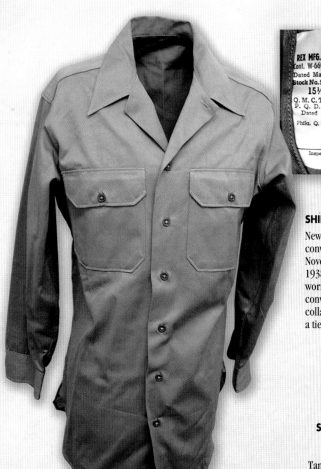

SHIRT, COTTON, KHAKI

New tan cotton shirt with convertible collar adopted in November 1941. It replaced the 1938-pattern which was to be worn with a tie. The new convertible design enabled the collar to be worn in garrison with a tie, or opened in the field.

SHIRT, COTTON, KHAKI, SPECIAL (STOCK No 55-S-1942/ 55-S-1958-7)

Tan cotton shirt with gas-proof features such as sleeve gussets and a buttoned gas flap on the chest. These were introduced in 1942 and warranted the 'Special' designation.

U.S. Army tin button used on early tan cotton trousers.

TROUSERS, COTTON, KHAKI, SPECIAL (STOCK No 55-T-12400/ 55-T-12650)

Tan cotton trousers with an added triangular antigas flap behind the fly (hence the 'Special' denomination).

TROUSERS, COTTON, KHAKI (STOCK No 55-T-10000/ 55-T-10672-65)

1937-pattern tan cotton trousers. These are straight-legged, with two side pockets, two hip pockets and a front watch pocket.

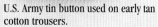

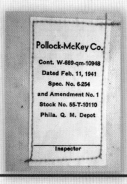

6. Winter service and field dress

At the end of the Thirties, the enlisted men's winter field and service uniform was made up of the wool service coat, shirt and trousers.

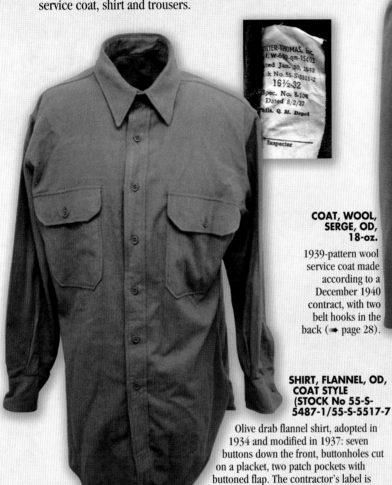

COAT, WOOL, SERGE, OD, 18-oz.

1939-pattern wool service coat made according to a December 1940 contract, with two belt hooks in the back (➡ page 28).

SHIRT, FLANNEL, OD, COAT STYLE (STOCK No 55-S-5487-1/55-S-5517-7

Olive drab flannel shirt, adopted in 1934 and modified in 1937: seven buttons down the front, buttonholes cut on a placket, two patch pockets with buttoned flap. The contractor's label is sewn on the rear right-hand tail. The shirt was replaced as of November 1941 by a similar garment with a convertible collar.

TROUSERS, WOOL, SERGE, OD, LIGHT SHADE (STOCK No 55-T-81995-20/ 55-T-82267-30)

1937-pattern straight wool trousers, standardized in 1938 for most arms and services. Like the tan cotton trousers, they have two side and hip pockets and a front watch pocket, together with a 5-button fly.

OVERCOAT, WOOL, MELTON, OD, ROLL COLLAR, 32-oz. (STOCK No 55-O-8876/ 55-O-9140)

Enlisted men's double-breasted wool overcoat, standardized in 1939: two slanted side pockets, two shoulder straps and a buttoned half-belt in the back. Mainly worn with the Service uniform and off-duty, it was however issued in quantity to combat troops for the winter campaign of 1944-45 (➡ page 46).

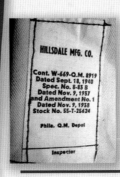

7. Field dress

The Army-wide introduction of the new 1941-type field jacket brought out a clear distinction between the Service uniform (garrison and off-duty uniform) and the Field (combat) uniform.

JACKET, FIELD, OLIVE DRAB (FIRST PATTERN)

Short windbreaker-type jacket in windproof and water-resistant cotton poplin with a flannel lining. Adopted 7 October 1940 following the prewar studies under General Parsons (CG of the IIIrd Army Corps), it was meant to replace the wool service coat (➡ page 28, 35) in the field. Characteristics: buttoned tabs at the waist and sleeves, front closure by a slide fastener hidden behind a buttoned placket, two wide pleats in the back, buttoned tab under the collar. This first pattern also calls for buttoned flaps on the slanted pockets, and no shoulder loops.

JACKET, FIELD, OD (SECOND PATTERN) (STOCK No 55-J-200/55-J-304)

Second pattern field jacket specified in May 1941: pocketflaps were deleted and shoulder loops added. It was gradually replaced by the M-1943 Field Jacket (➡ page 38), whose development begun in 1942.

SHIRT, FLANNEL, OD, COAT STYLE, SPECIAL (STOCK No 55-S-5652-2/ 55-S-5668-7)

Convertible collared flannel shirt with gas-proof features such as sleeve gussets and a buttoned gas flap on the chest. Two plastic buttons are sewn at the back under the collar for the attachment of the woolen antigas hood (➡ page 221)

TROUSERS, WOOL, SERGE, OD, LIGHT SHADE, SPECIAL

1937-pattern wool trousers dated 1942, with an early anti-vesicant 'Special' feature: a triangular green flannel flap has been added behind the fly.

JACKET, FIELD, LINED, ETO (FIRST PATTERN)

A locally developed and manufactured jacket, made in Great Britain as of May 1943. Copied on the British Battledress blouse, it was to be worn in the winter instead of the standard field jacket (➡ page 36). It was developed by the ETO Commanding General, BG Robert Littlejohn. The slanted breast pockets had been taken after the first type field jacket; the material, waist tab and buckle being copied on the British BD blouse. A wide gas flap buttons behind the front closure. The first batches were issued to the 29th Division in England for field trials.

JACKET, FIELD, LINED, ETO (SECOND PATTERN)

The final pattern was manufactured in Britain starting July 1943. It differs from the 1st pattern by its breast patch pockets, buttoned tabs at the waist, and shoulder straps. The gas flap had been done away with. General Eisenhower decided for its issue in March 1944 and 300,000 jackets were ordered from British firms. Mass production of its improved variant in the States, the M-1944 Wool Field jacket (or 'Ike' jacket) would not be sufficient until the end of the war (➡ page 28).

TROUSERS, ENLISTED MEN, ETO

British-Made wool trousers, in thicker material than the standard American garment, probably procured to be worn in the field with the ETO Field Jacket. They also differ by the two hip button-through patch pockets.
(Photo Militaria Magazine, Coleman collection)

TROUSERS, WOOL, SERGE, OD, LIGHT SHADE, SPECIAL (STOCK No 55-T-86606/ 55-T-86820)

These standard pattern wool trousers (17 April 1943 Specification) now featured a gas flap in matching material behind the fly.

The M-1943 uniform

During the fall of 1942, and due to numerous complaints about the issue combat uniform, the U.S. Army started to develop a 'universal' combat uniform, that would replace, namely: the olive drab field jacket (➡ page 36), the Arctic jacket (➡ page 46), the Mackinaw coat (➡ page 48), the wool overcoat (➡ page 35) as well as many specialized garments (for paratroopers, armor crews, mountain troops, etc.). The new M-1943 outfit would include about 20 new items, such as: cotton sateen jacket and trousers with their respective removable liners for warmth, a field cap and pile cap, buckle boots, high-neck sweater. New articles of equipage were also standardized at the same time: a new poncho/tent section, a mummy-shaped sleeping bag, etc.

These items were tested by the QMC at the summer of 1943 and then issued for field evaluation to units of the 3rd Infantry Division on the Anzio beachhead.

The new field uniform proved satisfactory and was then requisitioned accordingly by the Italian theater quartermasters. In NW-Europe however, General Littlejohn, supported by General Eisenhower had scheduled to issue the new M-1944 wool field jacket as the basic element of the next winter's fighting outfit, together with the woolen overcoat. In the States, meantime, the OQMG (Office of the Quartermaster General) tried to prescribe its new M-1943 jacket. Due to bad planning in Europe and other supply mishaps, the new uniform was not delivered in bulk before January 1945.

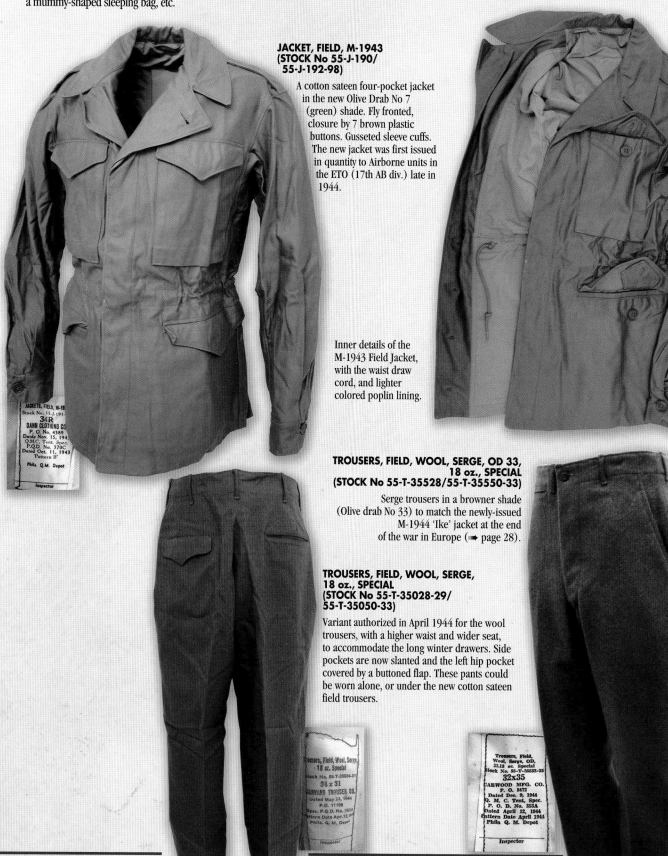

JACKET, FIELD, M-1943 (STOCK No 55-J-190/ 55-J-192-98)

A cotton sateen four-pocket jacket in the new Olive Drab No 7 (green) shade. Fly fronted, closure by 7 brown plastic buttons. Gusseted sleeve cuffs. The new jacket was first issued in quantity to Airborne units in the ETO (17th AB div.) late in 1944.

Inner details of the M-1943 Field Jacket, with the waist draw cord, and lighter colored poplin lining.

TROUSERS, FIELD, WOOL, SERGE, OD 33, 18 oz., SPECIAL (STOCK No 55-T-35528/55-T-35550-33)

Serge trousers in a browner shade (Olive drab No 33) to match the newly-issued M-1944 'Ike' jacket at the end of the war in Europe (➡ page 28).

TROUSERS, FIELD, WOOL, SERGE, 18 oz., SPECIAL (STOCK No 55-T-35028-29/ 55-T-35050-33)

Variant authorized in April 1944 for the wool trousers, with a higher waist and wider seat, to accommodate the long winter drawers. Side pockets are now slanted and the left hip pocket covered by a buttoned flap. These pants could be worn alone, or under the new cotton sateen field trousers.

The jacket's instruction label should be readable after laundering. It states that in cold weather, the jacket ought to be worn over the Pile field jacket.

JACKET, FIELD, PILE, OD (STOCK No 55-J-382-260/55-J-382-430)

A poplin shell lined in brown artificial fur ('pile'), with knit cuffs and stand collar. Front closure by six large plastic buttons held into cord loops.

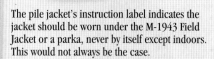

The pile jacket's instruction label indicates the jacket should be worn under the M-1943 Field Jacket or a parka, never by itself except indoors. This would not always be the case.

JACKET, FIELD, M-1943

Jacket made according to Spec 370D of 23 February 1944. It differs mainly from the former pattern (Spec 370C of Oct. 1943) by the instruction label sewn on the lining below the collar. Insignia are for a Captain in the 2d Infantry Division. The matching hood is illustrated on page 63.

TROUSERS, FIELD, COTTON, OD (STOCK No 55-T-34028-28/55-T-34044-32)

Cotton sateen field trousers in the Olive Drab No 7 (green) shade, introduced in August 1943. The pockets and lining are cut from unbleached white cotton. In the winter, the trousers were meant to be worn over a special pile liner (as the jacket) but this was quickly replaced by the standard wool serge trousers with suspenders. The field trousers are therefore cut one inch wider at the waist. A buttoned tab on each side enables the waist to be tightened when the trousers are worn alone. Similar tabs at the ankle gather the trouser legs to tuck them in the new 'Boot, combat, service' ('Buckle boots'). *(Photo by Militaria Magazine, Le Poilu collection, Paris)*

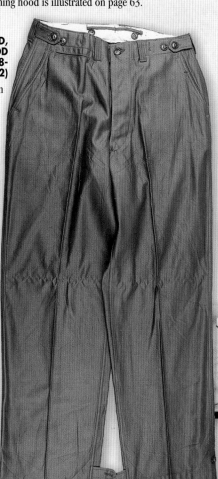

Instruction label for Trousers, field, cotton. On green HBT pockets and lining, this label is either sewn on or ironed-on in black letters.

Variant of the cotton field trousers made in the Uniform twill cotton material used on the khaki cotton trousers (➡ page 34). The lining and pockets are cut from green herringbone twill. The instruction label is sewn onto the right hand hip pocket. The waist tabs button towards the front but this was reversed according to the last wartime spec (Spec. 371C of February 22, 1945). All buttons are the tack type, in blackened metal.

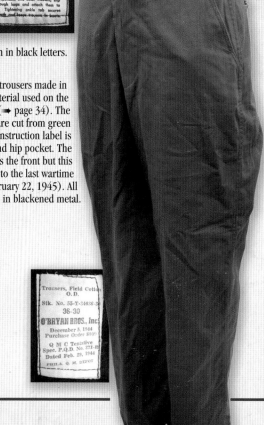

8. The Herringbone Twill fatigue uniform

In May 1941, the War Department announced that the older fatigue dress in blue denim would be phased out and replaced with new garments in green herringbone twill (HBT). The two-piece HBT fatigues were also worn as the Summer/tropical combat dress. Impregnated with an anti-vesicant compound, it was issued in Europe for the D-day invasion.

The blackened metal tack-on button used on most HBT clothing.

JACKET, HERRINGBONE TWILL (SPEC. 45B, 2 NOVEMBER 1942)

1942-pattern HBT jacket in the early light green color. It now has larger cargo pockets on the chest, with side pleats for expansion, the hem is plain.

JACKET, HERRINGBONE TWILL (STOCK NO 55-J-414/55-J-494) (SPEC. No 45, 3 APRIL 1941)

Early 1941-pattern fatigue jacket in light green HBT material. It has two pleated shirt-style pockets, a narrow band at the hem, and adjusting tabs and buckles at the waist.

Another type of metal tack-on button used on HBT clothing.

TROUSERS, HERRINGBONE TWILL (STOCK NO 55-T-38001-78/ 55-T-38108-10)

1941-pattern HBT trousers in the early light green color. These closely follow the pattern of the khaki summer trousers (➡ page 34), except for the material and the tack-on metal buttons. The contractor's label indeed bears the wrong specification, Spec 6-254 being for the khaki cotton trousers.

TROUSERS, HERRINGBONE TWILL, SPECIAL (STOCK NO 55-T-43310/ 55-T-43469) (SPEC. 42A, 30 OCTOBER 1942)

1942-pattern fatigue trousers still in the early light green color. Their only pockets are the two large cargo pockets on the thighs, with flap closure. The 'Special' designation means there is a triangular antigas flap behind the fly.

Another type of metal tack-on button used on HBT clothing, this time with a hollow center and floral pattern.

JACKET, HERRINGBONE TWILL, SPECIAL (STOCK NO 55-J-532-30/ 55-J-542-30) (SPECIFICATION No 45B, 2 NOVEMBER 1942)

'Special' HBT shirt with gas flap behind the front closure, and two buttons under the collar for attaching the antigas woolen hood (➡ page 221).

JACKET, HERRINGBONE TWILL, SPECIAL, OD SHADE 7 (SPEC. No 45D, 12 MARCH 1943)

Same jacket as at left, but in the new darker green color (Olive drab shade No 7). A white cutter's tag (➡ page 22) is still stapled on this mint example.

TROUSERS, HERRINGBONE TWILL, SPECIAL, OD SHADE 7 (SPEC. No 42C, 10 MARCH 1943)

HBT trousers identical to those on previous page, but in the new dark green color. Olive drab No 7 had been chosen in January 1943 for all HBT clothing and cotton field uniforms, as well as for most army webbing and canvas equipment.

TROUSERS, HERRINGBONE TWILL, SPECIAL, OD SHADE 7 (SPEC. No 42C, 10 MARCH 1943)

Variant of the trousers at left: the cargo pockets feature a pleat down the middle and not on the rear side. This time-saving feature – which can also be observed on some jackets – was an option for manufacturers.

9. The Normandy invasion

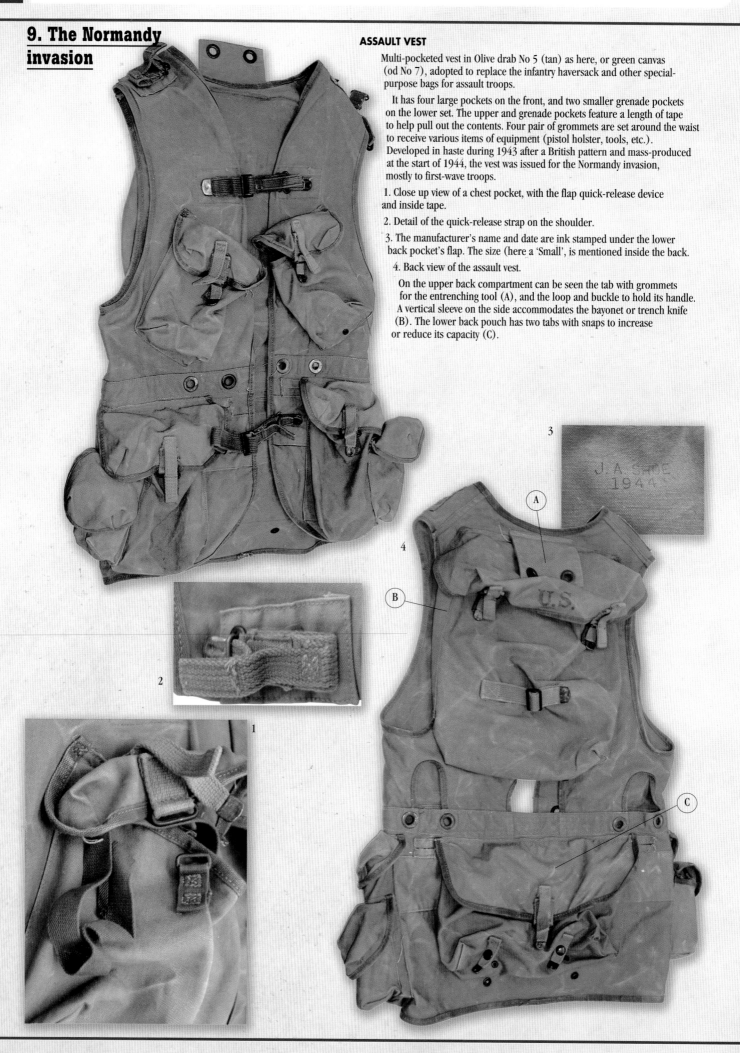

ASSAULT VEST

Multi-pocketed vest in Olive drab No 5 (tan) as here, or green canvas (od No 7), adopted to replace the infantry haversack and other special-purpose bags for assault troops.

It has four large pockets on the front, and two smaller grenade pockets on the lower set. The upper and grenade pockets feature a length of tape to help pull out the contents. Four pair of grommets are set around the waist to receive various items of equipment (pistol holster, tools, etc.). Developed in haste during 1943 after a British pattern and mass-produced at the start of 1944, the vest was issued for the Normandy invasion, mostly to first-wave troops.

1. Close up view of a chest pocket, with the flap quick-release device and inside tape.

2. Detail of the quick-release strap on the shoulder.

3. The manufacturer's name and date are ink stamped under the lower back pocket's flap. The size (here a 'Small', is mentioned inside the back.

4. Back view of the assault vest.

On the upper back compartment can be seen the tab with grommets for the entrenching tool (A), and the loop and buckle to hold its handle. A vertical sleeve on the side accommodates the bayonet or trench knife (B). The lower back pouch has two tabs with snaps to increase or reduce its capacity (C).

10. Amphibious operations

The white arc on this M1 steel helmet is the specific marking of the Engineer Special Brigades on D-day in Normandy.

WADERS, OVER-THE-SHOE (STOCK No 72-W-5000/ 72-W-5020)

Combination rubber boot and overall, worn for unloading landing craft or construction work in deep water.

BOOTS, KNEE, WADER (STOCK No 72-B-343-505/ 72-B-343-555)

Rubber boots with a waterproof canvas top that is tightened above and below the knee. These are worn over the leather boots, to work in shallow water.

BOOTS, RUBBER, KNEE, M-1937 (STOCK NO 72-B-1261/72-B-1271)

Brown or black rubber boots worn by engineers for working in the surf or for bridging operations.

LIFE, PRESERVER, BELT

Standard US Navy M-1926 preserver, provided to all Army personnel on troop transports and landing craft for amphibious operations. It could be quickly inflated thanks to two CO_2 cylinders located near the front buckle. Two rubber tubes with a metal valve allow for mouth inflation.

11. The two-piece camouflage HBT uniform

Developed for jungle fighting, this outfit was briefly issued in limited quantities for the Normandy fighting (for instance to personnel of the 41st Armored Infantry Battalion/2d Armored Div.) The uniform is partially reversible: although each side of the fabric shows a different dominant shade, pockets are present on the greener side only.

JACKET, HERRINGBONE TWILL, CAMOUFLAGE (STOCK NO 55-J-497-10/55-J-497-95)

The HBT jacket in camouflage material (Spec. 375, 3 June 1943) differs from the regular green jacket (➡ page 41) by the following details: plastic buttons (all hidden to prevent snagging) and reinforcing patches at the elbow.

Close-up of the anti-gas flap on the chest.

Close-up of the anti-gas gusset behind the trouser fly, the latter being secured by 5 plastic buttons.

TROUSERS, HERRINGBONE TWILL, CAMOUFLAGE (STOCK NO 55-T-38112-31/ 55-T-38119-33)

These trousers are also slightly different from the green fatigue trousers (➡ page 41): the gas flap is sewn on both sides of the fly, the cargo pockets are closed with fly buttonhole tabs, buttoned tabs for gathering the leg are placed at the ankle, and oblong patches are sewn on the knees.

The buttoned tightening tabs at the ankle.

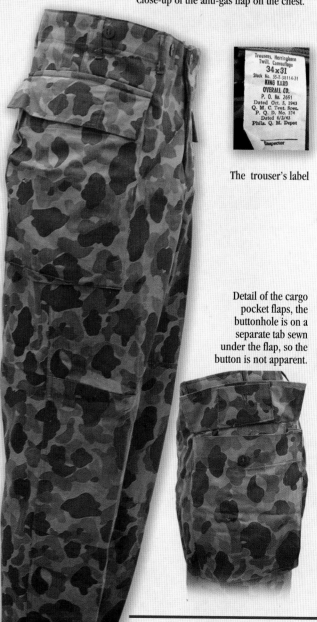

The trouser's label

Detail of the cargo pocket flaps, the buttonhole is on a separate tab sewn under the flap, so the button is not apparent.

12. Rainwear

RAINCOAT, SYNTHETIC RESIN COATED, OD, DISMOUNTED (STOCK NO 72-R-4050/72-R-4056)

Raincoat issued to all troops (except mounted soldiers). Introduced in 1942, this pattern was made in synthetic resin coated cotton cloth to save on rubber. It replaced the M-1938 rubberized raincoat and the older 1935 oil treated cloth raincoat (Raincoat, Oil Treated, Dismounted). The raincoat closed down the front with 5 large plastic buttons, a long rectangular gas flap bore the contractor's label.

The mounted troops raincoat had a longer vent down the back.

PARKA, WET WEATHER (STOCK NO 72-P-2510/72-P-2525)

Parka in synthetic resin coated cotton cloth, slip-on type, with four spring-loaded hooks and eyes on the chest. Hood and waist provided with draw cords. This item was made and issued the war throughout.

TROUSERS, WET WEATHER (STOCK NO 72-T-8010/72-T-8040)

Water-resistant bib front trousers, with cemented seam construction. The garment had two adjustable suspenders buckled on two metal tack-on buttons, a large thigh pocket at right and a draw cord in the leg hem.

PONCHO, SYNTHETIC RESIN COATED, OD

Rain garment developed late in 1942, originally to replace the raincoat in tropical regions. It could also be used as a sleeping bag and shelter half. The earlier 'Poncho, Lightweight, od' made of nylon was briefly manufactured in 1944.

13. Cold-weather clothing

JACKET, FIELD, OD, ARCTIC (STOCK NO 55-J-330/55-J-371)

Field jacket in wind and water resistant twill, lined with blanket-like material. This longer jacket was similar to the Olive Drab Field Jacket (➡ page 36). Tightening tabs at the wrists and waist were fitted with buckles instead of buttons. Standardized in 1941 for extreme cold climate regions, it was replaced by the M-1943 jacket (➡ page 38).

A plastic overcoat button.

The Kersey-lined trousers were cut following the same pattern as the standard serge trousers.

TROUSERS, KERSEY-LINED (STOCK NO 55-T-39425/55-T-39545)

These trousers were to be worn with the Arctic jacket pictured above. They were classified as Limited Standard in 1943, and replaced by the cotton field trousers and wool field trousers combination (➡ pages 38-39).

OVERCOAT, WOOL, MELTON, OD, ROLL COLLAR, 32 OZ. (STOCK NO 55-O-8900/55-O-9115)

This enlisted men's overcoat was introduced in 1939 (➡ page 35), and modified in 1942: to save on critical brass, green plastic buttons (still embossed with the US coat of arms) were used.

MASK, FACE, WOOL, FELT, OD (STOCK NO 73-M-100)

Extreme cold mask in olive drab wool felt, lined with white material. Elastic webbing holds the mask on the head, the neck and shoulder piece is closed on the back by two buttons.

TOQUE, WOOL-KNIT

Introduced in 1941, replaced as of 1943 by the Pile field cap (➡ page 63).

Below.
Label of a home-made wool toque, donated to soldiers by the American Red Cross.

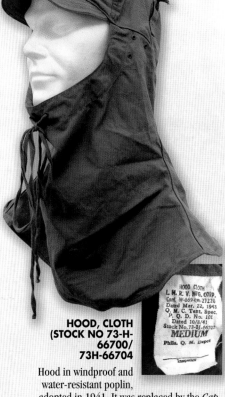

HOOD, CLOTH (STOCK NO 73-H-66700/ 73H-66704)

Hood in windproof and water-resistant poplin, adopted in 1941. It was replaced by the *Cap, Field, Pile* (➡ page 63) in 1943. The hood cloth, part of the cold weather clothing described on previous page, was worn over the wool-knit toque.

OVERCOAT, PARKA TYPE, REVERSIBLE, WITH PILE LINER (STOCK NO 55-O-3132-36/ 55-O-3132-46)

Cold climate garment with an olive drab and a white snow camouflage side. A removable liner could be added. The overcoat closed with a zipper and a buttoned placket, it had two slanted pockets and two large patch pockets with flaps below the waist, on the green side only. Snaps located on the front panels could be used to gather the hem around the legs. The hood could be made less capacious thanks to snaps at the back. This new pattern developed in 1943 replaced the older 1941-vintage sheepskin or alpaca lined parka type overcoats.

Removable liner for the reversible parka-type overcoat, in brown artificial fur ('Pile') with knit wristlets.
(Militaria Magazine photo, Coleman collection)

14. The Mackinaw coat

**COAT, MACKINAW, OD
(STOCK NO 55-C-33090/55-C-33190)**

This garment was similar to a late WW1 pattern, altered in 1938. This early model was made from greenish duck (canvas) lined in blanket material, it also called for a shawl collar faced with wool and a belt.

After 1941, a thinner poplin material was used, together with a lighter wool lining. In the Spring of 1942, another variant was introduced, its shawl collar was no longer faced with wool (➡ volume 2 page 44).

**COAT, MACKINAW, OD
(STOCK NO 55-C-33100/55-C-33190)**

The last pattern of Mackinaw (Spec. of 19 April 1943) has no belt. The insignia are for a Corporal in the 1st Infantry Division.

**'COAT, MACKINAW,
ENLISTED MEN'
(BRITISH MADE)**

The British-made Mackinaw was cut from cotton twill, in a stronger shade than the US-made garment. The belt buckle and plastic buttons are also distinctive.

15. Snow camouflage items

During the winter of 1944-45 in NW-Europe, the Army suffered from a severe shortage of white camouflage garments. As a stop-gap measure, it obtained 15,000 suits from the British. These smock and trousers are illustrated below.

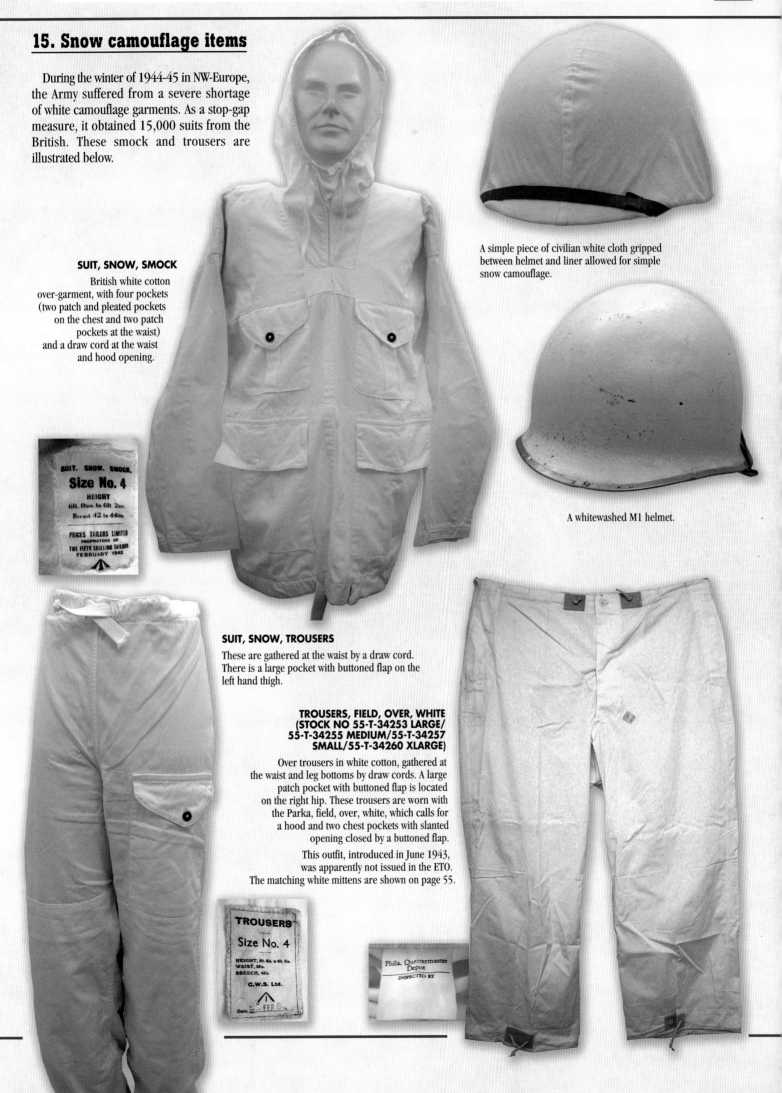

SUIT, SNOW, SMOCK

British white cotton over-garment, with four pockets (two patch and pleated pockets on the chest and two patch pockets at the waist) and a draw cord at the waist and hood opening.

A simple piece of civilian white cloth gripped between helmet and liner allowed for simple snow camouflage.

A whitewashed M1 helmet.

SUIT, SNOW, TROUSERS

These are gathered at the waist by a draw cord. There is a large pocket with buttoned flap on the left hand thigh.

TROUSERS, FIELD, OVER, WHITE (STOCK NO 55-T-34253 LARGE/ 55-T-34255 MEDIUM/55-T-34257 SMALL/55-T-34260 XLARGE)

Over trousers in white cotton, gathered at the waist and leg bottoms by draw cords. A large patch pocket with buttoned flap is located on the right hip. These trousers are worn with the Parka, field, over, white, which calls for a hood and two chest pockets with slanted opening closed by a buttoned flap.

This outfit, introduced in June 1943, was apparently not issued in the ETO. The matching white mittens are shown on page 55.

16. Misc. officers' clothing

JACKET, FLYING, TYPE A-2

A leather jacket adopted in 1931 for flying personnel, classified Limited standard in April 1943. It was sometimes worn by officers of other arm or services than the Air Force.

The A-2 jacket's tag is also a reminder that during WW2, the Air Forces were indeed still part of the U.S. Army. The label also indicates the garment's nomenclature, manufacturer and contract No.

OVERCOAT, FIELD, OFFICER'S

Belted coat made of two-ply water-resistant poplin material, with a button-in woolen liner.

During the summer of 1942, the QMC considered replacing the EM wool overcoat and raincoat (➡ pages 35, 45-46) with a similar coat but, due to the vast quantities of wool overcoats in stock, the new garment was standardized in December 1942 for officers only.

SHIRT, FLANNEL, OD, OFFICER'S

An olive drab flannel shirt for field wear, it has shoulder loops with cross stitching at the shoulder and a button near the collar.

'OVERCOAT, OFFICERS, USA, ETO' (BRITISH MADE)

Long officer's double breasted wool overcoat adopted in 1926: open notched collar, two vertical pocket openings at the waist, half-belt in the back with two buttons. This is the early-war coat prescribed with the service uniform (➡ pages 30-31), it was replaced by the Overcoat, short, M-1926, itself superseded by a newer M-1943 pattern. Illustrated here is a 1944 British-made garment.

Above.

OVERCOAT, SHORT, OFFICER'S, M-1926

This was initially an optional garment, which could be worn in formation only if all attending officers had the same coat. It had a shawl collar, two lower patch pockets, and an integral belt held by two large buttons.

OVERCOAT, SHORT, OFFICER'S, M-1943

A tailor-made version of the 1943 regulation coat, which provides for an open and notched collar and the deletion of the belt.

The tailor's label.

Another label, sewn in the right inside pocket, indicates that the coat has been ordered in November 1943 by one CT Heater.

17. Wool knit items

SWEATER, SLEEVELESS
(STOCK NO 55-S-64434/55-S-64450)

This knit sweater is adapted from a WW1 pattern and was worn during the whole of WW2.

SWEATER, HIGHNECK
(STOCK NO 55-S-64234/55-S-64252)

A new pattern of sweater developed together with the M-1943 outfit (➡ pages 38-39), based on the layering principle. The soldiers kept warm by wearing, under a cotton wind-resistant jacket, warm winter underwear, the flannel shirt, the sweater and Pile jacket (➡ page 39).

(Militaria Magazine)

18. Scarves

MUFFLER, WOOL-KNIT

A wool knit item in Olive drab. This one has been knit by a volunteer in an American Red Cross chapter.

Officer's muffler.

19. Trouser belts and suspenders

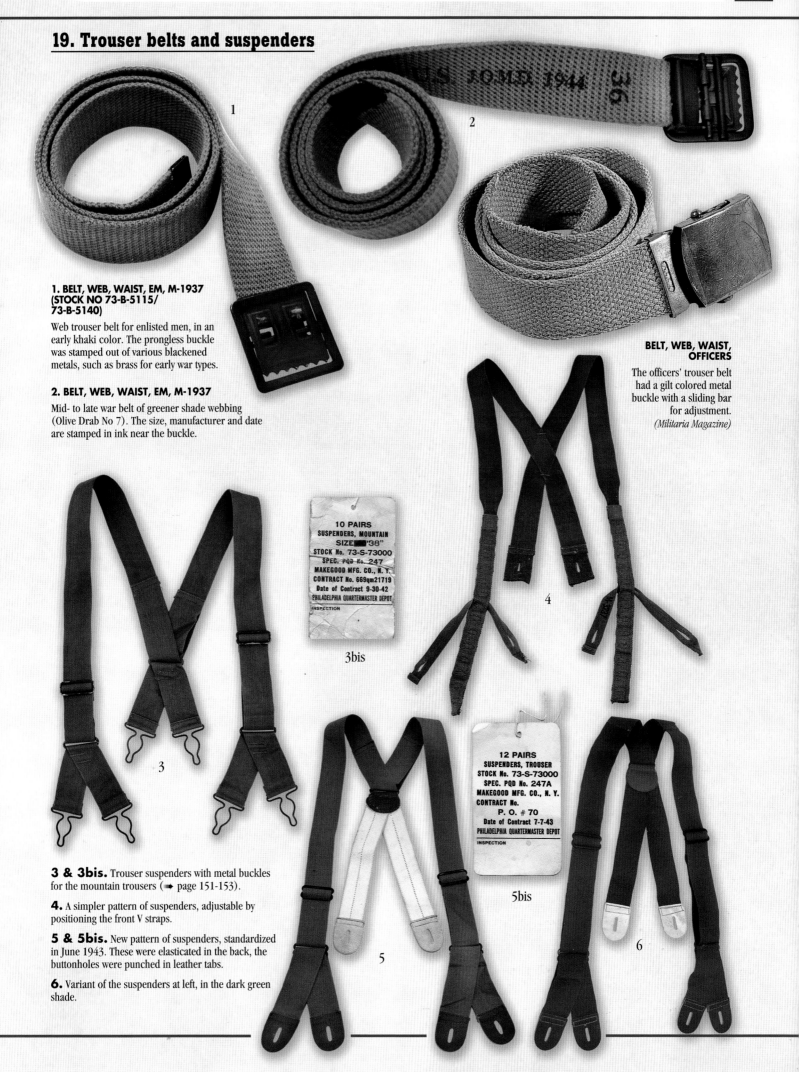

1. BELT, WEB, WAIST, EM, M-1937 (STOCK NO 73-B-5115/ 73-B-5140)

Web trouser belt for enlisted men, in an early khaki color. The prongless buckle was stamped out of various blackened metals, such as brass for early war types.

2. BELT, WEB, WAIST, EM, M-1937

Mid- to late war belt of greener shade webbing (Olive Drab No 7). The size, manufacturer and date are stamped in ink near the buckle.

BELT, WEB, WAIST, OFFICERS

The officers' trouser belt had a gilt colored metal buckle with a sliding bar for adjustment.
(Militaria Magazine)

**10 PAIRS
SUSPENDERS, MOUNTAIN
SIZE ██ "38"
STOCK No. 73-S-73000
SPEC. PQD No. 247
MAKEGOOD MFG. CO., N.Y.
CONTRACT No. 669qm21719
Date of Contract 9-30-42
PHILADELPHIA QUARTERMASTER DEPOT
INSPECTION**

3bis

4

**12 PAIRS
SUSPENDERS, TROUSER
STOCK No. 73-S-73000
SPEC. PQD No. 247A
MAKEGOOD MFG. CO., N.Y.
CONTRACT No.
P. O. # 70
Date of Contract 7-7-43
PHILADELPHIA QUARTERMASTER DEPOT
INSPECTION**

3

5bis

5

6

3 & 3bis. Trouser suspenders with metal buckles for the mountain trousers (➡ page 151-153).

4. A simpler pattern of suspenders, adjustable by positioning the front V straps.

5 & 5bis. New pattern of suspenders, standardized in June 1943. These were elasticated in the back, the buttonholes were punched in leather tabs.

6. Variant of the suspenders at left, in the dark green shade.

20. Gloves and mittens

GLOVES, WOOL, OD, LEATHER PALM (STOCK NO 73-G-43850/73-G-43885)

Standard issue winter gloves, not to be used as work gloves.

SIZE 9
CONT. NO.
W-H-G09-QM-35207
WING GLOVE CO.

GLOVES, LEATHER, HEAVY (STOCK NO 73-G-30500/ 73-G-30515)

Sturdy leather gloves for heavy construction and handling work. Available in two sizes. L5732 is the soldier's abbreviated serial number.

GAUNTLETS, BARBED-WIRE (STOCK NO 73-G-2050)

Work gloves with reinforced palm. Available in a single size, these were for handling barbed wire.

MITTENS, ASBESTOS, M-1942 (STOCK NO 37-M-394)

Mittens designed for protection when changing machine gun barrels. An extreme heat of 700° F can be withstood for about 15 seconds.

MITTENS, SHELL, TRIGGER FINGER
(STOCK NO 73-M-3610)

Poplin windproof mittens for mountain and cold climate operations, with a leather palm, worn over the wool mittens at right. The index finger is left free to activate the weapon's trigger. These were issued until stocks were exhausted, and superseded by the pattern shown below.

STOCK NO. 73-M-3620
5 Prs. Mittens, Shell, Trigger-finger, Type 1
Size Men's
Jos. N. Eisendrath Co.
July 10, 1943 - Cont. No. W 199 qm-34591
Q. M. C. Tent. Spec. C. Q. D. No. 105
Chicago Quartermaster Depot

Paper tag tied to a bundle of 5 pairs of Mitten shells made in July 1943.

MITTENS, INSERT, TRIGGER FINGER
(STOCK NO 73-M-2705/73-M-2720)

Wool mittens worn inside the mittens, shell.

Below.

MITTENS, SHELL, TRIGGER FINGER, TYPE 1 (STOCK NO 73-M-3620)

This shows a few differences in construction from the older model: the trigger finger is now located on the back of the hand and a strengthening piece of webbing tape has been added lengthwise inside the cuff.

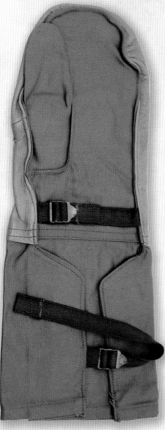

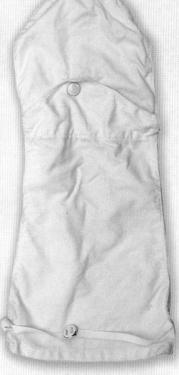

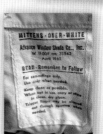

MITTENS, OVER, WHITE
(STOCK NO 73-M-3250)

Single size camouflage gloves slipped over other gloves or mittens.

21. Underwear

**DRAWERS, COTTON, SHORTS, WHITE
(STOCK NO 55-D-420/55-D-450)**

Issue drawers in the early white color, and
mother-of-pearl buttons.

**UNDERSHIRT, COTTON, SUMMER,
SLEEVELESS, OD
(STOCK NO 55-U-4830/55-U-4862)**

Cotton jersey vest, worn under the
flannel shirt.

**DRAWERS, COTTON, SHORTS, OD
(STOCK NO 55-D-400/55-D-415)**

Same pattern, in od cotton with green-
brown plastic buttons.

UNDERSHIRT, WINTER, 50-PC COTTON, 50-PC WOOL, WHITE (STOCK NO 55-U-7828/55-U-7862)

Wool and cotton blend long-sleeved undershirt, in the early unbleached white shade. The later issue was in Olive drab.

DRAWERS, COTTON, SPECIAL

Part of the anti-vesicant clothing, these long drawers feature a gas-proof gusset behind the back adjusting vent.

DRAWERS, WINTER, 50-PC COTTON, 50-PC WOOL, OD (STOCK NO 55-D-526/55-D-540)

Long johns in olive drab cotton and wool blend.

The size of the winter drawers is adjustable at the waist by a vent with a string and grommets.

22. Service shoes

SHOES, SERVICE, COMPOSITION SOLE (TYPE II)

The 1939 regulation shoe was made of chrome-tanned russet leather, with toe cap, leather sole and heel. In 1941, the QMC adopted a new nomenclature for footgear and the original shoe became the 'Shoe Service Type I.' A rubber heel was added in October 1940, together with a rubber tap shortly afterwards (Shoes Service, Type II, composition sole - as illustrated here).

SHOES, SERVICE (TYPE III)

Shoe made according to the Type II pattern but in flesh-out leather, with rubber heel and integral sole. Adopted in February 1943, this model also calls for a reinforcing rivet on each side, where the uppers and quarter merge, and for two rivets at the top of the back stay.

SHOES, SERVICE, REVERSE UPPER

June 1943 pattern: the boot shaft is slightly lower, the toe cap is deleted. The same year, cotton laces were replaced by more durable and rot-proof nylon laces.

1. The markings inked or embossed in the top of the shaft indicate the size and width, date of contract, etc. The Boston QM Depot was tasked with the development of all Army footwear.

BOOTS, SERVICE, COMBAT

A Service shoe fitted with an integral cuff, authorized in November 1943 to replace the shoe and leggings, as well as the parachute jumper boots (➡ page 139). Early 'Buckle boots' were made with 'Type III' service shoes then 'Shoes, Service, Reverse Upper'. The cuff, in tanned leather lined with OD or white canvas, is tightened on the leg by two straps and buckles. The integral sole, including the instep, is made of reclaimed black rubber.

2. The leather cuff bears the size and width of the shoe, embossed in the leather, as well as the other customary information in ink (maker, date and No of contract...).

23. Leggings and socks

LEGGINGS, CANVAS, M-1938, DISMOUNTED

Canvas leggings, in a light shade of Olive drab. These were issued in 4 sizes as of 1939, for field use with the Service shoe. The hooks and grommets were in brass at the beginning of the conflict, then in blackened metal.

LEGGINGS, CANVAS, M-1938, DISMOUNTED (STOCK NO 72-L-61883/72-L-61903)

1942-dated leggings in darker Olive drab, with blackened metal fittings.

LEGGINGS, CANVAS, M-1938, DISMOUNTED, OD NO 7 (STOCK NO 72-L-61920-72/L-61929)

Late-war (November 1944) leggings in green canvas, they are also shorter by 3 inches.

SOCKS, WOOL, SKI

Thick unbleached wool socks worn over the cushion sole socks or other socks. Originally developed for mountain troops, they were widely issued during the winter of 1944-45 for wear with cold climate footwear such as the Shoe pacs (➡ page 60-61).

SOCKS, WOOL, CUSHION SOLE, OD

Wool (65%) and cotton (35%) socks of a new pattern introduced in 1943 for wear with the Service shoe. They have been made more resistant and comfortable by reinforcing the sole, from heel to toe, with a soft 'lock' weave.

24. Cold climate footwear

BOOTS, BLUCHER, HIGH TOP
(STOCK NO 72-B-128-8/72-B-133-18)

High boots in greased leather, smooth leather sole, laced through eyelets on the uppers and hooks on the shaft. These were at first authorized for Alaskan stations, then issued to troops operating in the Aleutians in 1943, but proved inadequate. However, due to the shortage of cold weather footgear in NW Europe at the beginning of 1945, Blucher boots were issued in some quantity at this time.

OVERSHOES, ARCTIC, ALL RUBBER
(STOCK No 72-O-398/72-O-422)

Prewar model fully made of rubber. The overshoes are closed by four spring-loaded hooks and flat buckles. Owing to the rubber crisis, they were not made after 1940. Worn in mud and snow over the Service shoe and leggings, these were not advisable for sustained marching.

OVERSHOES, ARCTIC, CLOTH TOP
(STOCK NO 72-O-275/72-O-295)

Second pattern overshoes, with rubber enclosing sole and water resistant canvas top. Owing to difficulties in the mass-production of the new Shoe pacs (➡ page 61), overshoes were issued as a substitute until the end of the war.

United States Rubber Products, Inc.
All Rubber 4 Bkle. Overshoe
Contract W155 QMECW 163
Dated July 5, 1935
Stock No. 72-O-402
Spec. tentative July 6, '34 Class B
SIZE 6
BOSTON Q. M. DEPOT

Label glued inside the early rubber overshoes.

**SHOE PAC, HIGH (16 INCHES)
(STOCK NO 72-S-8400/72-S-8420)**

High boots with greased leather top and rubber enclosing sole and uppers. Three models, according to their height, were issued early in the war. They were worn over several pairs of thick wool socks. The removable and insulating insole was made of wool felt, or wool and bovine hair. The shoe pacs were suitable for marching in snow and mud.

**SHOE PAC, 12-INCH, M-1944
(STOCK NO 72-S-8790/72-S-8824)**

New model of shoe pac adopted in 1944. The top was made of two pieces of leather sewn together, a steel shank was added under the sole for arch support. A wide rib at the top of the heel helped secure the several patterns of snow shoes (➡ page 155).

Removable insulating wool and bovine hair insoled issues with every pair of shoe pacs.

10 NARROW

GOODYEAR RUBBER CO.
CONT. W-19-07-QM-1890
MAY 24 1944 N SIZE
BOSTON CH DEPOT 10

Markings inked on the inside top of the boot shaft: this pair was made by the Goodyear Rubber Co. according to a 24 May 1944 contract. The size is a 10 N (for Narrow).

SHOE PACS

YOUR FEET
CAN BE
COMFORTABLE
IN
ARCTIC
COLD

READ CAREFULLY

This instruction leaflet was handed out with every new pair of Shoe pacs.

SHOE PACS

WHEN WORN

SHOE PACS are used in cool, wet-cold, or snowy climate.

HOW WORN

Wear with TWO pairs of socks, wool, ski and ONE pair of insoles, felt. Wear the SMALLER of the two sizes of socks next to the foot and the LARGER size over it. EXAMPLE: Size 11 sock is worn next to the foot and size 12 is worn over it. When pulling on the SECOND sock take care to prevent the FIRST sock from pulling too tight over the toes of the foot.
Two sets of socks are provided.

GRADE FOR FITTING

SHOE PACS are supplied in WHOLE (not half sizes) and in THREE WIDTHS, narrow (N), medium (M), and wide (W). Narrow corresponds to A, B, and C service shoe widths, medium to D and E and wide to EE and wider. WHOLE sizes will fit same WHOLE sizes as service shoes. For all half sizes with next HIGHER WHOLE SIZE.
EXAMPLE: Size 9 medium SHOE PAC will fit 8-1/2O service shoe size; The fit should be SNUG but never TIGHT.

CARE OF SOCKS AND SHOE PACS

Keep socks and inside of SHOE PAC DRY. Otherwise, there is danger of frozen feet or trench foot. Wear the two sets of the ski socks on alternate days, always giving one set a chance to dry out. Do not dry SHOE PACS near an open fire. Do not place them ON or TOO close to radiator or steam pipe. Apply dubbing once per week to the leather tops without getting it on RUBBER BOTTOM.

25. Headgear

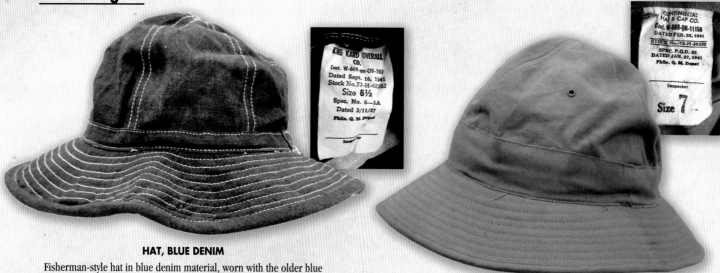

HAT, BLUE DENIM

Fisherman-style hat in blue denim material, worn with the older blue denim dungarees. Replaced in 1941 by the light green HBT hat introduced with the new fatigue dress.

HAT, FIELD, COTTON, KHAKI
(STOCK NO 73-H-38300/73-H-38334)

This hat was authorized in January 1941 to be worn with field dress instead of the garrison cap. It was issued first during the Summer of 1941 pending the delivery of the new HBT fatigue/training outfit. Its manufacture ceased in July 1941.

HAT, HERRINGBONE TWILL
(STOCK NO 73-H-42308/73-H-42340)

New fatigue hat introduced in January 1941 with the two-piece light green HBT fatigues (⟹ page 40). According to regulations, it was worn with the brim turned down. The hat was issued to all personnel except Armored troops and motor mechanics, who had a specific cap (⟹ page 128). It became limited standard in July 1943.

CAP, WOOL, KNIT, M-1941
(STOCK NO 73-C-64660/73-C-64680)

Olive drab cap, standardized in February 1942 for wear in cold weather under the steel helmet (⟹ page 64). Nicknamed 'Beanie', it has a short stiff brim and a turn-down to cover the ears. It was gradually superseded by the Cotton Field Cap of 1943.

CAP, FIELD, COTTON, OD, WITH VISOR
(STOCK NO 73-C-16010/73-C-16035)

Poplin shell cap, with an internal flannel-lined curtain that could unfold over the ears and nape. Authorized in August 1943, it was tested among other components of the new M-1943 outfit. It was also meant to replace various caps (Cap wool knit, Cap ski, Helmet combat winter, pages 129 & 152). This early-manufacture cap (6 June 1944 Purchase order) has two ventilation grommets on the side, the instruction label is sewn inside the crown piece.

Instruction label of the Cotton field cap.

CAP, FIELD, COTTON, OD, WITH VISOR

Late-war manufacture cap (7 February 1945 Purchase order): the side grommets have been deleted ; the instructions are now ironed-on in black.

HAT, RAIN
(STOCK NO 73-H-55010/73-H-55025)

Rainproof hat in oil-treated cloth, issued with the early war rain jacket and trousers. The ear flaps are lined in white felt, the chin straps button under the chin.

CAP, WINTER, OD

A World War One pattern hat, in cotton duck lined with wool material, mostly seen on service troops. Slightly modified before the war, this was issued until 1943 and replaced by the Pile field cap.

Thanks to its deep ear flaps that cover the ears and neck, the Pile field cap was much valued in winter, and by vehicle drivers. It could also be worn under the steel helmet.

CAP, FIELD, PILE, OD
(STOCK NO 73-C-16350/73-C-16375)

A cold climate cap in windproof and rainproof poplin, lined with wool material. The turned-up visor and ear flaps are covered with artificial fur ('Pile'). This was adopted in August 1943 with the new M-1943 combat uniform. It replaced the Winter cap, Lambskin-lined cap, Fur cap, Wool knit toque and Cloth hood (➡ page 47).

The hood's instruction label.

HOOD, JACKET, FIELD, M-1943

A hood in cotton sateen made according to Spec. No 44A of June 2 1944. Available in three sizes (S, M and L), it was held onto the shoulder loop buttons of the M-1943 Field Jacket (➡ pages 38-39). Usually worn under the steel helmet, it could also be buttoned on the officers' field overcoat (➡ page 50).

26. Steel helmets

The new liner introduced in 1936 for the M-1917A1 steel helmet.

STEEL HELMET, M-1917A1

A British WW1 pattern adopted in 1917 by the U.S. Army. The helmet was upgraded in 1936 with a new leather liner, and a buckled webbing chinstrap. It was replaced by the M1 helmet.

HELMET, STEEL, M1

Steel helmet with movable chinstrap loops, an improvement implemented as of October 1943.

First type chinstrap loops.

Close-up on the movable chinstrap loop. The hinge is welded in three spots.

HELMET, STEEL, M1

Adopted in June 1941. The steel shell is painted in a rough Olive drab finish. The anti-magnetic stainless steel rim was introduced in December 1942. The rim was welded at the front of the visor. After 1944, it became optional for manufacturers to weld the rim at the back of the helmet but it appears that most helmets worn in the ETO are the front-welded rim type. The two-part chinstrap is tacked on welded loops. These loops were however prone to breaking and were replaced by movable loops in welded hinges, welded with two then later three spots. The steel shell was worn over the liner shown on opposite page.

Steel helmet with the horizontal white bar in the back, an ETO marking to distinguish NCOs.

M1 steel helmet with welded-on rank insignia for a Major.

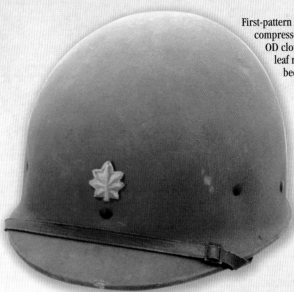

First-pattern helmet liner, in compressed fiber covered in OD cloth. A Major's oak leaf rank insignia has been painted on.

LINER, HELMET M1, NEW TYPE

Second pattern (1943) helmet liner, in compressed canvas impregnated with synthetic resins. It is only painted OD on the outside.

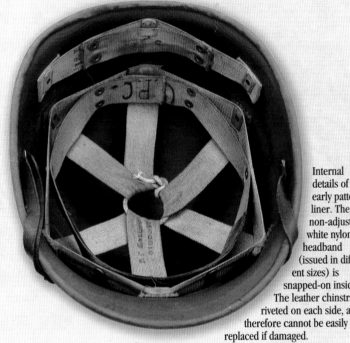

Internal details of the early pattern liner. The non-adjustable white nylon headband (issued in different sizes) is snapped-on inside. The leather chinstrap is riveted on each side, and therefore cannot be easily replaced if damaged.

Inner details of the second pattern liner. The leather chinstrap is replaceable, the headband is lined with leather and adjustable thanks to a buckle at the back. It is held on the liner suspension by six flat metal clips.

The vertical white bar on the back of this helmet liner identifies an officer.

This helmet liner bears the markings for an NCO in the 1262nd Engineer Combat Battalion. Belonging to the 1st (US) Army, this battalion started operating in France in January 1945.

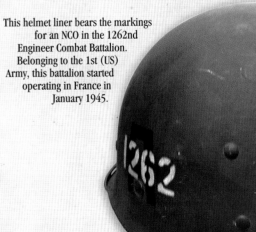

Steel helmet nets

A British type fine-mesh net, gathered closely on the helmet shell thanks to a lace knotted at its base.

A wide-mesh net, cut from a larger vehicle camouflage net.

Instruction label for the 1943 helmet net with band.

NET, HELMET, with BAND

USES:— 1. To break up the helmet silhouette.
2. To secure camouflage foliage to helmet.
3. To prevent glare.

ADJUSTMENTS FOR VARIOUS USES:

1. Without foliage:
To put on helmet net, place net on ground with rubber band on its upper side. Place helmet, without its liner, upside down on top of net, with back of helmet close to the connection of band to net. Slip band around outside of helmet brim. Fold front edges (see Fig. 1) or all edges (see Fig. 2) of net inside helmet brim, with helmet chin-strap going into the two slots cut in opposite sides of net. Put in liner helmet to grip net between helmet and liner.

Elastic band under net.

Connection of band to net in rear.

If desired to break up distinctive outline of head and neck, allow net in rear of chin-strap to hang loosely.

OVER

FIG. 1

NET, HELMET, WITH BAND

Standard issue net, which appeared together with the new M-1943 combat uniform. The loose ends are gripped between the helmet shell and liner. The integral neoprene elastic band was for attaching foliage.

2. With foliage:
To secure camouflage foliage most easily, place band outside helmet and over net. Select foliage of type around you. Place leaves with their top sides outward. Avoid using big, shiny leaves.

Connection of band to net in rear.

Avoid wearing too much camouflage foliage at a time on helmet.

FIG. 2

3. To aid concealment of head silhouette and face while observing helmet may be turned so that loose net, usually hanging in rear of helmet, covers face.

FIG. 3

OVER

27. Eyeshields and goggles

EYESHIELD, M1 (AIR SPRAY)

Expendable acetate eyeshields against sprayed vesicant gases, and usually kept within the gas mask bag (➡ page 216-221). These were however often used against the wind and dust. Four unfolded eyeshields were stored flat in a thick paper case, two being of the clear type, and two being tinted dark green.

STOCK NO.
74-G-76-38

Type II, Goggle, M-1943, Complete, with non-polarizing Celluloss Acetate lenses with green tint color, to be used for protection against dust, wind, excessive light and glare.

To clean the lens use a clean, soft cloth and clean gently to avoid scratching the surface. Clean goggle regularly to avoid an accumulation of dust and dirt throughout goggle.

GOGGLES M-1943 (GREEN TINT)

Green tinted goggles against the glare, issued in a plain paper case with Stock No (74-G-76-38) and instructions. A third pattern, with red-tinged lenses (Stock No 74-G-76-45) was given to machine gunners in order to follow the trajectory of tracer bullets.

GOGGLES M-1943 (STOCK NO 74-G-76)

Goggles worn to protect the eyes from the wind and dust, with clear acetate lenses. The marking 'US 1943' is inked on the inside of the leather 'frame'. Case is in green imitation leather.

GOGGLES, POLAROID, ALL PURPOSE, TYPE 1021

Foam-rubber frame with clear plastic shield introduced in 1942. The imitation leather case holds a spare shield in thick green tinted acetate.

GOGGLES, VARIABLE DENSITY

Goggles for ground forces anti-aircraft gunners, made by Polaroid. The front knob adjusts the filtration lenses' density according to ambient light, and allows for aiming at aircraft coming in from the sun. The metal storage box also contains an instruction sheet for field repairs.

GOGGLES, M-1944 (STOCK NO 74-G-77)

Black rubber moulded mask with set-in replaceable wide shield, offering enhanced vision compared to the Type 1021 goggles. Stored in a stout cardboard box with metal reinforced angles.

Note. The M-1943, Polaroid and M-1944 goggles were issued to most combat arms and certain personnel (drivers, etc), as well to armored and motorized troops (➡ page 126)

1. Suspenders

SUSPENDERS, BELT, M-1936

Webbing suspenders with adjustable straps and hooks. These were used to support the pistol or cartridge belts, and for carrying the M-1936 canvas field bag (➡ page 70) on the back.

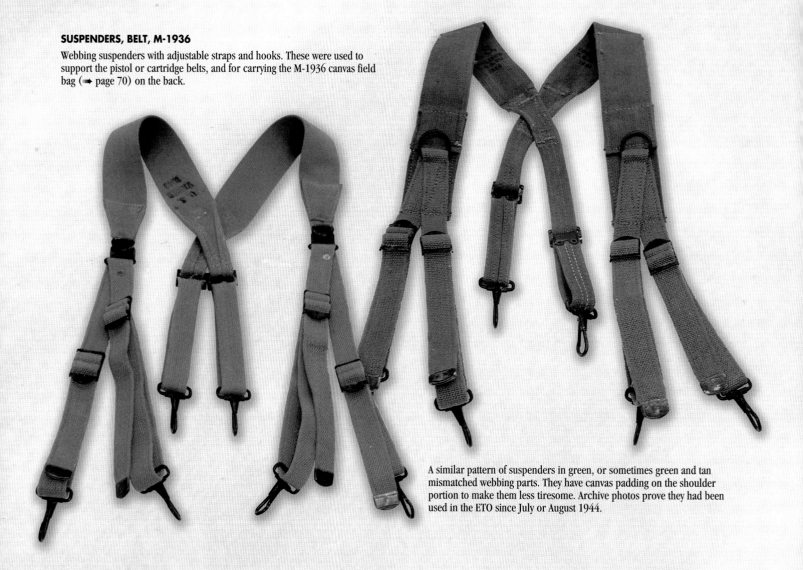

A similar pattern of suspenders in green, or sometimes green and tan mismatched webbing parts. They have canvas padding on the shoulder portion to make them less tiresome. Archive photos prove they had been used in the ETO since July or August 1944.

2. Pistol belts

BELT, PISTOL OR REVOLVER, M-1936

Webbing belt issued, among others, to all personnel armed with handguns, carbines and submachine guns, as well as to medics. This tan colored belt, dated 1942, has blackened brass fittings. The top row of grommets is for the suspenders' hooks, the bottom row for securing various items of equipment thanks to special bent wire hooks.

Rear view of a pistol belt, exposing its markings, and the length adjusting system (right).

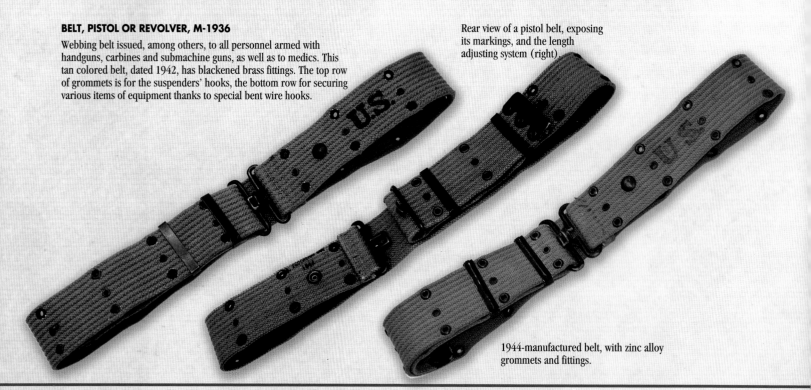

1944-manufactured belt, with zinc alloy grommets and fittings.

3. Haversacks and field bags

A. The M-1928 Haversack

This was the standard haversack for dismounted troops throughout the war. Made of canvas, it could be used as a light assault pack, or as a complete field pack when the lower part (Pack carrier) was added.

1. HAVERSACK, M-1928

The pouch on top of the main flap held the meat can and cutlery. The intrenching tool was hooked under this, on a two-grommeted tab. The bayonet was carried in the same fashion on the left side of the haversack. This particular haversack has been made by Boyt in 1942.

2. The haversack viewed from the back, showing the main straps and the two shorter straps in the back, all hooked to the belt. The M1910 haversack had only one such strap in the back.

3. The main compartment is closed by a lower flap and horizontal straps, the top flap with the meat can pouch would then be pulled down and tied with the vertical strap at bottom. The haversack normally contained 6 C-ration cans and the toilet set. The raincoat was folded under the flap.

4. HAVERSACK, M-1928 (BRITISH MADE)

1944-manufactured haversack, in a greener shade and with British style buckles and hooks. Local production of US military equipment allowed Britain to pay back part of its lend-lease debt during the war. It also saved on shipping space from the States and sometimes helped to alleviate production backlogs of some American companies.

5. CARRIER, PACK, M-1928

Strapped to the bottom edge of the haversack, the pack carrier held the 'blanket roll': blanket, spare underwear, tent pole, pins and cord, neatly rolled inside the shelter half. (➡ page 110)

B. The M-1936 Field bag

BAG, CANVAS, FIELD, OD, M-1936

Field bag issued in lieu of the haversack to officers and other personnel such as airborne troopers and armored crews. It was carried on the back with the M-1936 suspenders (➡ page 68), or slung on the side with its special strap (Strap, carrying, od, Bag, canvas, field, see opposite page). This light olive drab example is 1942-dated.

There is a small pocket on one side of the bag, closed by a metal tack-on button.

MYRNA SHOE INC.
1943

Variation in thick water-resistant treated material. Manufacturer and date are mentioned under the flap.

C. Ammunition bags

BAG, CARRYING, AMMUNITION, M1

Canvas bag for carrying all sorts of ammunition: boxed ammo for machine guns, rifle clips, carbine magazines, and especially hand and rifle grenades. Shown here is a 1943-vintage bag with its carrying strap.

STRAPS, CARRYING

Left: Strap, carrying, od, Bag, canvas, field. Strap provided with the M-1936 Field bag, it could also be used together with the Ammunition bag. Replaced by the General purpose strap.
Below: Strap, carrying, general purpose. It could be hooked on a variety of bags: M-1936 field bag, Ammunition bag, M-1938 dispatch case (➡ page 87). The dark green strap illustrated is dated 1944.

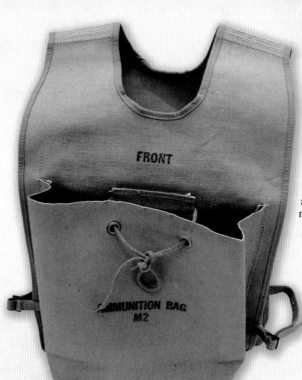

BAG, AMMUNITION M2

A large canvas vest given to ammunition carriers of crew-served weapons. Its large front and back pockets held various loads, such as boxed MG ammo, bazooka rockets or mortar shells. Manufactured in tan or green canvas, this item does not bear any marking of date or manufacturer.

British-made Ammunition bag M1 and strap, both dated 1944.

D. The M-1943 Pack

Tested as a replacement for the M-1928 haversack, it was in fact a variation of the 1942 Jungle pack, which was made of camouflaged canvas. The pack shown here is the final version, slightly roomier, in green material. It was issued in some quantity in Europe in 1944, and was finally superseded by the two-part combat pack of late 1944.

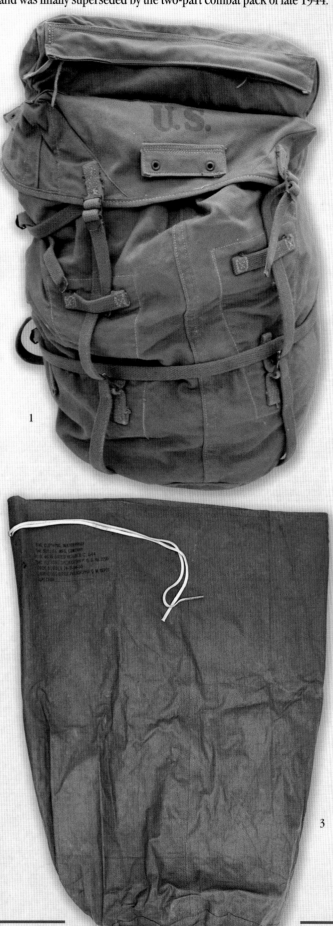

1. Front view of a 1944-dated jungle pack, showing the various straps and buckles for adjusting the inner capacity, as well as attaching a blanket, poncho or raincoat. The pouch with a zippered opening on the top flap held the meat can or a first-aid kit. The grommeted tab on the flap was for the entrenching tool carrier. The was another on the right side for a bayonet or machete.

2. This back view shows the suspenders that hook onto the front of the belt, and the shorter straps for fastening in the back, as with the M-1928 Haversack.

3. BAG, CLOTHING, WATERPROOF

Bag issued with the Jungle and M-1943 packs to protect some of their contents (in amphibious assaults for instance). This bag could be used with the Barrack and Duffel bags (➡ page 115) as well.

BAG, CLOTHING, WATERPROOF
THE SUNLITE MFG. COMPANY
P. O. 4600 DATED OCTOBER 17, 1944
QMC TENTATIVE SPECIFICATION P. Q. D. No. 229D
STOCK NUMBER 74-B-54-50
CONTRACTING OFFICE PHILADELPHIA Q. M. DEPOT
INSPECTOR

E. The Pack, field, combat

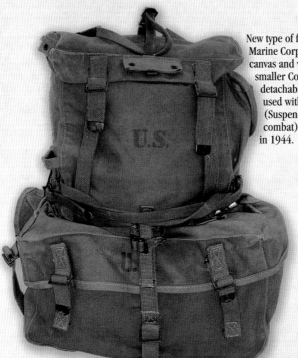

New type of field pack inspired by the Marine Corps 1941 pack. Made of green canvas and webbing, it is in two parts: the smaller Combat pack, and the detachable Cargo pack. The pack was used with special suspenders (Suspenders, Pack, field, cargo and combat) which were also authorized in 1944.

The complete M-1944 Field pack, fitted on its special suspenders. These three items are dated 1944.

PACK, FIELD, COMBAT

Two grommeted tabs are sewn to the top flap: one on the front for the entrenching tool, and another on the right side for the bayonet. The Blanket roll (blanket rolled into the shelter half) could be tied horseshoe-fashion on the pack thanks to 3 straps and buckles, on the flap top and both sides of the pack. The combat pack, which has a waterproof 'throat' above its opening, held basic personal items such as rations, meat can and cutlery, spare underwear and toilet articles.

PACK, FIELD, CARGO

This is held under the combat pack by four quick-release tabs and buckles. On the later and almost identical M-1945 Pack, the cargo pack was held by regular straps and buckles. The cargo pack has a carrying handle on top and was usually kept with unit baggage. It contained non-essential items such as spare shoes, trousers, shirts and underwear.

SUSPENDERS, PACK, FIELD AND COMBAT

These were issued with the M-1944 pack, used much in the same way as the previous M-1936 suspenders with the Field bag.

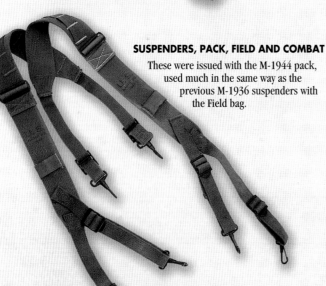

Instruction sheet handed out with the M-1944 combat pack.

F. Waterproof bags

These rubberized bags were used to protect signal and other equipment against water during amphibious operations. There were five types according to their capacity.

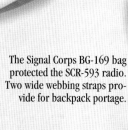

BAG, WATERPROOF, SPECIAL PURPOSE

Small capacity bag, dated 1944. It was slung on the side with its adjustable webbing strap.

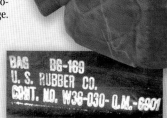

The Signal Corps BG-169 bag protected the SCR-593 radio. Two wide webbing straps provide for backpack portage.

The BG-159 bag was used for carrying the BD-71 telephone switchboard.

An extract from the QM 3-4 Catalog showing the 5 different types of rubberized bags.

G. Packboards

THE YUKON PACKBOARD

An early-war design taken after a local Alaskan pack. A wooden and canvas frame supports heavy loads lashed on with cord strung on the side hooks. It was used mainly in steep, difficult terrain to resupply front line troops. The various loads could be radios, heavy weapons, ration and ammo boxes, water and gasoline cans, telephone wire reels, etc.

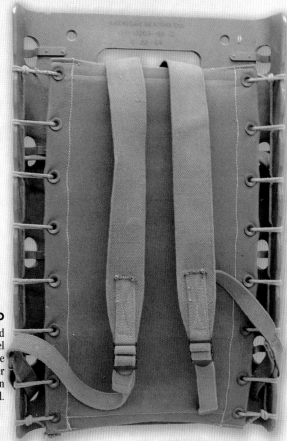

PACKBOARD, PLYWOOD

Second type packboard in shaped plywood ; a wide canvas panel laced on the sides cushions the back. Introduced as a simpler alternative to the Yukon packboard.

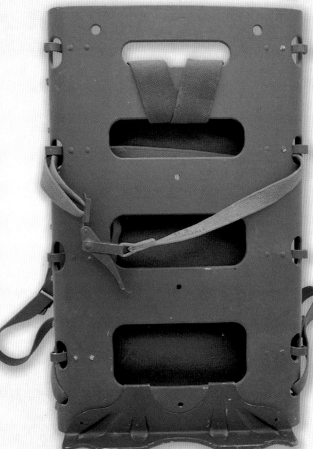

A light metal 'Attachment, packboard, plywood, cargo' could be hung on three alternate positions on the back of the packboard, in order to place the load as high on the shoulders as possible. One or more 'Strap, quick-release, packboard, Type 1' secure the load.

These shoulder pads could be slipped on the suspenders of the various packs to render portage less tiresome.

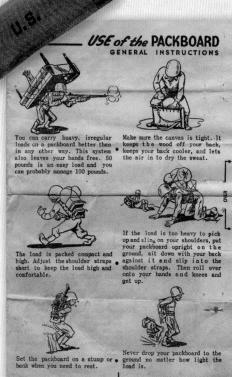

Comic-style instructions sheet for the Packboard, plywood.

3-INDIVIDUAL EQUIPMENT

4. Canteens, canteen cups and canteen covers

1. CANTEEN, M-1910

Model of 1910, 1942-dated canteen, with aluminium body and cap. The canteen fits into the cup (opposite page), whose handle is folded underneath, and carried in its cover (➡ pages 78-79).
(Photo Militaria Magazine, Coleman collection)

2. CANTEEN, M-1942

Canteen in enameled metal made in two parts, with a horizontal solder seam. The plastic cap is the first type, serrated from top to bottom (the second type has a strengthening rim at the bottom). This kind of canteen was only made in 1942 to save on aluminium. There is also a variation with a vertical solder seam.

3. Manufacturer markings on the base of three M-1942 enameled canteens.

4. CANTEEN, PLASTIC

Metal saving canteen in an orange-tinged translucent plastic (Ethocel). These were made in 1943-44, by the injection molding process. Third type cap.

5. The date and manufacturer's name are molded on the base of the plastic canteen.

6. CANTEEN, STAINLESS STEEL

New pattern of canteen standardized in 1943. This 1943-vintage example is fitted with a first type cap.

7. CANTEEN, STAINLESS STEEL

Another canteen, made in 1944 and with a 3rd type plastic cap, the top being recessed to protect the chain rivet.

8. CANTEEN M-1910

Aluminium canteen made after 1943 and the end of the critical metals shortages. This 1944-dated example has a 3rd type cap.

9. CANTEEN M-1910

Canteen in a bright aluminium alloy. A production variant with a horizontal solder seam, dated 1945.

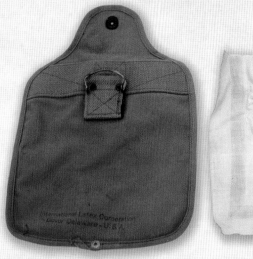
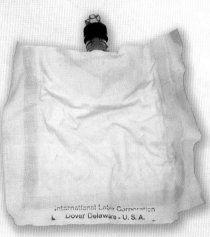

CANTEEN, COLLAPSIBLE, TWO-QUART

An experimental soft plastic canteen, tested with the new M-1943 outfit. It is shown here with the instructions label and a detachable hook to allow for positioning on a belt or pack. These canteens, made only by the International Latex Corporation (➡ page 112), are undated.

The collapsible canteen calls for a removable inner plastic bladder fitted with a hard plastic spout and stopper. The carrier is made of OD canvas. The special wire buckle on the back engaged on the detachable hook shown at left, which itself was affixed to the belt. This quick-release device proved unsatisfactory as the cover would often slip from the hook and become lost. An improved cover was designed with a permanently fixed hook. The final pattern of collapsible canteen was introduced in 1945, with a long carrying strap.

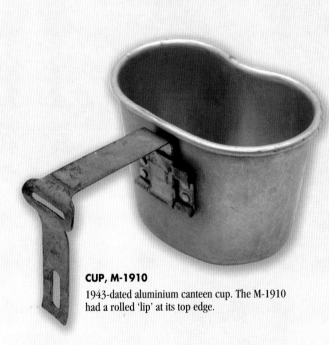
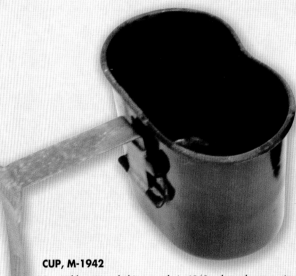

CUP, M-1942

Cup in blue enameled iron made in 1942 only, at the same time as the enameled canteen. As of 1943, iron cups were zinc or tin coated.

CUP, M-1910

1943-dated aluminium canteen cup. The M-1910 had a rolled 'lip' at its top edge.

Example of markings, stamped on the cup's folding handle.

CUP, STAINLESS STEEL

1944-dated cup, with sharp lip.

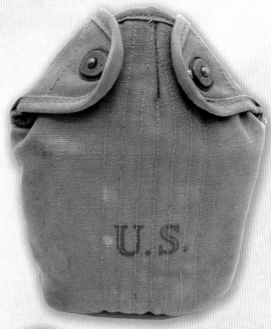

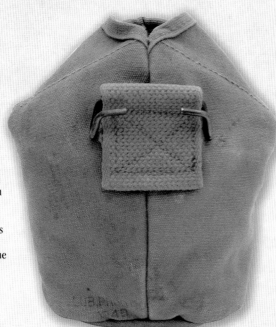

COVER, CANTEEN, DISMOUNTED, M-1910

An early canteen cover made in 1940, with a brass hook. This pattern, with a distinctive assembly seam in the back, was produced until 1942. Canteen covers were lined with gray-blue wool scraps for insulation.

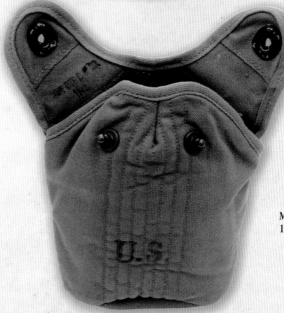

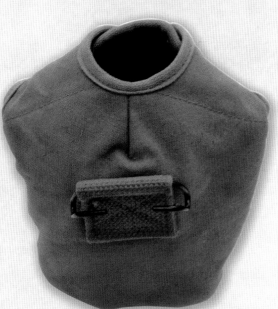

M-1910 canteen cover made in 1942, with the new side seam.

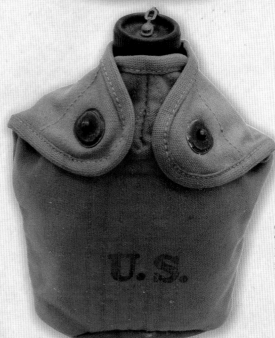

Cover manufactured in 1945. The web loop that secures the hook is reinforced with a wide rectangular tab.

COVER, CANTEEN, MOUNTED, M-1941

Cover for horsed troops, fitted with an adjustable strap that hooked on one of the saddle bags. This cover was sometimes used by paratroopers as it made the canteen attachment more secure.

COVER, CANTEEN, MOUNTED, M-1941 (BRITISH MADE)

This British-manufacture can be told by its four seams on the front (instead of seven). The extension strap ends with a quick release tab and buckle.

COVER, CANTEEN, MOUNTED, M-1917

Older pattern cover, but made in Britain in 1944. It has a similar quick-release arrangement as the cover depicted above right.

Cavalry extension strap fitted with a larger snap hook.

5. First-aid packets and pouches

The first-aid packet provided to American soldiers in World War Two had been developed during the twenties by the Medical Department Equipment Laboratory, at Carlisle Barracks (Penn.), and was thus designated 'First-aid packet, US Government Carlisle model.' During the fall of 1941, it was decided to add a small paper packet of sulfanilamide crystals inside the metal box containing the bandage. During the war, only the outer packaging was modified.

1. FIRST-AID PACKET, CARLISLE MODEL

Brass stamped box, in two parts, painted OD and closed by a metal strip crimped on the side. This packet, pre-dating the fall of 1941, does not have the sulfanilamide packet. The white linen bandage is wrapped in oiled paper.

2. In order to save on precious brass, the box was stamped out of tin as soon as the end of 1941. The enclosed sulfanilamide packet is indicated on the bottom of the box.

3. Contents of the first-aid packet

Instructions are inked in red on the white linen bandage. The gas proof box is made of tin. The opening strip is at top left. The red and white paper packet contained sulfanilamide crystals which were sprinkled on the wound.

4. After it was decided to add the sulfanilamide, the remaining stock of packets including the crystals, while not bearing this information on the bottom, were painted in bright red.

5. Variation packet enclosed in a green plastic box, with brass tear-to-open strip. Using plastic saved on

tin, which was needed for canned foodstuffs and lubricant containers.

6. As a further measure to conserve strategic metals, a new waxed cardboard outer box was introduced in 1943. The bandage was protected against moisture, dirt and war gases inside a laminated tin foil and paper wrapping

7. A new bandage in a brownish color replaced the previous white linen bandage. It was kept inside the same laminated wrapping, and then further protected by a two-piece waxed cardboard box.

A first-aid pouch was issued to every soldier, it was officially hooked on the right rear side of the belt. The pouch held the first-aid packet and wound tablets (➡ page 227)

POUCH, FIRST-AID PACKET, M-1910

Older pattern pouch in OD canvas, with two 'Durable' type snaps. It was used during WW1 and still manufactured by the Jeffersonville QM Depot (JQMD) in 1942.

(Right hand side photo by Militaria Magazine, Coleman collection)

POUCH, FIRST-AID PACKET, M-1924

New webbing pouch introduced to accommodate the Carlisle model packet. It is closed by a single 'Lift-the-dot' snap fastener.

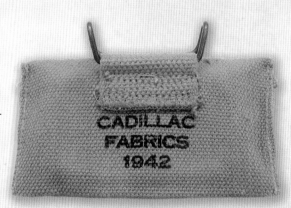

POUCH, FIRST-AID PACKET, M-1924

A pouch also manufactured in 1942 by the Jeffersonville QM Depot. It has a deeper and pointed flap. The red inked letters CS stand for 'Combat Serviceable': this piece of equipment is satisfactory for issue, even if slightly used.

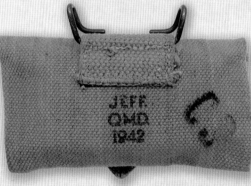

POUCH, FIRST-AID PACKET, M-1942

New pouch adopted to accommodate the larger cardboard box packet and the sulfadiazine pills.

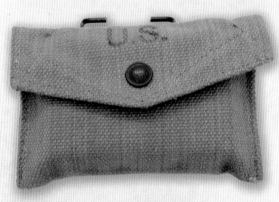

POUCH, FIRST-AID PACKET, M-1942 (BRITISH MADE)

The webbing and snap fastener are distinctively British, as well as the markings under the flap.

6. Tools

CARRIER, SHOVEL, INTRENCHING, M-1910

1943-made carrier, with khaki body and green trim.

SHOVEL, INTRENCHING, M-1910

Same pattern as used during the Great War, with 'T' shaped handle. Markings are stamped onto the wood handle and the metal socket that connects the head to the handle.

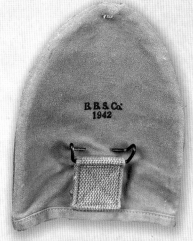

CARRIER, SHOVEL, INTRENCHING, RUCKSACK

A variant where the double hook has been set further down. When carried on a rucksack or pack, the shovel handle would not protrude under its base.

(Photograph by Martin Brayley)

CARRIER, SHOVEL, INTRENCHING, M-1943

Early pattern of carrier, the double hook is fixed.

SHOVEL, INTRENCHING, M-1943

New pattern folding shovel. The manufacturer's markings (here *Ames 1944*) are stamped on the underside of the helve, near the screw collar.

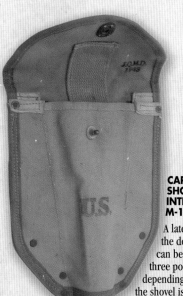

CARRIER, SHOVEL, INTRENCHING, M-1943

A later variation, the double hook can be placed in three positions, depending on whether the shovel is worn on the belt or on a pack.

1. PICK-MATTOCK, INTRENCHING, M-1910 AND CARRIER
Both tool and carrier are dated 1943. The pick is carried dismantled in two parts.

2. AXE, INTRENCHING, M-1910 AND CARRIER
Both are dated 1942. The carrier has the double hook on the back.

3. MACHETE, 18″ BLADE, M-1942
The sheath is in webbing, reinforced with rivets and a metal throat.
Suspension hook is missing here.

4. WIRE CUTTERS, M-1938
Both tool and carrier are dated 1942.

5. A variation of wire-cutters with strengthened head. Carrier is closed by a flap.

6. British-made variation carrier, 1944 dated.

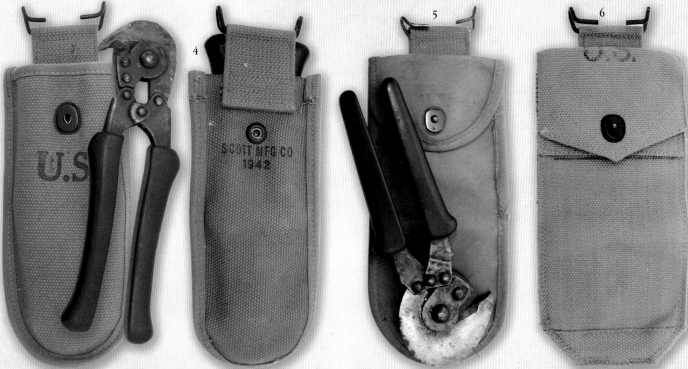

7. Fighting knives

KNIFE, TRENCH, M-1918 (TRENCH KNIFE MK I)

A trench knife with 'knuckles' cast handle and double-sided blade. The scabbard is made of two crimped stamped metal halves, copper coated and painted black. It has two riveted wire hooks for the belt on its back, the markings are LF & C 1918. The original trench-duster knife was apparently a French-made design for the AEF (hallmarked 'Au Lion'), and the American-manufactured knife illustrated here was probably not delivered before the armistice. It was however used during the Second World war and issued preferably to shock troops, until superseded by the M3 trench knife in 1943, when it was declared Substitute standard.

KNIFE, BOLO, M-1917

This could be used as a short machete or in close combat. Its wide tapered blade, in blued steel, bears the manufacturer's marking: *Plumb St Louis 1918*. The M-1917 wood scabbard is covered with a canvas and leather sheath, marked on its tip: *Brauer Bros 1917*.

KNIFE, COMMANDO, CATTARAUGUS 225Q

This knife has a 6" Bowie-style blade and a tempered steel pommel. The grip is fashioned out of leather washers. Made by the Cattaraugus Cutlery Company, this is one of many civilian hunting knives donated to the Army or bought by soldiers prior to the adoption of the M3 trench knife.

KNIFE, FIGHTING, PAL RH 36

Parkerized 6-inch blade, aluminium pommel, leather handle. In the early forties, the PAL Cutlery Co. bought out Remington Cutlery and carried on its range of hunting knives. The initials RH on the blade are for *Remington Hunting*.

KNIFE, FIGHTING, EGW

Another civilian hunting knife, made by the EG Waterman Co. It has a distinctive 7 3/8" polished steel blade.

Knife, Trench, M3

The regulation M3 knife and its M6 leather scabbard were introduced in March 1943. The 6 3/4" blue or gray-parkerized blade bears on one side the manufacturer and year (always 1943 in this marking format). Later, this would be shortened to the manufacturer's name and on the later batches this would be transferred to the hilt. The pommel always has the Ordnance Dept. flaming bomb as an acceptance mark.

The M3 knife was manufactured in 1943-1944, by nine firms only: Aerial Cutlery Company, Boker H & Company, Camillus Cutlery Company, Case WR and Sons Cutlery Company, Imperial Knife Company, Kinfolks Incorporated, PAL Blade and Tool Company, Robeson Cutlery Company and Utica Cutlery Company. It was superseded in May 1944 by the M4 bayonet, intended for the M1 carbine. The M4 was not apparently issued in numbers in the ETO before VE-Day.

The M6 leather scabbard was made in 1943 only. It was replaced by a new plastic scabbard authorized in July 1943, the 'Scabbard, trench knife, M8.' This was upgraded as the M8A1 as of April 1944 by the addition of the standard belt hook. Many M8 scabbards were also modified this way.

KNIFE, TRENCH, M3 WITH SCABBARD M6

An early knife, blade-marked 'US M3 Imperial.' The leather M6 scabbard is marked 'US M6 Milsco 1943.'

KNIFE, TRENCH, M3 WITH SCABBARD M8

Knife made by Kinfolks Incorporated, with an M8 plastic and webbing scabbard.

The sole marking on the blade is the manufacturer's, the missing date indicates a post-1943 order.

The Ordnance Dept. flaming bomb on the pommel is the official acceptance mark.

On this late-manufacture knife (1944), the manufacturer's name (PAL) is stamped on the hilt. The scabbard is an M8, to which a belt hook has been added.

PAL marking on the hilt.

8. Optical and map-reading equipment

1. FLASHLIGHT, TL-122B AND TL-122C

Two plastic flashlights, operating on two BA-30 dry batteries. A small push-button above the main switch enables Morse code communication. Multi-colored filters and a spare bulb are located within the screw-on cap.

2. TYPE E BINOCULARS

Marked '*US Army Signal Corps, Military Stereo 6 x 30.*' The leather case has a compass on its lid. This is the WW1 pattern issued until 1941-42 and replaced by the M3.

3. BINOCULARS, M3, 6X30, AND CARRYING CASE M17

Standard ground troops binoculars, 6 x 30, the figure 6 stands for magnification, and 30 for the diameter of the lens in millimeters. The leather case is marked '*Case Carrying M17*' on the lid, and '*D 44160*' on the front.

4. COMPASS, PRISMATIC, M-1938 AND CARRYING CASE

5. COMPASS, WATCH-TYPE

Pocket-type compass already provided during the First World War. The initials US are engraved on the lid.

6 & 7. COMPASS, LENSATIC, AND CARRYING CASE

Standard issue compass, simpler and cheaper than the M-1938. The case is made of waterproofed canvas, it is hooked on the right front of the belt. (See also the wrist compass ➡ page 142)

7. Detail of the lensatic compass markings.

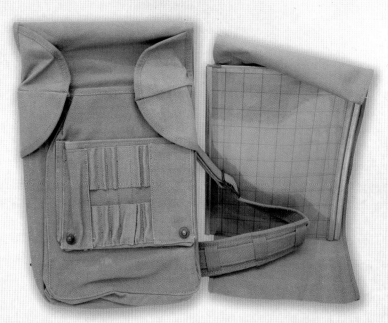

The map case has two large compartments, as well as small pockets and slots for pencils, erasers, etc. A clear plastic insert (right) with red grid lines is used with military maps.

CASE, CANVAS, DISPATCH, M-1938

Issue map and document case. The special strap, with shoulder pad, is hooked on two rings located on the back of the case (➡ page 131).

Like all US Army maps, this large-scale road map has been prepared and printed by the Corps of Engineers.

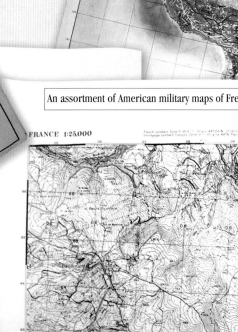

An assortment of American military maps of French regions and localities.

The Ordnance Department

The Ordnance Dept. was tasked with providing weapons and vehicles, and their maintenance. It also issued ammunition, and recovered all friendly or enemy ordnance materiel left on the battlefield.

Ordnance department
officer collar insignia

At Camp Pittsburgh (Mourmelon, France) on June 21, 1945, soldiers of the 156th Field Artillery (44th Division) are preparing M1 carbines for shipment to the Pacific.
(National Archives)

1. Flare guns

Pyrotechnic pistol manufactured by the International Flare Signal Co in September 1943. The frame is made of brass and the barrel of steel.

Flare gun made in zinc by Sklar in 1943.

1.537 in. flare cartridges, of the type provided to aviation units:
Signal, aircraft, double star, Green-green, AN-M39
Signal, aircraft, single star, Yellow, AN-M44
Signal, aircraft, double star, Red-green, AN-M41

2. .45 caliber M-1917 Revolver (Smith & Wesson)

On this early war shot taken in the States, a soldier from a signal crew is armed with a World War One vintage .45 caliber revolver. This was replaced in 1942 by the new M1 carbine. The work uniform is the pre-war blue denim dungarees.
(National Archives)

REVOLVER, CALIBER .45, SMITH & WESSON M-1917
Double action six-shooter, with side opening cylinder and hand ejector, made by Smith & Wesson and Colt in 1917-1919. In order to fire the service .45 Caliber rimless cartridge, Joseph Wesson patented the 'half-moon' clip that held three rounds for loading the gun and extracting the spent cases.

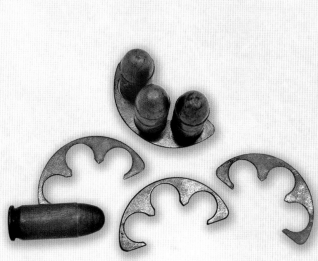

'Half-moon' clips for the .45 Caliber rimless cartridge.

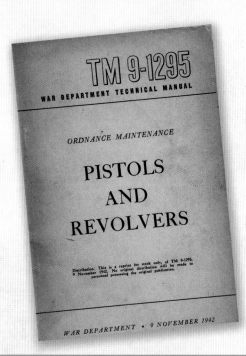

HOLSTER, REVOLVER, CAL .45, M-1909
Leather holster for the M-1917 Smith & Wesson revolver, and the M-1907 and M-1917 Colt revolvers.

M-1917 three-pocket ammunition pouch for six .45 caliber revolver clips. It was worn on the pistol belt thanks to a wide loop at the back.

3. Automatic pistol, M-1911 and M-1911A1

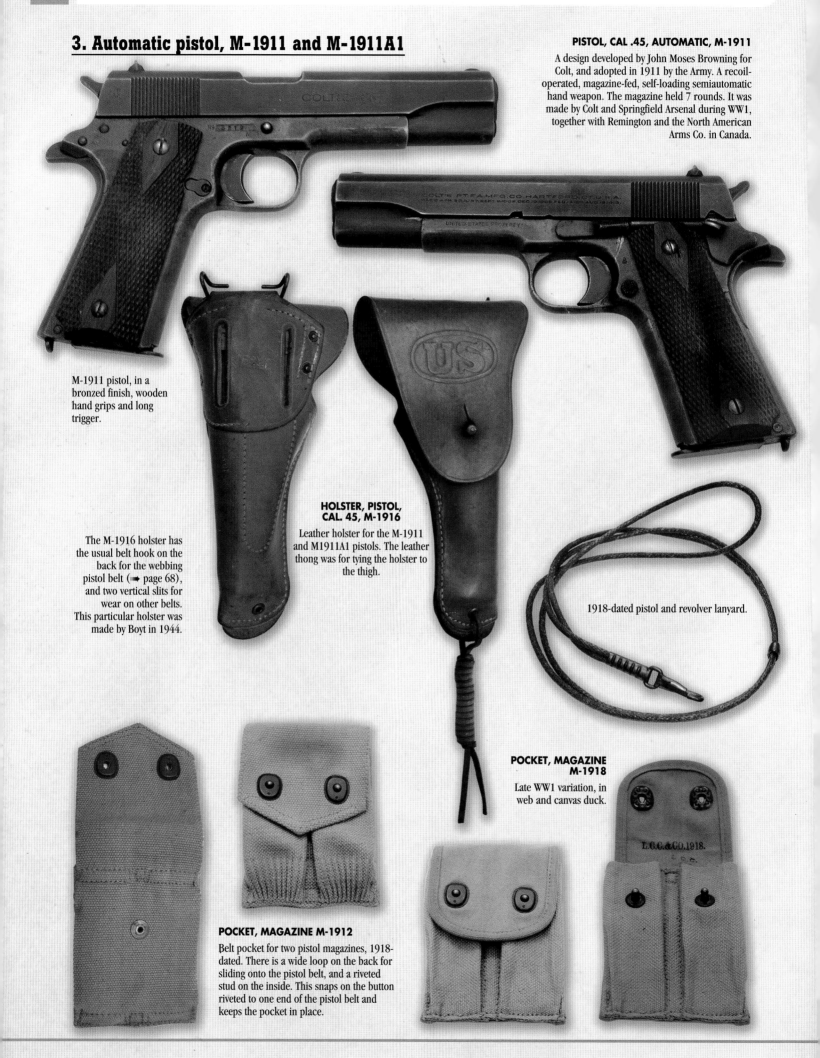

PISTOL, CAL .45, AUTOMATIC, M-1911

A design developed by John Moses Browning for Colt, and adopted in 1911 by the Army. A recoil-operated, magazine-fed, self-loading semiautomatic hand weapon. The magazine held 7 rounds. It was made by Colt and Springfield Arsenal during WW1, together with Remington and the North American Arms Co. in Canada.

M-1911 pistol, in a bronzed finish, wooden hand grips and long trigger.

HOLSTER, PISTOL, CAL. 45, M-1916

Leather holster for the M-1911 and M1911A1 pistols. The leather thong was for tying the holster to the thigh.

The M-1916 holster has the usual belt hook on the back for the webbing pistol belt (➡ page 68), and two vertical slits for wear on other belts. This particular holster was made by Boyt in 1944.

1918-dated pistol and revolver lanyard.

POCKET, MAGAZINE M-1918

Late WW1 variation, in web and canvas duck.

POCKET, MAGAZINE M-1912

Belt pocket for two pistol magazines, 1918-dated. There is a wide loop on the back for sliding onto the pistol belt, and a riveted stud on the inside. This snaps on the button riveted to one end of the pistol belt and keeps the pocket in place.

PISTOL, CAL .45, AUTOMATIC, M-1911A1

Improved version of the WW1 pistol introduced in the Twenties: extension of the grip safety, shortening and knurling of the trigger ; a clearance cut on both sides of the receiver into which fits the finger tip of a right-handed or left-handed shooter, a raising and knurling of the mainspring housing; and the widening of the front sight. During the Second World War, the M-1911A1 was manufactured mainly by Colt, Remington Rand and Ithaca, and in smaller quantities by Union Switch & Signal and Singer. By 1945, more than 2.5 million M-1911 and M-1911A1 pistols had been made.

M-1911A1 pistols were parkerized, with plastic hand grips. Note how the mainspring housing at the back of the grip is raised and knurled.

.45 CALIBER AMMUNITION

1. Cartridge, Ball, Cal .45, M-1911 (Headstamped FA 18)
2. Cartridge, Ball, Cal .45, M-1911 (WCC 43)
3. Cartridge, Dummy, Cal .45, M-1921 (FA 44).

1   2   3

HOLSTER, PISTOL, M3

Shoulder holster in leather, introduced in 1942 for Airforce pilots but also used by other arms and services of the US Army. This specimen was made by Enger-Kress in 1943. The other pattern is the M7 (➡ page 131)

COVER, WATERPROOF, PISTOL OR PERSONAL EFFECTS SPEC. P. Q. D. NO. 377B STOCK NO. 74-C-310-38 THE VISKING CORP. DECEMBER 13, 1944   P. O. 3547 PHILADELPHIA Q. M. DEPOT

INSPECTOR

COVER, WATERPROOF, PISTOL OR PERSONAL EFFECTS (8"X 18")

An article issued for amphibious operations.

Pistol lanyard, marked Hickock 1943.

Pistol magazine pocket, M-1912-type, but British-made in 1944 of webbing material.

POCKET, MAGAZINE, DOUBLE-WEB, M-1923

New type magazine pocket, with a single 'Lift-the-dot' fastener. This one was made by Avery in 1942.

4. U.S. Carbine, M1

On the eve of World War Two, the US Army was looking into a light weapon that would fit between the pistol and rifle for personnel whose main task was not close range combat (such as: mortar and MG crews, vehicle drivers, signal crews, etc.). The Winchester prototype was chosen in October 1941 as the standard Carbine, Caliber .30, M1. It was a gas-operated, self-loading shoulder weapon, fed by a straight 15-round magazine. More than six million carbines were manufactured between 1941 and 1945, by various concerns, such as: Winchester, Rock Ola, Inland, Saginaw, Underwood or IBM.

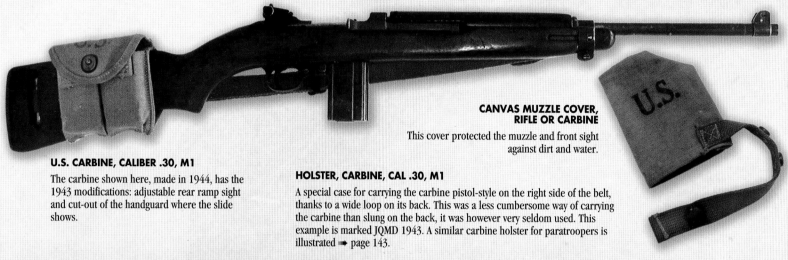

CANVAS MUZZLE COVER, RIFLE OR CARBINE

This cover protected the muzzle and front sight against dirt and water.

U.S. CARBINE, CALIBER .30, M1

The carbine shown here, made in 1944, has the 1943 modifications: adjustable rear ramp sight and cut-out of the handguard where the slide shows.

HOLSTER, CARBINE, CAL .30, M1

A special case for carrying the carbine pistol-style on the right side of the belt, thanks to a wide loop on its back. This was a less cumbersome way of carrying the carbine than slung on the back, it was however very seldom used. This example is marked JQMD 1943. A similar carbine holster for paratroopers is illustrated ➡ page 143.

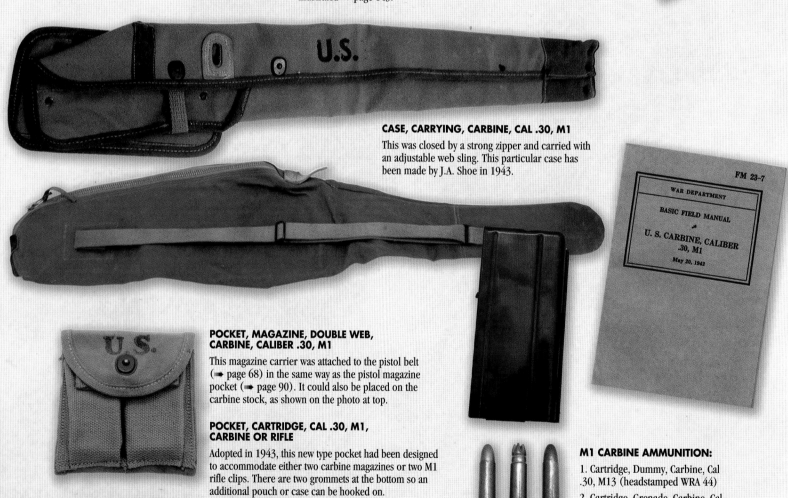

CASE, CARRYING, CARBINE, CAL .30, M1

This was closed by a strong zipper and carried with an adjustable web sling. This particular case has been made by J.A. Shoe in 1943.

FM 23-7

WAR DEPARTMENT

BASIC FIELD MANUAL

U. S. CARBINE, CALIBER .30, M1

May 20, 1942

POCKET, MAGAZINE, DOUBLE WEB, CARBINE, CALIBER .30, M1

This magazine carrier was attached to the pistol belt (➡ page 68) in the same way as the pistol magazine pocket (➡ page 90). It could also be placed on the carbine stock, as shown on the photo at top.

POCKET, CARTRIDGE, CAL .30, M1, CARBINE OR RIFLE

Adopted in 1943, this new type pocket had been designed to accommodate either two carbine magazines or two M1 rifle clips. There are two grommets at the bottom so an additional pouch or case can be hooked on.

50 CARTRIDGES
CARBINE, CALIBER .30 M1
AMMUNITION LOT W.C.C. C226
WESTERN CARTRIDGE COMPANY

M1 CARBINE AMMUNITION:

1. Cartridge, Dummy, Carbine, Cal .30, M13 (headstamped WRA 44)

2. Cartridge, Grenade, Carbine, Cal .30, M6 (headstamped LC 43). Crimped end round for grenade launching.

3. Cartridge, Ball, Carbine, cal .30, M1 (WCC 43).

Box of fifty .30 Caliber rounds for the M1 carbine, made by the Western Cartridge Company (WCC).

5. The M-1903 U.S. Rifle

The M-1903 Rifle, also known as the 'Springfield' Rifle was a bolt-operated, magazine-fed longarm, with a 5-round capacity in the standard .30-06 caliber. An American adaptation of the Mauser system, the '03 rifle was one of the two service rifles of World War One. During the Second World War, several variations were used by the Army: the M-1903 alt. 1905 (with a blade bayonet instead of a ramrod bayonet), the M-1903A1 (the small of stock is shaped in the way of a pistol grip), the M-1903A3 (simplified leaf sight located on top of the receiver, slightly forward of the bold handle), and M-1903A4 (sniper rifle, without front and rear sights, fitted with a Weaver telescopic sight).

U.S. RIFLE, CAL .30, M-1903

The M-1903 alt. 1905 rifle illustrated here has the standard M-1907 leather sling.

BAYONET, M-1905

New bayonet authorized in 1905 for the M-1903 rifle, with its M-1910 scabbard. The scabbard itself is fashioned out of wood and the outer cover is made of canvas and leather. The bayonet was carried on the belt or haversack thanks to the usual double hook. The M-1905 bayonet could also be affixed to the M1 rifle.

BELT, CARTRIDGE, CAL .30, M-1917, DISMOUNTED

Ammunition belt of WW1 vintage, in canvas and webbing. It held twenty 5-round clips of .30 caliber rifle ammunition.

DUMMY TRAINING RIFLE

A faithful reproduction of the M-1903 rifle given to new recruits for drill and basic musketry training. The manufacturer's markings (Victory Trainer PD Co. 1942) are embossed on the butt plate.

COMBINATION SCORE BOOK
FOR
U. S. RIFLES M1903 AND M1
AND
BROWNING AUTOMATIC RIFLE M1918A2

SLOW FIRE
RAPID FIRE
B.A.R SLOW FIRE
B.A.R RAPID FIRE

Dummy rounds (Cartridge, Dummy, Cal .30, M-1906), loaded into a 5-round stripper clip for the '03 Rifle.

BELT, CARTRIDGE, CAL .30, M-1918, MOUNTED

A belt for horsed troops, in canvas and webbing. It has nine pockets for rifle clips and a blank space for a .45 caliber pistol magazine pocket (➡ page 90).

6. The U.S. M-1917 rifle

In 1917, the U.S. government bought the patents for the Pattern 1914 rifle, made in the USA for the British Army. This new gun was easier and cheaper to produce than the M-1903 rifle and therefore became the primary American service rifle of World War One. Like the Springfield rifle, the M-1917 rifle was bolt-operated and magazine-fed with a 5-round capacity in the standard .30-06 caliber. During WW2, it was mainly used for Stateside troop training.

BAYONET, M-1917

The specific bayonet for the M-1917 rifle, with its second-type scabbard.

7. The U.S. Rifle, cal .30, M1

U.S. RIFLE, CAL .30, M1

In 1936, the United States Army pioneered the widespread issue of a semi-automatic rifle to combat troops when it chose the new M1 rifle. It was a gas-operated, clip-loaded shoulder weapon. The expendable 'en bloc' clip held 8 rounds in the standard .30-06 caliber. The M1 rifle had been developed for 15 years by a young engineer at the Springfield Arsenal: John C. Garand. In 1941-45, the M1 rifle was manufactured at Springfield (for a total of 3,519,471 rifles), and by Winchester (513,582). The rifle shown here was made in 1941, it has the new M1 web sling adopted in 1944.

1. BAYONET, M-1942

The M1 rifle could be fitted with the M-1905 bayonet (page 93) and also with the M-1942 bayonet, which differed by a larger pommel, its plastic serrated grips and a parkerized finish. The scabbard is an M3 in olive drab plastic, the throat is in chemically blackened metal and features the usual double hook.

2. BAYONET, M-1905 E1

These were shortened M-1905 or M-1942 bayonets for the M1 rifle, the tip is centered on the blade. The new scabbard is the M7. A shortened variant of the older M3 long scabbard was also used.

1

2

3

3. BAYONET, M1

Standard short bayonet introduced in March 1943. These new-made weapons can be told apart because the fuller stops short of the blade tip, which is not the case with the shortened blades of the older modified bayonets.

The M1 rifle clip held 8 rounds, here of the 'Cartridge, Ball, Cal .30, M2' variety.

BELT, CARTRIDGE, CAL .30, M-1923, DISMOUNTED

The standard WW2 rifle ammunition belt, in OD No 3 web. It could carry 10 M1 rifle clips, or 20 stripper clips for the M-1903 and M-1917 service rifles.

POCKET, CARTRIDGE, CAL .30, M1, CARBINE OR RIFLE

A new pocket designed to accommodate either two carbine magazines or two M1 rifle clips.

Expendable cotton bandoleer: its six pockets accommodated M1 rifle clips, or stripper clips, or carbine magazines.

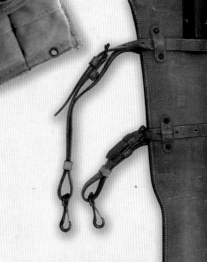

SCABBARD, RIFLE, M-1938

Russet leather scabbard, used to carry the M1 rifle in a vehicle or motorcycle.

GRENADE LAUNCHER, M7

This was attached to the muzzle of the M1 rifle, enabling it to project various types of grenades.

RIFLE GRENADE SIGHT, M15

It is shown here with its canvas carrying case and instruction sheet/range tables. The sight was attached to the left side of the stock and consists of a screwed-on mounting plate and movable sight. The sight could be mounted on the rifle or carbine.

1. GRENADE, RIFLE, ANTITANK (AT), M9 A1

Hollow charge antitank grenade, fired in a flat trajectory.

2. SIGNAL, GROUND, AMBER STAR, PARACHUTE, M21A1

A signal flare projected like a rifle grenade.

The typical rifle grenade container is made of thick bituminous cardboard.

3. GRENADE, PROJECTION ADAPTER M1

For antipersonnel effect, this adapter permits the launching of the standard MKII fragmentation hand grenade. (➡ page 100)

COVER, WATERPROOF, RIFLE OR CARBINE (8"X 56")

An elongated soft plastic sheath to protect the rifle or carbine in amphibious assaults. A white opaque variation was also provided.

CASE, CLEANING, ROD, M1

Tubular cleaning rod and accessories, taken down and carried in its canvas case. There is a double hook on the back for the belt.

CLEANER, RIFLE BORE

A convenient container that could be placed inside one of the cartridge belt pockets.

M1 RIFLE COMBINATION TOOL AND CLEANING ACCESSORIES, carried in the stock

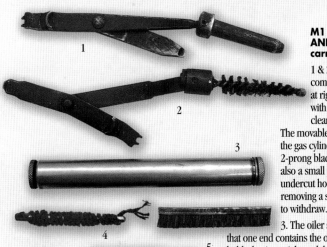

1 & 2. Two variations of the combination tool. The articulated tool at right is for cleaning the chamber, with either a slotted end for the cleaning patch (1) or a wire brush (2). The movable screw driver blade is for adjusting the gas cylinder screw and for other screws, the 2-prong blade is for the rear sight nut. There is also a small projection for drifting out pins. The undercut hook is the hand extractor, used for removing a spent case the extractor has failed to withdraw.

3. The oiler and thong case is partitioned so that one end contains the oil and oil dropper and the other holds the tip, weight and thong (4) and the brush (5).

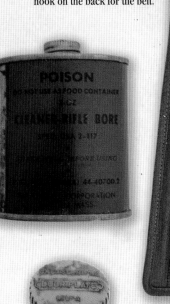

'Lubriplate' grease, used on specific points of the breech. It was also carried in the stock of the M1 rifle.

8. The Thompson Submachine guns

THOMPSON SUBMACHINE GUN, CAL .45, M-1928A1

A submachine gun with a delayed blowback action, firing the service caliber .45 ammunition. This model has the Cutts compensator at the muzzle, and a Lyman ramp sight. It was fed by stick magazines of 20 or 30-round capacity, or by the 50-round drum magazine.

THOMPSON SUBMACHINE GUN, CAL .45, M1A1

Simplified version of the Thompson SMG adopted in 1942: simple blowback action, fixed firing pin, strengthened stock that could not be dismantled without a special tool. The operating handle has been moved to the left side of the receiver. The compensator and cooling fins on the barrel have been deleted, and the Lyman sight replaced by a simple peep sight. This gun could only be fed by box magazines.

POCKET, AMMUNITION MAGAZINES

A web carrier for Thompson SMG 20-round magazines. There is a wide loop on the back for placing it on the belt. This particular carrier is dated 1942.

Heavy-duty canvas cover with zippered opening, to protect the Thompson SMG.

1942-dated shoulder bag for the 50-round drum magazine.

The M-1928A1 Thompson's 50-round drum magazine.

CASE, MAGAZINE, 30-ROUND, WITH SHOULDER STRAP

A canvas bag, dated 1943, for SMG magazines.

Right.
British made variant of the SMG magazine bag, dated 1943.

9. The M3 Submachine Gun

SUBMACHINE GUN, CAL .45, M3

The M3 was introduced in December 1943. Cheaply made of stamped and welded steel parts, it looked like a mechanic's grease gun, hence its nickname. It fired in automatic mode only and was fed by a 30-round straight magazine. In this picture, the stock is not extended.

The M3A1 was standardized in December 1944 and production began in 1945. The M3A1 did away with the cocking lever, it was not issued in the ETO before VE-Day.

July 1945 at Sissonne (France). Men from a Tank destroyer battalion are preparing Thompson submachine guns for shipment to the USA after VE-day.
(National Archives)

10. The Browning Automatic Rifle

BROWNING AUTOMATIC RIFLE, CAL .30, M-1918A2, WITH BIPOD

The BAR appeared at the end of World War One and was subsequently modified in 1937 and 1940. Following the introduction of the M1 rifle the BAR became the M-1918A2.

The BAR was an air-cooled, gas-operated automatic rifle, fed by a 20-round magazine of .30 caliber ammunition. There were two cyclic rates of automatic fire, normal and slow. Some automatic riflemen chose to take down the bipod as it made the gun unwieldy for close-range fire.

BAR take-down tool.

BELT, MAGAZINE, BAR, M-1937

Canvas and webbing ammunition belt for 12 BAR magazines. This one has been made by Boyt in 1941.

M-1918 BAR canvas bandoleer, for six magazines. It could be worn singly or in pairs, one for each side and accordingly marked 'Left' and 'Right.' This one is a left-side bandoleer, dated 1918.

11. The Browning M-1919A4 Machine Gun

BROWNING MACHINE GUN, CAL .30, M-1919A4

This .30 caliber machine gun functioned by short recoil of the barrel, with a vertical sliding breech lock. It was fed by fabric or metal link belts of 250 rounds. The MG is affixed here to a ground M2 tripod, while it could also arm a variety of vehicles and AFVs. A later model adopted in February 1943, the M-1919A6, fitted with a shoulder stock and bipod was used as a light machine gun.

Pressed steel ammunition box for 250 rounds of machine gun ammunition. In this case, cartridges are inserted into the canvas belt with a tracer for every four rounds of armor-piercing ammunition.

Special tool for removing ruptured casings from the MG breech.

.30-06 CALIBER AMMUNITION

1. Cartridge, Armor Piercing, Cal .30, M2 (headstamped FA 42, black tip)

2. Cartridge, Tracer, Cal .30, M1 (headstamped FA 43, red tip).

SLING, CARRYING, MACHINE-GUN AND AMMUNITION

Strong webbing strap with two hooks, for carrying the machine gun, or ammo boxes.

Plywood range table and canvas cover for MG crews.

M3 Machine for loading individual rounds in a textile MG belt.

COVER, TRIPOD MOUNT M1

A canvas cover to protect the head of the M2 MG mount when it was folded for transport on a vehicle.

Cover for a .30 caliber machine gun spare barrel.

12. The Browning Machine Gun, Cal .50, M2 HB

Combined breech and muzzle cover.

**BROWNING
MACHINE GUN,
CAL .50, M2 HB
(HEAVY BARREL)**

This heavy machine gun is mounted here in the antiaircraft mode, affixed to the M63 AA mount and fed by a 200-round box magazine. The weapon could also be mounted on the M1 ground mount and several other types of vehicular pedestals and mounts. Introduced in 1918, the .50 caliber machine gun remained in active service long after the Second World war.

RESTRICTED

FM 23-65

WAR DEPARTMENT FIELD MANUAL

BROWNING MACHINE GUN,

CALIBER .50 HB, M2

WAR DEPARTMENT · NOVEMBER 1944
RESTRICTED

Pressed steel box for 105 rounds of metal-linked .50 caliber ammunition.

Expendable metal links for the .50MG, packed by ten each.

Canvas bag for salvaging metallic belt links in vehicles.

Cartridge, Incendiary, Cal .50, M1.

Headstamped SL 43 (Saint Louis Ordnance Plant), light blue tip.

M2 Machine for loading .50 caliber rounds into disintegrating metal links and forming a complete belt for the heavy machine gun.

13. Hand Grenades

GRENADE, HAND, OFFENSIVE, MK III A1

A demolition device with concussive effect in enclosed spaces. The body was made of compressed fiber with sheet metal ends. A paper tape indicated the model, lot number and date of loading (here 1942). This grenade was fitted with the M6A2 or A3 fuze.

GRENADE, HAND, FRAGMENTATION, MK II A1

The explosion of the charge breaks the serrated cast iron body and sends lethal fragments within a wide radius. The MK II grenade was fitted with the M10 (A1, A2 or A3) detonating fuze. The grenade body was painted yellow early in the war, and painted or repainted in olive drab for camouflage purposes as of mid-1942. The yellow band left on the body just under the fuze identified an explosive device.

GRENADE, HAND, SMOKE, COLORED, M18

Chemical grenade, producing a colored smoke signal for 1 minute (yellow smoke here, but variants emit red, orange, blue, green, black or purple smoke). The sheet metal body is painted in blue-gray, like all chemical devices. The top part is pierced with six vents covered with tape, and painted in the smoke color. The fuze was the M200A1.

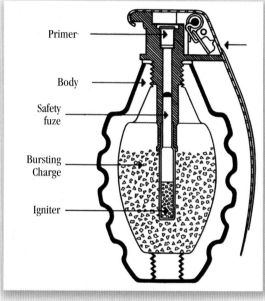

Primer

Body

Safety fuze

Bursting Charge

Igniter

Cut-out view of the MK II A1 fragmentation grenade

GRENADE, HAND, SMOKE, WP, M15

White phosphorus (WP) filled smoke grenade, cylindrical steel body with rounded bottom. Fuze was the M6A3.

A World War One vintage hand grenade chest carrier. It was introduced in 1918 and very seldom used in 1941-45.

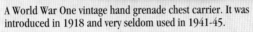

More often, infantrymen would carry grenades in the Ammunition Bag M1, which could accommodate 11 rifle grenades or 28 hand grenades, without their fiber containers.

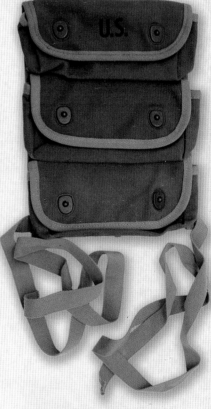

CARRIER, GRENADE, 3-POCKET

Two types of grenade carriers, both 1944-dated and apparently rarely used. They were hooked to the belt and tied to the thigh by tapes.

14. Booby traps

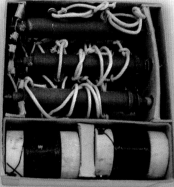

The M1 pull firing device was packaged by 5 units complete with standard base and two 80-ft spools of trip wire.

PULL-RELEASE TYPE FIRING DEVICE, M3

Packaged in the same way as the M1 device, one is attached here to a MKIIA1 fragmentation grenade.

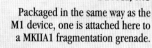

PULL TYPE FIRING DEVICE, M1

Cast alloy case with attached standard base that could be screwed on a hand grenade or demolition charge. Action is initiated by a 3 to 5 lb pull on the trip wire.

PULL TYPE WEAPONS FIRING DEVICE

A booby trap that activates a weapon. It was screwed on the trigger guard and locked on the trigger.

Spool of light and dark colored trip wire for booby traps.

PRESSURE TYPE FIRING DEVICE, M1A1

Cardboard box of 5 units, with several extension rods according to depth at which charge was buried. Action was initiated by a pressure of 20 lb or more.

1. RELEASE TYPE FIRING DEVICE, M1

Mechanical device with hinged plate release, held by a restraining weight of 2 lb or more.

2. RELEASE TYPE FIRING DEVICE, M5

A similar device, held by a restraining weight of 5 lb or more.

15. Land mines

MINE, ANTIPERSONNEL, M2 A1

Bounding fragmentation mine actuated by a pressure or pull-type firing device.

MINE, ANTIPERSONNEL, M3

Cast iron mine, triggered by a pressure or pull-type firing device.
(Musée de l'Infanterie, Montpellier)

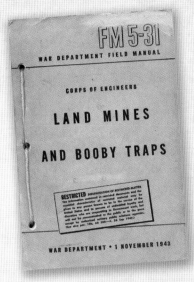

FM 5-31 was the Corps of Engineers manual describing all types of land mines and booby traps used by Allied and enemy armies.

ANTITANK MINE, M1

Steel-bodied mine, initiated by a pressure of 500 lb on the top fuze, or 250 lb on the side of the spider. This could be placed on top or under the mine before it was dug in. The M1 AT mine was packaged by 5 units in a wooden crate, together with 5 plates and fuzes. The M1 was superseded by the M1A1 fitted with a different fuze.

MINE, ANTITANK, HE, HEAVY, M6A1

This mine had two auxiliary fuze wells for boobytrapping.

An M6A1 AT mine in its metal carrying frame.

16. Rocket launchers

ROCKET LAUNCHER, 2.36 INCH, M1A1

The M1A1 rocket launcher ('Bazooka') was introduced in August 1943, being an improved variant of the M1 adopted in June 1942. It consists of a smooth bore steel tube, with a wooden stock and front grip, a crude bar sight and electrical ignition system. The web sling is the M1 also used with the M1 rifle (➡ page 94).

A contactor latch at the breech end holds the rocket and provides the ground terminal, the electrical circuit is prepared for ignition by attaching the long wire coming from the rocket venturi to a contact spring on the tube. The electrical circuit is completed, via two BA-30 dry batteries stored in the stock, by depressing the trigger.

Also shown is a High Explosive Antitank Rocket 2.36 inch, M6A1, painted in olive drab with yellow markings.
(Photo Militaria Magazine, D. Sacleux Collection)

MASK, FACE, LAUNCHER, ROCKET

An accessory introduced early in 1944. It was a modified pair of M-1943 goggles (➡ page 67) with an added curtain to protect the face against burning powder pellets from the bazooka rocket.

MASK, FACE, LAUNCHER, ROCKET
(Stock No.) 7B-M-126
Use this mask for protecting the face when firing the rocket launcher. Avoid scratching the precision surfaces of lenses by cleaning regularly with a soft cloth. Use very light pressure when cleaning.
SAVE CARTON FOR CARRYING CASE
AMERICAN OPTICAL CO., SOUTHBRIDGE, MASS.
CONT. NO. W19-078-QM 3229

BAG, CARRYING, ROCKET, M6

Canvas carrier for 3 rockets stored in their tarred fiber containers. Two inside partition straps hold the contents in place. Another pattern intended for paratroops had a strong snap hook for attaching the bag to the parachute harness, and two leg tie-tapes.

ROCKET LAUNCHER, M9A1

New type rocket launcher designed at the request of Airborne troops, designated M9 in June 1943. The new M9A1 with a strengthened coupling lock was authorized in September 1944. It is a two-piece unit, the metal stock permits firing in four positions. The firing device located in the grip is magneto-type, depressing the trigger generates the current.

Rocket launcher M9A1 in the carrying position.

17. the 60-mm mortar

FM 23-85

WAR DEPARTMENT

BASIC FIELD MANUAL

60-MM MORTAR, M2

SIGHT, M4

The M4 sight was used with both the 60-mm and 81-mm mortars. Its leather case (Case Carrying, M14) has a hand strap at the top, a double hook at the back for the belt, together with brass rings on the side for a leather shoulder sling.

PAD, SHOULDER, M2

An item issued to MG and mortar crews. These are usually undated but bear L ('left') and R ('right') markings.

LIGHT, AIMING POST, M14

Night sighting device. The lamp at left was clamped on the aiming post, and the other lamp, at right, would shed light on the mortar sight. Both were powered by 2 BA-30 single-cell batteries.

SHELL, HE, M49 A2, 60-MM MORTAR

High explosive mortar round, with M52 point detonating fuze. The complete round was carried in the bituminized fiber container at left.

60-MM MORTAR, M2

The mortar consists of 3 main parts for portage: the base plate, barrel and bipod. The M2 mortar was a French Brandt design whose patent had been leased by the US Army in 1938. The maximum rate of fire was 30 to 35 rounds per minute, range – 1,985 yards, weight of projectile – 3 to 4 pounds. The mortar fired high explosive or illuminating rounds, carried in the M2 Ammunition bag (➡ page 71).

18. The 81-mm Mortar, M1

81-MM MORTAR, M1

In the early thirties, the US Army was looking for a medium caliber mortar, and finally chose the French Brandt design. After extensive field testing, it bought the manufacturing rights in 1932. The range was about 3.300 yards, rate of fire 18 to 30 rounds per minute, weight of projectile 7 to 13 lbs.

Nomenclature plate on a mortar bipod manufactured in 1943. It is riveted on the top part.

Caliber of mortar

Kind of filler

Nature of shell

Ammunition lot number

Shell painted olive drab, yellow markings

SHELL, HE, M56, 81-MM MORTAR

With point-detonating fuze M53

19. Recoilless Rifle, 57-mm, M18

RECOILLESS RIFLE, 57-MM, M18

A light gun that could be fired from the shoulder, or affixed to the mount of the Browning M-1917A1 heavy water-cooled machine gun. Its shell has a perforated case whose high velocity gas ports counteract the recoil and rearward movement of the barrel. As with the bazooka, the loader must keep clear of the back blast zone behind the breech.
The 57-mm recoilless rifle was used for the first time in the ETO by the 17th Airborne Div. during operation 'Varsity' (the crossing of the Rhine) on March 24, 1945.

Weight – 45 pounds, weight of projectile – 2 3/4 pounds, maximum range – 4,340 yards.

Complete round for the 57-mm recoilless rifle.

Breech, muzzle and sight cover for the 57-mm recoilless rifle.

20. Artillery ammunition

AMMUNITION DATA CARD

Kind Charge, Spotting, M1A1, Black Powder Lot No. EAP-1- 2
Quantity in Lot
50-0-1C Amend. 1
Dwg. No. 82-3-228 Rev. January 30, 1945 Spec. No. 50-55-1 Amend. 2
Manufactured and Loaded by AUSTIN POWDER CO. CLEVELAND, OHIO Date
Contract No. W-33-019 Ord. 3955
Packed 20 Per Box
Remarks:
Certified to by Inspector
Cleveland Ordnance District

Data card packed together with most ammunition, here for black powder spotting charges: i.e. charges of low explosive used in practice ammunition to show the striking point of the projectile.

Ear wardens used by artillery crews, with their black plastic carrier.

Artillery time fuze setter.

Tarred fiber container for the M51A3 point detonating fuze, used with various ammunition, such as shells for the 4.5 in. gun, the 155 Howitzer M1 and Gun M1A1, and the 8 in. Howitzer.

Cut-out view of a 105-mm complete HE shell

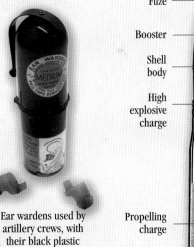

Fuze
Booster
Shell body
High explosive charge
Propelling charge
Primer

Markings found on a 3-inch gun armor-piercing shell

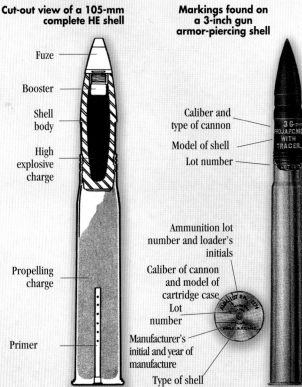

Caliber and type of cannon
Model of shell
Lot number
Ammunition lot number and loader's initials
Caliber of cannon and model of cartridge case
Lot number
Manufacturer's initial and year of manufacture
Type of shell

Shell type color markings
Olive drab shell, markings in yellow: explosive ammunition
Black, white markings: unfilled projectile
Gray, yellow markings: smoke shell
Gray, green markings and stripe: vesicant gas shell
Gray, green markings and 2 stripes: persistent vesicant gas
Gray, red markings and stripe: irritant gas
Gray, red markings and 2 stripes: persistent irritant gas
Blue, white markings: practice shell

Red, black markings: canister shell

Main abbreviations used in marking shells according to type
AP: Armor Piercing
AT: Anti Tank
BD: Base Detonating
HE: High Explosive
HV: High Velocity
NP: Napalm
P: Phosphorous
PD: Point Detonating
PI: Point Ignition
TM: Time Mechanical

A. Complete Round 105-mm Howitzer

Shell semi-fixed HE AT M67, Base detonating fuze M62.

Antitank, high explosive round for the M2A1 or M4 howitzers. The brass case is an M14 fitted with an M28A2 primer.

B. Cartridge, Drill, M12

Practice dummy round for the 90-mm gun. The dummy fuze is an M44A2. Of identical size and weight to an actual round, this was used for training artillerymen in loading and unloading the gun.

C. Brass M18 case with M31 primer for the 75-mm howitzer shell.

D. Brass M25 case with M32A2 primer for the 40-mm shell. It was fired by the anti-aircraft M1 Automatic gun, designed by Bofors of Sweden before the war.

E. Tarred fiber container for a complete 40-mm round.

F. Complete Round 37-mm Gun. Shell, Fixed, HE, M63. Fuze Base Detonating M58. The brass case has an M23A2 primer.

G. M2A1 brass case with M36 primer for the 20-mm ammunition.

21. Artillery laying equipment

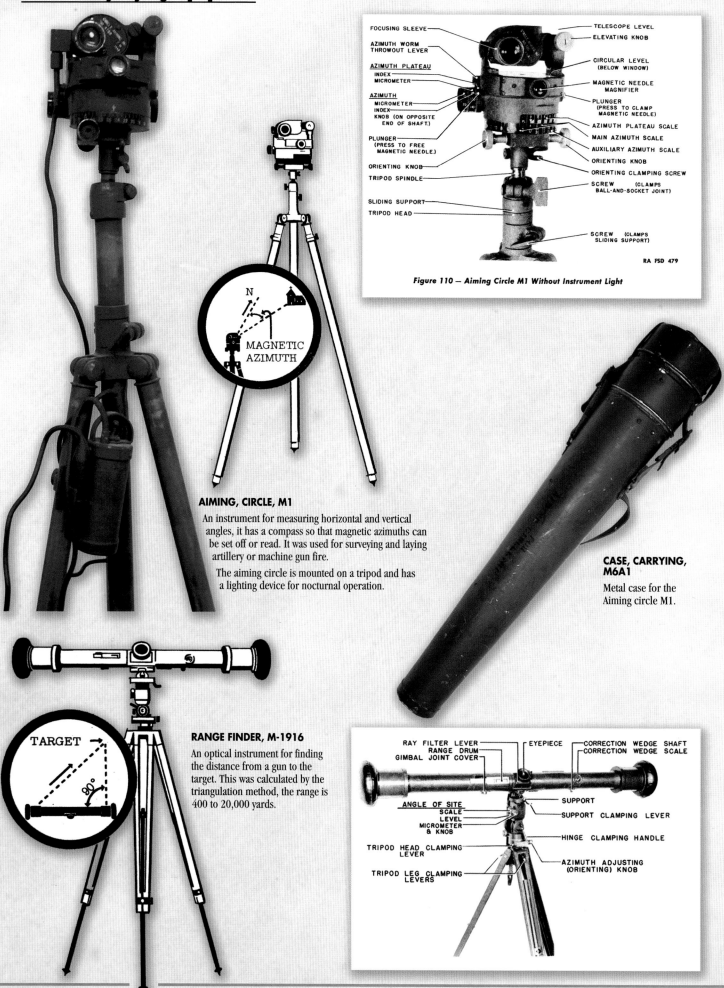

FOCUSING SLEEVE

AZIMUTH WORM
THROWOUT LEVER

AZIMUTH PLATEAU
INDEX
MICROMETER

AZIMUTH
MICROMETER
INDEX
KNOB (ON OPPOSITE
END OF SHAFT.)

PLUNGER
(PRESS TO FREE
MAGNETIC NEEDLE.)

ORIENTING KNOB

TRIPOD SPINDLE

SLIDING SUPPORT

TRIPOD HEAD

TELESCOPE LEVEL

ELEVATING KNOB

CIRCULAR LEVEL
(BELOW WINDOW)

MAGNETIC NEEDLE
MAGNIFIER

PLUNGER
(PRESS TO CLAMP
MAGNETIC NEEDLE)

AZIMUTH PLATEAU SCALE

MAIN AZIMUTH SCALE

AUXILIARY AZIMUTH SCALE

ORIENTING KNOB

ORIENTING CLAMPING SCREW

SCREW (CLAMPS
BALL-AND-SOCKET JOINT)

SCREW (CLAMPS
SLIDING SUPPORT)

RA PSD 479

Figure 110 — Aiming Circle M1 Without Instrument Light

N

MAGNETIC
AZIMUTH

AIMING, CIRCLE, M1

An instrument for measuring horizontal and vertical angles, it has a compass so that magnetic azimuths can be set off or read. It was used for surveying and laying artillery or machine gun fire.

The aiming circle is mounted on a tripod and has a lighting device for nocturnal operation.

CASE, CARRYING, M6A1

Metal case for the Aiming circle M1.

TARGET

80°

RANGE FINDER, M-1916

An optical instrument for finding the distance from a gun to the target. This was calculated by the triangulation method, the range is 400 to 20,000 yards.

RAY FILTER LEVER
RANGE DRUM
GIMBAL JOINT COVER

EYEPIECE

CORRECTION WEDGE SHAFT
CORRECTION WEDGE SCALE

ANGLE OF SITE
SCALE
LEVEL
MICROMETER
& KNOB

TRIPOD HEAD CLAMPING
LEVER

TRIPOD LEG CLAMPING
LEVERS

SUPPORT

SUPPORT CLAMPING LEVER

HINGE CLAMPING HANDLE

AZIMUTH ADJUSTING
(ORIENTING) KNOB

FT 3-R-2

FIRING TABLES
FOR
GUN, 3-INCH, M5 AND M7
(ANTITANK)
AND
GUN, 3-INCH, M3
(ANTIAIRCRAFT)
FIRING
SHELL, HE, M42,
PROJECTILE, APC, M62
AND SHOT, AP, M79
1943

ANGLE OF SITE
KNOB
MICROMETER
SCALE
LEVEL
RETICLE ROTATING RING
DIOPTER SCALES
AZIMUTH
KNOB
INTERPUPILLARY SCALE
THROWOUT LEVER
LEVEL
MICROMETER
SCALE

RA FSD 489

TELESCOPE, M-1915 A1

Tripod for the M65 BC scope.

TELESCOPE B.C.
M65
NO. 1191 G.I.R.
M.L.CO. 1944

Nomenclature plate for
the M65 BC scope.

CASE CARRYING M-18

BC (BATTERY COMMANDER'S) TELESCOPE M65

A BC scope is used for observing fire and measuring horizontal and vertical angles in calculating firing data.

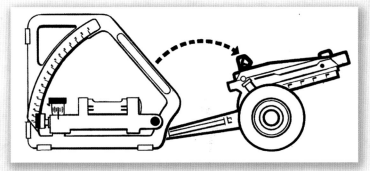

Location of the M1 quadrant on the Howitzer, Pack, 75-mm, M1A1.

GUNNER'S QUADRANT, M1

Instrument used for laying the gun in elevation. It measures the vertical angle which the axis of the bore makes with the horizontal. The M1 quadrant was used with most US field artillery pieces. Its leather carrying case was the M18.

1. Bivouac equipment

These GIs from the 44th Division are pitching pup tents for an inspection during stateside training early in the war.

TENT, SHELTER, HALF, NEW TYPE

As part of his issue, every soldier had a shelter-half, usually rolled into the haversack's pack carrier (➡ page 69). The new type tent authorized in late 1942 had two closed ends, whereas the early war type had only one.

A two-man tent could be pitched by buttoning together two shelter halves, and two tents pitched end-to-end accommodated four soldiers.

The shelter half accessories were:

1. A folding 'Pole, Tent, Shelter, Half.' This was replaced as of 1944 by the 'Pole, Tent, Single, Section.' The complete pole was made of three assembled sections of olive drab painted wood

2. Five wood tent pins

3. A 'Guy, Tent, Shelter Half'

4. Five 'Foot Stop, Tent, Shelter Half', i.e. cord loops slipped into metal grommets at the base of the tent to stake it down.

BLANKET, WOOL, OD, M-1934

The issue olive drab blanket. Two were issued to troops sleeping outdoors.

COT, FOLDING, CANVAS

The manufacturer's markings are ink-stamped onto both the wood structure and the canvas part.

ROLL, BEDDING, WATERPROOFED, M-1935

An item issued to officers for carrying a tent,
blankets and other bedding articles,
as well as spare clothing in several inner compartments.
It also doubled as a ground sheet.

1. BAG, SLEEPING, M-1940

Early type sleeping bag, made of padded
fabric. For carrying, it rolled up inside the
attached bag sewn at the top, closed
by a drawstring.

2. COVER, BAG, SLEEPING, M-1940

A waterproof cover for the M-1940 sleeping
bag. The use of dark green material is
noteworthy for an item made as early
as August 1942.

3. BAG, SLEEPING, WOOL

New mummy-shaped wool bag standardized in
February 1944. It was as warm as the two
blankets previously issued to troops in
the field.

4. LINER, BAG, SLEEPING

A cotton washable liner for all the mummy-
shaped sleeping bags (wool bag, mountain
and arctic bags). It features a muslin veil to
protect the face.

5. CASE, WATER REPELLENT, BAG, SLEEPING

A green cotton cover for all types of mummy-
shaped bags.

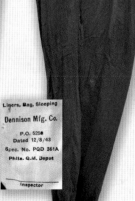

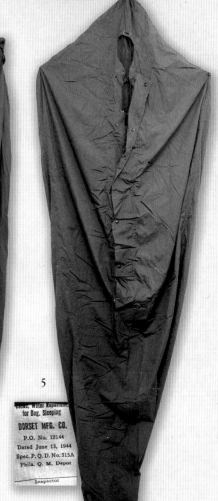

BUCKET, WATERING, CANVAS

Two sizes of canvas buckets. Initially used by mounted troops, these were issued to most arms and services.

BAG, CANVAS, WATER, STERILIZING, POROUS, COMPLETE WITH COVER AND HANGER

The 'Lister bag' used in the field for purifying well-water. A vial of lime hypochlorite was emptied in the bag and the water then stirred with a clean wooden stick. There were five taps on the sides for drinking or filling canteens. The bag usually hung from a tree limb, or was supported above ground by three wooden poles

LANTERN, GASOLINE, LEADED FUEL

This particular lantern has been made by Coleman in 1944 (➡ volume 2, page 77).

A 5-gallon water jerrycan. The W (water) initial and manufacturing date (1942) are embossed under the handles.

Another jerrycan for water, with screw-on cap. The W initial is stamped on the side. The manufacturer and date are indicated on the underside of the can.

A 5-gallon water bag portable on the back thanks to its haversack-style web harness and hooks. When in use, it was suspended upside down. The inner soft plastic bladder has a plastic tap, covered by a screwed-on plastic cup tied with a metal chain. This piece of equipment was made by the International Latex Corporation (➡ page 77) in 1945.

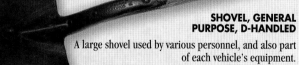

SHOVEL, GENERAL PURPOSE, D-HANDLED

A large shovel used by various personnel, and also part of each vehicle's equipment.

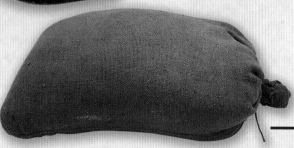

Sand bag made of jute material.

2. Garrison life

THE SECOND WORLD WAR ERA 'STARS AND STRIPES'

During the war, the US National flag showed the 13 stripes of the original founding states, and 48 stars for the 48 federated states of the Union in 1941-45.

SLING, COLOR, WEB, OD

A special sling for color bearers, in olive drab web. The metal plate for the flag pole is leather-padded in the back.

COMBAT INFANTRY BATTALION 1

COMBAT INFANTRY COMPANY 2

1. Flag streamer authorized in 1943 and tied to the staff of infantry battalion guidons in which at least 65% of the personnel held the Combat Infantryman Badge (➡ page 20). An 'Expert Infantry Battalion' streamer was introduced at the same time.

2. Guidon streamer for Combat Infantry Companies.

Information and orientation booklets handed out to recruits undergoing training at an Infantry Replacement Training Center (left), and the Fort Meade No 1 Army Ground Forces Replacement Depot (right).

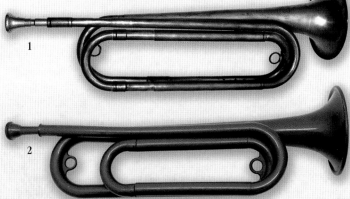

1. TRUMPET, G, WITH SLIDE TO F

A brass instrument with two loops for a sling or unit tabard. It was played by the company bugler for the customary calls (from 'reveille' to 'retreat').

2. TRUMPET, G, WITH SLIDE TO F, PLASTIC

A brass-saving bugle made of Tenite, a plastic material patented by the Eastman Tennessee Corporation. This was adopted in 1943.

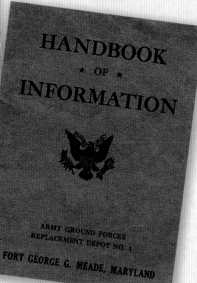

The TL-66A blowtorch was a Signal Corps tool.

MARKING OUTFIT, STAMPING, METAL

This was used to stamp the abbreviated Army service number on certain metallic pieces of equipment. It contains 37 dies, a brass hammer, a small anvil and two templates, one for marking the meat can and embossing the identification tags (➡ page 255), and one for marking eating utensils.

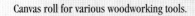

Canvas roll for various woodworking tools.

Wooden crate for a complete Carpenter's tool set No 2. One of these was issued to each infantry rifle company.

Army shoe repair slip, with several detachable tabs.

JACKET, DOG, WATER REPELLENT

Made of cotton lined with wool, it was available in 3 sizes.

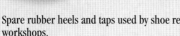

Spare rubber heels and taps used by shoe repair workshops.

BAG, BARRACK, OD

Two were issued to every soldier (labeled 'A' and 'B'). After the introduction of the better duffel bag, it was used as a laundry bag.

BAG, BARRACK, M-1929

Issue prewar and early-war bag, made of blue denim material. This was superseded by the olive drab barrack bag.

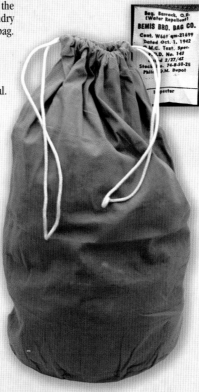

BAG, DUFFEL

A larger and sturdier bag in green canvas, adopted in 1943. It had a shoulder strap and the neck closure could be padlocked. This 1944-dated bag once belonged to John C. Hart and bears his complete name and serial number. One can still observe the Transport Quartermaster bar code painted on every piece of unit baggage. This helped when unloading ships and forwarding equipment to the right unit.

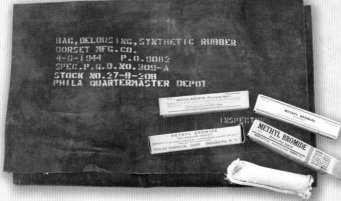

BAG, DELOUSING

A synthetic rubber bag used to disinfest lousy clothing.
An ampule of lice poison (Methyl bromide) was popped into the bag before it was closed tight.

Two duster cans of insecticide ('louse') powder.

1. Button stick/brush and private purchase polishing cloth for burnishing brass uniform buttons.

2. A personal shoe kit, an example of many that could be purchased on the civilian market or from a Post Exchange.

3. Two tins of shoe polish, in the regulation 'russet' shade.

4. A tin of dubbin. This issue boot grease was a compound of oils and tallow, applied to protect shoe leather against mildew and to improve its water-repellency.

3. Personal Hygiene

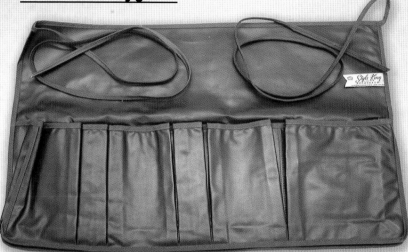

Metal soap box.

A private-purchase toiletry set in water resistant cloth, that could be tied around the waist like an apron so all contents were within reach.

Washcloth in OD material.

Issue soap, and a private purchase black plastic box.

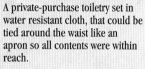

A canvas issue wash basin (page 119).

Plastic comb, tweezers and nail file. Only the comb was government issue.

Issue olive drab huck towel.

Regular and large-size shaving mirrors, with a colored plastic frame.

Black plastic safety razor (PX merchandise)

Post exchange counter display box for 'Mollé' brushless shaving cream.

Another apron-style grooming kit. A much simpler pattern made in HBT fabric and donated by the American Red Cross, it was usually filled with a razor and blades, toothbrush, etc.

Two types of shaving brushes.

Various commercial brands of shaving cream, usable with or without brush. Some packages indicated an exclusive manufacture for the Armed forces.

Haemostatic pencil for shaving cuts.

The 'Burma shave' cream tube came together with a leaflet of the famous jingles played on the radio with this brand's advertising.

Official issue 'Star' brand plastic safety razor and blades.

BAG, CANVAS, VALUABLES, NUMBERED, WITH TAG, METAL IDENTIFICATION

This bag was used when taking advantage of the mobile showers and laundries. The soldier's valuables were deposited with a clerk before showering and exchanging dirty clothing for clean or new items. The numbered metal token was hung around the neck and traded for the bag contents at the end of the line.

A Gillette brand razor and Pal blades.

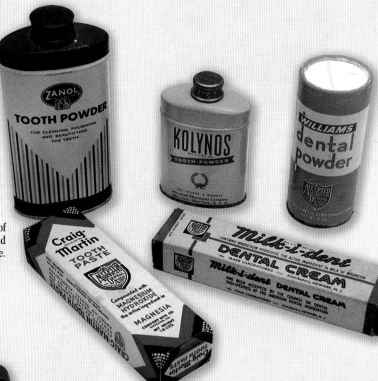

Different types of tooth powder and toothpaste.

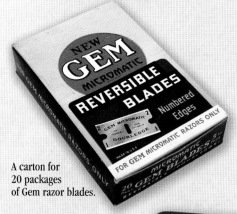

A carton for 20 packages of Gem razor blades.

Toothbrushes and plastic brush case.

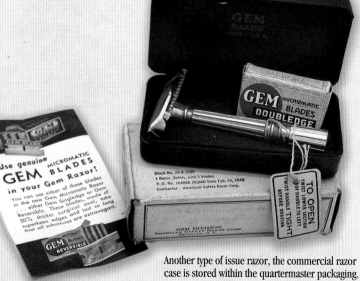

Another type of issue razor, the commercial razor case is stored within the quartermaster packaging.

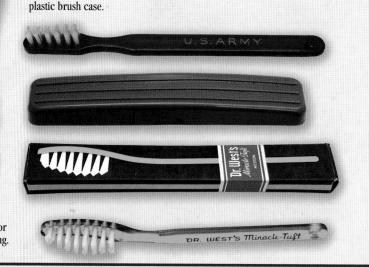

Another amenity bag given by the American Red Cross: a plain pouch with drawstring closure (➡ page 117).

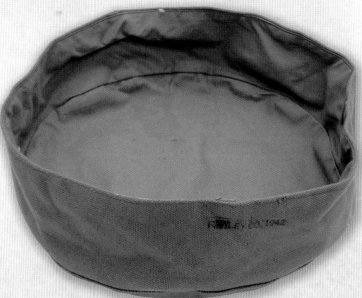

Large collapsible canvas wash basin (➡ page 116).

Issue sunburn preventive cream.

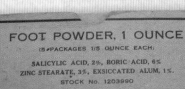

Foot powder, in paper packages and metal box dispenser. This was issued by the Medical Department.

Two types of commercial talcum-powder dispensers.

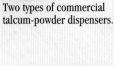

Handkerchief in olive drab cotton, one of 4 issued to each recruit.

1

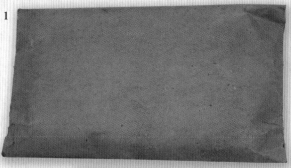

2

1. Toilet paper in a moisture resistant envelope, packed with - among others - the Ten-in-One ration (➡ page 178). 2. The smaller packet was contained in the K-ration box (➡ page 177).

4. Administrative equipment, paperwork

DESK, FIELD, FIBER, COMPANY

Field desk issued together with one 'Fiber, Chest, Record' (right) to each organization for filing unit records. The desk contained stationery and office supplies, various manuals and regulations, service records and current Morning and Sick reports, as well as duty rosters.

CHEST, RECORD, FIBER, (TYPE I)

A chest for filing all non-current documents.

This field desk bears painted-on Transport Quartermaster (TQM) markings: colored bars and unit code number. These were used for operations involving naval transport, in order to keep track of unit baggage. In this case, the markings are for a French Army ordnance heavy maintenance battalion of 1944-45.

CHEST, RECORD, FIBER, (TYPE II)

A similar chest, with the same stock number, but with a slightly different arrangement of contents.

DESK, FIELD, FIBER, HEADQUARTERS

A larger field desk, for regimental headquarters. It held copies of all three battalions personnel files.

Metallic folding camp chair

Folding wood camp table, dated 1944.

55D2 radio set for recreational purposes, manufactured in 1943. It replaced the H100/URR set and could be hooked on military as well as civilian networks.

An ML 102D type barometer and its case, 1944-dated.

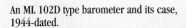

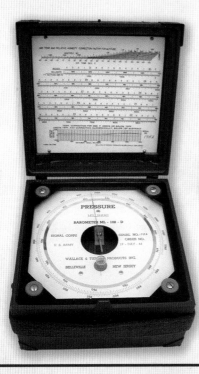

CASE, CANVAS, MAP, ROLL TYPE

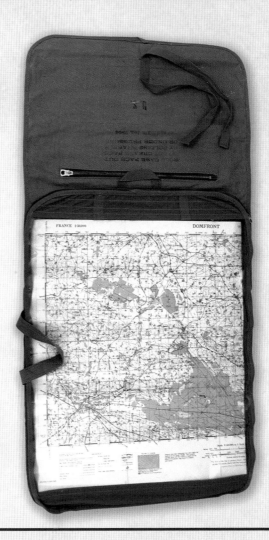

An ingenious canvas case that allowed map reading without completely unfolding the map. The map was protected under a clear plastic sheet.

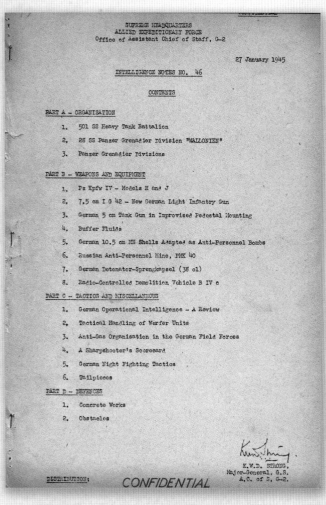

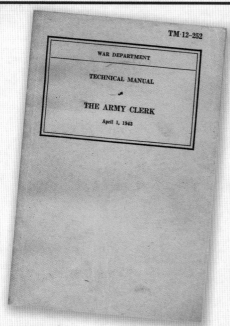

A confidential intelligence bulletin released by the SHAEF G-2 (Major-General Strong) on January, 27, 1945. Its contents deal mainly with several German units' organization, weapons, equipment and tactics.

TM 12-252 was the Technical Manual for Army clerks who kept all personnel records: morning reports, duty rosters, furloughs, pay, etc.

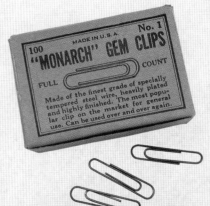

Official envelopes for routine War Department correspondence.

A small loose-leaf folder.

Spare typewriter ribbon.

TYPEWRITER, PORTABLE, WITH CARRYING CASE

Portable typewriter for unit clerks, issue model made by Corona.

Various brands (Velvet, Dixon, Corona, Ditto) of color pencils for mapping work.

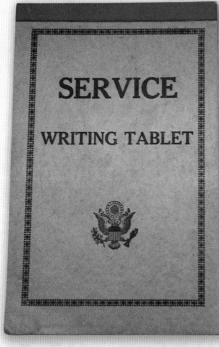

White cray sticks.

Writing pad, lead pencil and eraser.

5. Mail

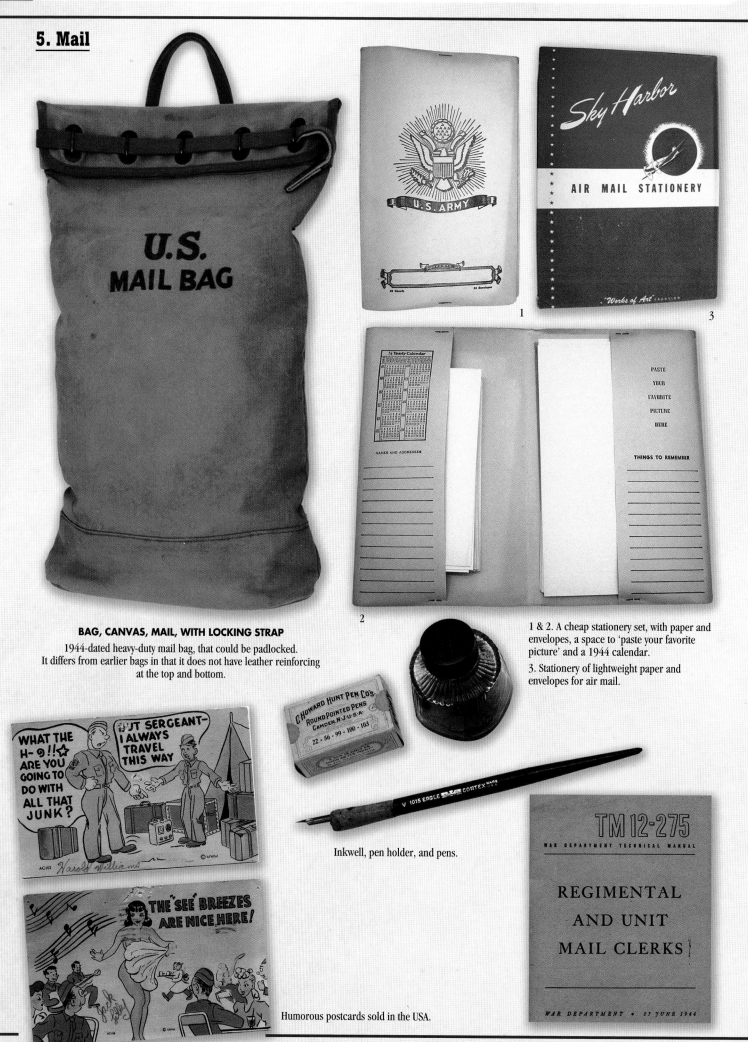

BAG, CANVAS, MAIL, WITH LOCKING STRAP

1944-dated heavy-duty mail bag, that could be padlocked.
It differs from earlier bags in that it does not have leather reinforcing
at the top and bottom.

1 & 2. A cheap stationery set, with paper and envelopes, a space to 'paste your favorite picture' and a 1944 calendar.

3. Stationery of lightweight paper and envelopes for air mail.

Inkwell, pen holder, and pens.

Humorous postcards sold in the USA.

V-Mail

In order to save on shipping space and for expediting the Armed Forces mail, the US Army instituted V-Mail in 1942. The soldier overseas wrote his letter on a special form measuring 11 x 8.5 in. This was then photographed on 16 mm film by the theater V-Mail processing center. The microfilm, with negatives for about 1,800 letters per roll, was then shipped or flown to the States, where individual letters were reproduced as 5 x 4 in. photo prints and forwarded to the soldier's family or friends.

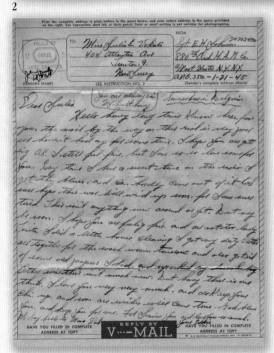

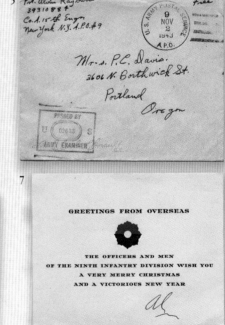

3. The obverse of the V-Mail form bears the instructions for use and the addressee.

4. A V-Mail letter as received by the addressee: a 5 x 4 in. black and white photo print.

5. Soldiers' letters sent by regular mail, although with the free mailing privilege of Armed forces personnel. They have been passed by the unit censor.

1. Writing set of 12 V-mail forms.

2. A V-mail letter in its original form. It has the oblong military censorship stamp and the place of writing is indicated as "somewhere in Belgium."

6. An example of blue envelope. This was available to an enlisted man as a cover for personal mail which would be censored by the Chief base censor and not by an officer in his unit.

7. A greetings card for 1944 sent by a soldier in the 9th Infantry Division's 15th Engineer Battalion. The card was mailed on November, 2, 1943, just before the unit left Italy for England.

1. A short history of U.S. armored troops

The modest armored elements created between the wars in America were still attached to infantry or cavalry formations. The first actual armored units were formed and trained under the aegis of the Armored Force, established on July 10, 1940. The Armored Force would eventually field 16 Armored Divisions, all sent to the European front. The 2d and 3d Armored Divs were organized as 'heavy' divisions of 14,620 men, retaining the regimental structure for its two tanks units and single armored infantry component. All other divisions were 'light' divisions (10,537 men), calling for 3 tank battalions and 3 armored infantry battalions. This structure enabled an easier tactical use. The numerous independent tank battalions also activated were attached on an almost permanent basis to each infantry division.

On General George S. Patton's initiative, Cavalry groups made up of lightly armored and mobile units were created to fulfill reconnaissance missions.

And lastly, tank destroyer units equipped with towed or self-propelled guns were organized to seek and destroy enemy armored threats. These TD battalions were usually used as Army reserve, but the self-propelled units were often individually attached to infantry divisions in order to provide close range artillery support.

2. Armored units patches

1. & 2. Officer's branch insignia for the Armored Force, Tank Destroyer units, and the Cavalry.

3. The Armored Force shoulder patch was worn by training centers as well as independent battalions.

4. & 5. Armored Corps (I to IV) were created and briefly functioned in 1940-42 in the U.S., only I Armored Corps saw combat in North Africa.

6 to 20. Armored divisions were identified by a Roman numeral on the generic Armored Force patch.

21. The 'Tanker' lozenge-shaped patch was a non-regulation insignia sometimes worn by combat crews.

22 & 23. Two variations of the Tank Destroyer Force's patch.

3. Clothing and equipage

A. Early-war uniforms

Note. The breeches and boots shown here were worn early in the war by cavalrymen and other mounted troops, motorcyclists and personnel of the early armored units.

BREECHES, COTTON, KHAKI (STOCK NO 55-B-30029/ 55-B-30830)

Model of 1926 riding breeches, early-war manufacture with zinc buttons. The matching shirt is shown page 34.

BREECHES, WOOL, ELASTIQUE, OD, 18 OZ (STOCK NO 55-B-45496-20/ 55-B-45697-30)

Whipcord fabric breeches, model of 1926. In 1937, the US Army chose trousers as the universal-issue garment. Breeches were however retained by mounted units until 1944, when the horse was finally phased out. See page 35 for the matching wool shirt

BOOTS, LEATHER, LACE, LEGGING TOP (STOCK NO 72-B-829/72-B-846-72)

New pattern cavalry boots introduced in 1940. The legging top was tightened with 3 straps and buckles. This kind of high boot was worn all the war long by several high-ranking officers, such as General Patton.

BOOTS, LEATHER, LACED, EM (STOCK No 72-B-373/72-B-598-35)

Cavalry boots authorized in 1931 and worn at the beginning of the war, by motorcyclists among others. Made in russet leather with a toe cap, leather sole and rubber heel. These were laced up to the top through grommets and hooks. Inset: close up on the inked markings inside the boot shaft.

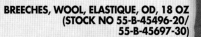

6 - ARMORED TROOPS

B. The herringbone twill outfit

The one-piece overalls and cap were introduced as work clothing for motor mechanics of all branches, and as combat garb for armored troops.

CAP, HERRINGBONE TWILL, OD No 7 (STOCK NO 73-C-25725/73-C-25759)

This late-war cap, made in 1945, only differs by its stronger green (Olive drab No 7) shade.

Cap, Herringbone Twill,
O. D. 7
OMAHA CAP & HAT
MFG. CO.
P. O. No. 10779
Dated Jan. 13, 1945
Spec. No. 6-326
Dated Nov. 27, 1943
Stock No. 73-C-25743
Phila. Q. M. Depot

Inspector
Size 7¼

CAP, HERRINGBONE TWILL (STOCK No 73-C-25605/ 73-C-25639)

A work cap adopted in 1941. This 1943-manufactured example retains the initial light green shade.

Caps, Herringbone Twill
Size 7½
Acme Uniform Cap Co.
Cont. W-669-QM-28272
Dated April 24, 1943
Spec. P.Q.D. No. 18-B
Dated April 8, 1941
Stock No. 73-C-25623
Phila. Q. M. Depot

SUIT, WORK, ONE-PIECE, HERRINGBONE TWILL, OD (STOCK No 55-S-49846-30/ 55-S-49888)

Light green HBT material overalls, made according to December 1938 (altered in April 1942) specs. It has two breast patch pockets (the right one with a partially sewn shut flap), two side slanted pockets with button-through closure, a watch pocket and two hip patch pockets. All buttons are tack-type, black lacquered with the usual star design (➡ page 40).

Blue Bell - Globe Mfg. Company
Cont. No. W669-QM-1853
Dated 5-13-42
Stock No. 55-S-49850
Size 36R
Spec. No. BBB-S-786
Dated Dec. 19, 1938
Phila. Q. M. Depot

SUIT, HERRINGBONE TWILL, OD NO 7, ONE-PIECE, SPECIAL (STOCK No 55-S-45525/55-S-45580)

Second pattern HBT coveralls, according to a September 1943 spec. The material is now dark green and an antigas flap has been added down the front. The right-hand side breast pocket, the watch pocket, the side slanted pockets and the left hip pockets have been done away with. The two large patch pockets located on the upper thighs and hips are covered with wide oblique flaps. Like the earlier pattern, the suit has a vertical pocket on the right leg to carry a screwdriver, wrench or other tool. All buttons are the customary black tack type.

Suit, H.B.T., O.D.
7 Special, One Piece
Stock No. 55-S-45534
34R
H. LANG CO.
Cont. W-36-030-qm-5584
Dated May 25, 1944
Q. M. C. Tent. Spec.
P. Q. D. No. 928
Dated 9/21/43
Phila. Q. M. Depot

Inspector

C. Winter combat clothing

The QMC developed a specific cold weather combat uniform in 1941 for armored troops. This Winter combat uniform was composed of a cloth helmet, bib-type trousers, and a zippered jacket. All these items were made of Olive Drab No 3 uniform twill, lined with blanket-like (kersey) material. They were tested in the field during the winter of 1941-1942, then improved and adopted in the spring of 1942.

HELMET, COMBAT, WINTER (STOCK NO 73-H-64405/ 73-H-64425)

First-type helmet lined with wool scraps covered with facing material (Spec. No 25 of February 10, 1941). The second model (Spec. No 25A, March 27, 1942) has an apparent blanket lining. This warm head cover was worn under the crash helmet (➡ page 130).

Inset, a first-type Winter combat helmet's contractor's label.

TROUSERS, COMBAT, WINTER (STOCK NO 55-T-600/ 55-T-680)

First type trousers in wool lined twill, with adjustable but non-detachable suspenders. The leg bottoms can be gathered with tie tapes. The side openings are zippered and give access to the trousers worn underneath.

JACKET, COMBAT, WINTER (STOCK No 55-J-100-55-J-130)

This 'tanker's jacket' has a full-length zipper on the front, knit collar, cuffs, and waistband. The first-type jacket had two patch open-topped pockets on the front, replaced on this second pattern (Specification 26A, 26 March 1942) by two classic inner, slanted opening pockets. The winter combat jacket was originally slated for issue to armored crews, it was nevertheless worn by other combat soldiers, and especially by officers.

Second pattern winter combat trousers, introduced in 1942, with a zippered fly opening slightly off-center, suspenders attached by special buckles and tack-on metallic buttons. The leg bottoms are gathered by snap-on tabs.

D. The tank helmet

Lining details of a crash helmet manufactured by the Sears Saddlery Company.

HELMET, TANK

The crash helmet for armored troops was the result of a 1938 project for tank and armored vehicle crews, who were then attached to either the infantry or cavalry. The Armored Force had not been established and both arms promoted their own tank tactics and specialized equipment. A patent was registered in 1941 and widespread issue of the new crash helmet began the same year.

The vulcanized fiber shell has ten ventilation holes, a wide attached neck piece protects the back of the head against blows, the flexible side flaps house the R-14 round earphones. As the helmet as it is offered no ballistic protection, the M1 helmet shell (➡ page 64) could be positioned over it.

The headset HS-18, with two R-14 Signal Corps receivers was fitted in the tanker's crash helmet, as well as inside some soft aviation flying helmets.

The CD-307 cord with a JK-26 jack and PL-55 plug was used as an earphone lead with either the R-14s or the HS-30.

The SW-141 switch allowed for two-way conversation, by connecting the throat mike to the armored vehicle's radio and intercom system. It was suspended from the neck with a length of string or leather thong.

The T-30 throat microphone, widely used in the noisy environment of armored vehicles, was held on the neck by an elasticated strap.

The T-17 hand microphone was used with several army radios, and by armored crews.

The HS-30 headset: HB-30 headband, R-30 receivers, and CD-620 cord. These simple general issue earphones could be worn with the crash helmet, and under M1 steel helmet.

E. Armored troops equipment

GOGGLES, RESISTAL, M-1938

Issue goggles for armored troops at the beginning of the war, they are a pattern registered by the Harry Buegeleisen Co. The hallmark 'Resistal HB NY' is embossed on the metal frame. Contrary to a similar pattern for the Airforce, these goggles are not lined with chamois leather on the inside of the face piece. Armored crews were also provided with later-type goggles (➡ page 67).

HOLSTER, PISTOL, M7

Shoulder holster for the M-1911A1 pistol, used by tank crews, among others. Compared to the M3 holster (➡ page 91), the M7 has an additional adjustable chest strap.

DUST, RESPIRATOR, M1

A special mask introduced in April 1941. The faceform is made of shaped rubber with a felt filter on the cheeks, an outlet valve and an elasticated headnet.

M-1938 DISPATCH CASE

Map case for mounted troops, this one was made by Boyt in 1942. It has added straps to keep it close to the body or steed.

4. Vehicle equipment

A. First aid kits

MOTOR VEHICLE FIRST AID KIT (12-UNIT)

This was issued on a scale of one each for four vehicles.

An instructions and contents sheet was glued inside the box lid.

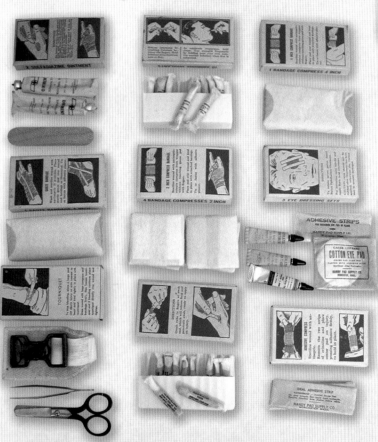

Left.
Detail of some of the contents
of the vehicle first aid kit.

MOTOR VEHICLE FIRST-AID KIT (24-UNIT)

Large sized kit, for armored vehicles.

GAS CASUALTY FIRST AID KIT

Special kit carried in unit vehicles and issued one for
every 25 men.

B. Signal equipment of armored units

THE SCR-610

SCR-610 radio components:

– 1 BC-659A transmitter and receiver

– 1 PE-120 A power supply unit

– 1 FT-250 K mounting

– 1 AN-29 C antenna for ground operation

– 1 whip antenna for vehicular use: MP-48 mast and 4 sections (M-450, M-451, M-452, M-453)

– 1 TS-13 handset.

Range: 5 miles. Mounted on vehicles (jeeps, trucks, half tracks, scout and armored cars).

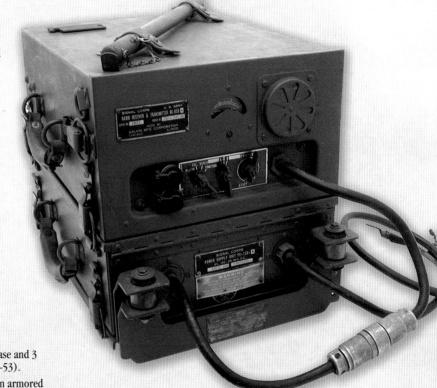

THE SCR-528

Components of the SCR-528 tank radio:

– 1 BC-604 transmitter

– 1 BC-603 receiver

– 1 BC-605 interphone amplifier

– 1 FT-37 mounting

– 1 antenna (MP-37 mast base and 3 sections: MS-51, MS-52, MS-53).

Range: 5 to 18 miles. Used in armored units for short and medium range tactical communication.

The markings printed on a flag set cardboard container indicate this was a Signal Corps item.

FLAG, SET, M-238

A set of 3 color bunting signal flags for optical communications within tank units. These were wagged by the tank commander from his cupola.

The colored flags (red, orange and green) are tied to MC-270 wood poles, and carried in the CS-90 canvas cover. The strap and D-ring on the back of the carrier are for attaching the set to the vehicle.

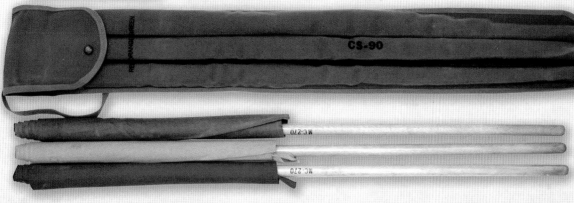

C. Motor transport equipment and radio maintenance

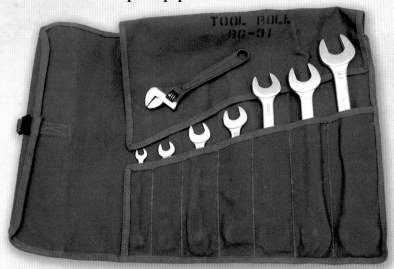

BG-31 TOOL ROLL

A tool roll of wrenches for Signal Corps use (BG is a Signal Corps item nomenclature, for bags).

5-gallon gasoline jerrycan, the initial G is embossed on one side. The date (1943) and manufacturer are stamped on the underside.

An M32 recovery tank from B/25th Tank Battalion (14th Armored Division) in Batzendorf (France), 9 February 1945.
(National Archives)

TUBE, FLEXIBLE NOZZLE

A nozzle that screws on in place of the jerrycan's cap, for filling up a vehicle without spilling.

Battery tester.

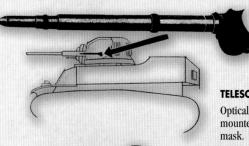

TELESCOPE, M70

Optical aiming sight for the M3 Light and M4 Medium tanks. This was mounted on the mantlet alongside the main gun. Note the padded rubber mask.

D. Vehicle-related documents

TM 21-300
WAR DEPARTMENT TECHNICAL MANUAL

DRIVER SELECTION

TRAINING AND

SUPERVISION,

WHEELED VEHICLES

WAR DEPARTMENT · FEBRUARY 1945

TM 10-460

ATTITUDE
KNOWLEDGE · ABILITY
JUDGMENT · HABITS
EXPERT DRIVING
KEEPS 'EM ROLLING
PHYSICAL FITNESS · MENTAL FITNESS

DRIVER'S MANUAL
UNITED STATES ARMY

Standard Form No. 26
Approved by the President
June 10, 1927

DRIVER'S REPORT—ACCIDENT
MOTOR TRANSPORTATION

INSTRUCTIONS TO DRIVERS

In case of injury to person or damage to property:
 A. Stop car and render such assistance as may be needed.
 B. Fill out this form, ON THE SPOT, so far as possible.
 C. Deliver this report promptly to your immediate superior.

Failure to observe these instructions will result in disciplinary action.

1. Name of Government driver:

2. Stationed at

3. Make and type of Government vehicle

4. Service number

5. Name and address of owner of other vehicle (or owner of property damaged)

6. Name and address of driver of other vehicle

7. License of other vehicle : State
 No.

8. Place of accident : City
 Street

DRIVER'S DAILY PREVENTIVE MAINTENANCE SERVICES
Perform these services according to the instruction in TM 37-2810, or vehicle operator's manual.

BEFORE OPERATION SERVICE

DURING OPERATION SERVICE

AT HALT SERVICE

AFTER OPERATION SERVICE

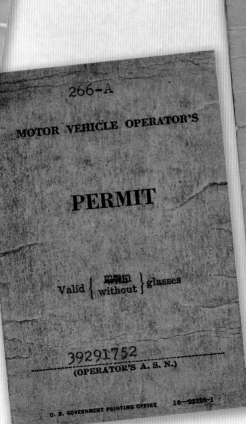

266-A

MOTOR VEHICLE OPERATOR'S

PERMIT

Valid { with / without } glasses

39291752
(OPERATOR'S A. S. N.)

U. S. GOVERNMENT PRINTING OFFICE   16—22236-1

O. O. Form No. 7360
(Approved Dec. 7, 1942)
(Old Q. M. C. Form No. 228)

2 September, 19 43
(Date of issue)

Frank R Aten
(Operator's signature)

I CERTIFY THAT   Frank R. Aten, Pvt.
(Name and rank)

has demonstrated proficiency in driving (par. 16, A/R 850–15) the types of vehicles listed below as per signed authentication.

TYPE VEHICLE	AUTHENTICATION (Signed by a commissioned officer)
Car, halftrack	
Car, passenger	*George C Price 2nd Lt QMC*
Motorcycle	
Tank, heavy	
Tank, light	
Tank, medium	
Tractor	
Truck-tractor (semitrailer)	
Trucks, cargo, ¼–¾-ton	*George C Price 2nd Lt QMC*
Trucks, cargo, 1½–2½-ton	*George C Price 2nd Lt QMC*
Trucks, cargo, 4-ton and larger	
Trucks, amphibian (all)	
Vehicle, wheeled, combat	
Special	

16—22236-1

The regulation US Army driver's licence. This one has been given in Sept. 1943 to a private, who qualified for driving cars (jeeps), weapons carriers and trucks, up to a payload of 2.5 tons (GMC).

1. History and organization

By June 1940, the American War Department had been so impressed by the success of German airborne troops in Europe that it authorized a Parachute Test Platoon. Selected men of the 29th Infantry were chosen as cadre for the unit, commanded by Major William Lee. The platoon proved its mettle very quickly in several manoeuvres, and the War Department created the 501st Parachute Infantry Battalion (PIB) in October 1940. At the same time, the Army also experimented with glider-borne assault troops.

The 502nd, 503rd and 504th PIBs were established in 1941, as well as the 550th Airborne Infantry Battalion. In February 1942, the four battalions were expanded into regiments, and in March, the Airborne Command was created to oversee the training and administration of such units. The 82d and 101st Airborne divisions were activated in August 1942, the 17th in April 1943 and the 13th in August 1943.

The 1944 Airborne division called for three Parachute infantry regiments and one Glider infantry regiment, plus numerous airborne support units (artillery, signals, engineers, etc.). The first combat operation for US parachute troops occurred in November 1942 during operation 'Torch', when 2/503 PIR was dropped near Oran. Airborne units were then committed to several campaigns in Sicily, Italy, Normandy, Southern France, the Netherlands, during the battle of the Bulge and in Germany.

Brigadier-General Anthony C. McAuliffe, artillery commander of the 101st Airborne Division, delivers a speech to soldiers of the 327th Glider Infantry Regiment and airmen of the 53rd Troop Carrier Wing, before leaving for Holland on D+1 of operation 'Market-Garden' (September 18, 1944).
(National Archives)

2. Badges and insignia
(next page)

– Shoulder sleeve insignia
1. 82nd Airborne Division
2. 101st Airborne Division
3. 501st Parachute Infantry Regiment
4. 508th Parachute Infantry Regiment
5. 509th Parachute Infantry Regiment
6. 13th Airborne Division
7. 17th Airborne Division
8. Airborne command
9. Pathfinders (lower sleeve)
– Garrison cap insignia
10. Parachute Infantry. Non-regulation insignia which appeared early in 1941, worn on the left side by enlisted men (➡ page 29).
11. Glider-borne artillery. Officer's pattern worn on the right side as of April 1942 (➡ page 31).
12. Regulation garrison cap insignia for all airborne personnel, authorized spring 1943 (enlisted men's insignia).

– Qualification badges
These were pinned on the left breast, above the service ribbons.
13. BADGE, PARACHUTIST'S
Adopted in 1941, the badge was awarded by commanding officers of airborne units to soldiers who had completed the prescribed proficiency tests, or who had taken part in at least one combat jump.
14. BADGE, GLIDER
Badge for glider-borne troops, awarded under the same conditions as the Parachutist's badge.
– Wing ovals (embroidered on fabric, or made of cut-out pieces of material).
These were in the battalion or regiment colors, and the wings were pinned onto them. Ovals were worn only with the service uniform (garrison, leave).
15. 504th PIR oval.
16. Oval for the HQ/82nd Airborne Division.

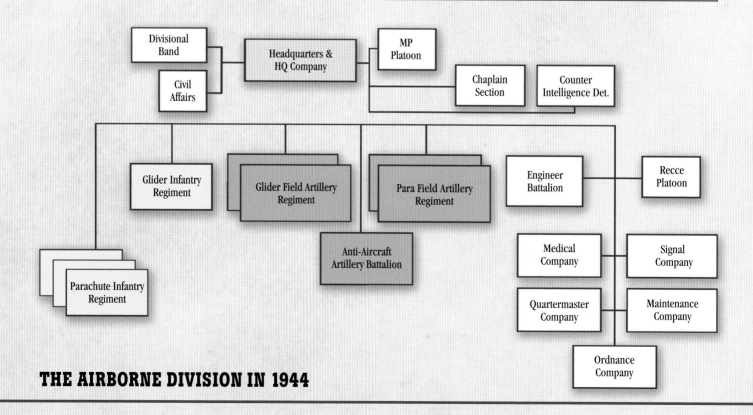

THE AIRBORNE DIVISION IN 1944

1

2

3

4

5

6

7

8

9

10

11

12

13

14

15

16

3. Paratrooper uniforms

The jump suit

The first American military paratroopers wore the early-war HBT one-piece suit (➡ page 128) for training. As this was unsuitable for actual combat, a new uniform was introduced early 1941. Made of Olive drab shade No 3 uniform twill, this was composed of a belted coat and trousers, featuring large expanding pockets on the breast and thighs. The first-pattern uniform had a single snap closure for these pockets. The second pattern jump uniform, which appeared in 1942, had two snaps on the cargo pockets. Glider-borne troops were not issued the jump uniform, but wore the standard field uniform of the time.

After the early airborne operations in the Mediterranean, the jump uniform was deemed overall satisfactory, except for its durability. For the Normandy operation of June 1944, reinforcing patches of canvas were sewn on the elbows and lower pockets' bellows of the coat, and at the knees and pockets of the pants. Twin straps let in at the inseam helped keep the thigh pockets contents from bulging. Reinforcing patches were usually cut from greenish waterproofed material, which turned gray after laundering. More than 90% of all jump suits were thus reinforced before D-Day. At the end of the summer of 1944 however, the specific jump suit was replaced by the universal-issue M-1943 field uniform (➡ pages 38-39).

The M2 switch-blade knife (➡ page 142) was carried in the coat, inside a special pocket under the collar, closed on both sides by a short zipper.

1. Both breast pockets have a narrow slit on top of the flap to insert a pencil, or to hang a grenade by its safety lever, or a torch by its clip (➡ page 86).

2. A loop (one of 3) on the small of the back holds the belt in place.

3. The cuffs are closed by 'Durable' type metal snaps (also used on the collar, shoulder loops and pockets), which usually bear the marks 'United Carr' or 'Scovill.'

4. Four ventilation holes are located under the arm.

COAT, PARACHUTE JUMPER (STOCK NO 55-C-35808/55-C-35862)

This wind and rain-resistant coat was adopted in December 1941. It closes down the front with a zipper, from the collar down to slightly under the waist. The integral belt has a prongless bar buckle. This particular coat has slanted breast pockets for easier access, this was only a manufacturer's variation.

TROUSERS, PARACHUTE JUMPER (STOCK NO 55-T-40499/55-T-40563)

Pattern specified in February 1942. It has two side pockets, a watch pocket, two hip pockets, and two large expanding pockets on the thighs.

The tapered legs help inserting the trousers in the jump boots (➡ page 139). The left hip pocket has a button-through closure. The lining and pockets are cut from off-white cotton.

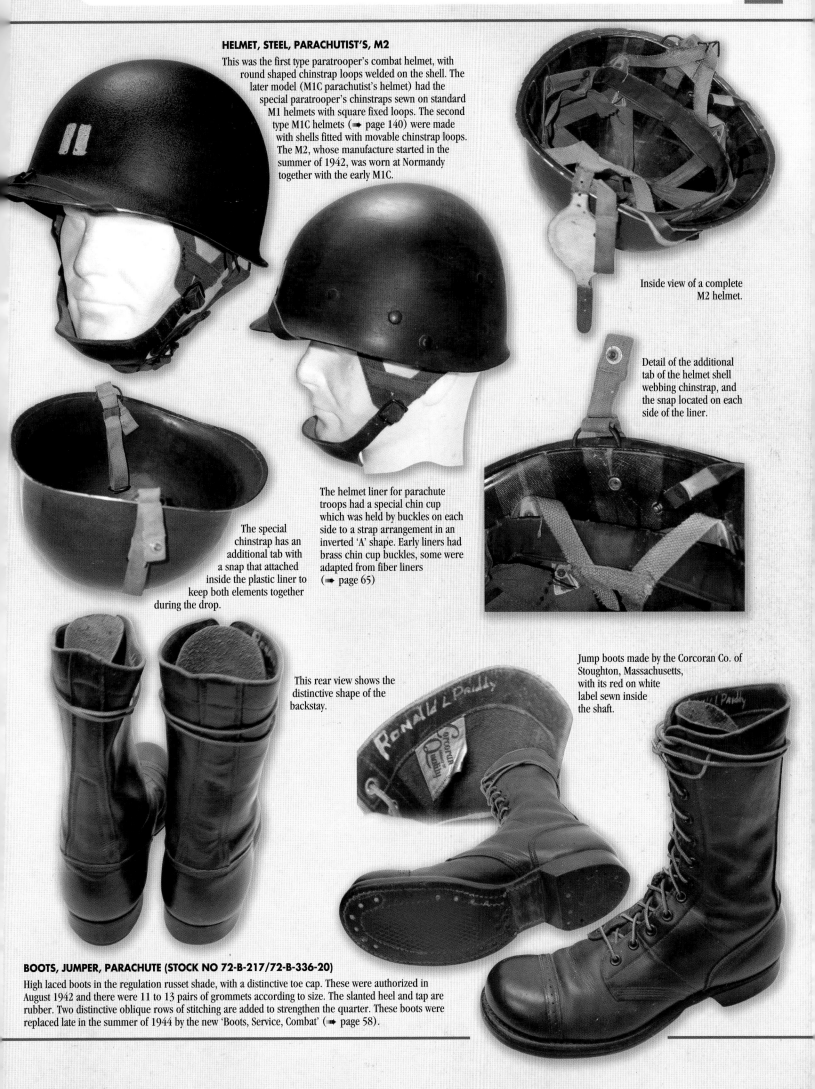

HELMET, STEEL, PARACHUTIST'S, M2

This was the first type paratrooper's combat helmet, with round shaped chinstrap loops welded on the shell. The later model (M1C parachutist's helmet) had the special paratrooper's chinstraps sewn on standard M1 helmets with square fixed loops. The second type M1C helmets (➡ page 140) were made with shells fitted with movable chinstrap loops. The M2, whose manufacture started in the summer of 1942, was worn at Normandy together with the early M1C.

Inside view of a complete M2 helmet.

Detail of the additional tab of the helmet shell webbing chinstrap, and the snap located on each side of the liner.

The special chinstrap has an additional tab with a snap that attached inside the plastic liner to keep both elements together during the drop.

The helmet liner for parachute troops had a special chin cup which was held by buckles on each side to a strap arrangement in an inverted 'A' shape. Early liners had brass chin cup buckles, some were adapted from fiber liners (➡ page 65)

This rear view shows the distinctive shape of the backstay.

Jump boots made by the Corcoran Co. of Stoughton, Massachusetts, with its red on white label sewn inside the shaft.

BOOTS, JUMPER, PARACHUTE (STOCK NO 72-B-217/72-B-336-20)

High laced boots in the regulation russet shade, with a distinctive toe cap. These were authorized in August 1942 and there were 11 to 13 pairs of grommets according to size. The slanted heel and tap are rubber. Two distinctive oblique rows of stitching are added to strengthen the quarter. These boots were replaced late in the summer of 1944 by the new 'Boots, Service, Combat' (➡ page 58).

HELMET, STEEL, PARACHUTIST'S, M1C

The second pattern paratrooper's helmet was introduced during the fall of 1943 and issued widely after the Normandy operation. The shell had movable chinstrap loops (➡ page 64).

Inside view of the helmet. The leather chin cup was replaced by simpler web straps during the summer of 1944.

Liners manufactured later in the war to fit inside paratrooper helmets had greener web 'inverted A' straps, with larger stamped metal buckles for the chin cup.

Close-up on the movable chinstrap loops. The tab and snap system for keeping the shell and liner together is apparent.

The web chinstrap remained the same with all types of paratrooper helmet shells.

GLOVES, HORSEHIDE, RIDING, UNLINED (STOCK NO 73-G-22010-73-G-22050)

These leather gloves developed for mounted troops were also issued to all ranks of paratrooper units.
(Photo Militaria Magazine)

Flag armband in coated material, affixed by two safety pins. This was issued to all assault troops for the North African invasion of November 1942 (operation 'Torch'). For the Normandy operation of June 1944, a rectangular flag in muslin was issued to airborne troops only, but the older armband was sometimes cut out around the flag, this being crudely sewn on the right upper arm.

CAP, MECHANIC'S, WINTER, TYPE A-4

A knit cap for Airforce mechanics, that was sometimes obtained by paratroopers.

Below.

Olive drab knit skull cap, worn under the steel helmet in the same manner as the M-1941 wool knit cap (➡ page 62). This non-issue item was donated to soldiers by religious or other welfare committees, here the Christian Science War Relief Committee.

Cotton field trousers issued together with the M-1943 field jacket (➡ page 39), and locally modified for paratroopers by the addition of two large cargo pockets on the thighs. These were made of heavy-duty canvas, and often fitted with long tie tapes around the leg.

M-1943 field jacket badged up for a Corporal in the 17th Airborne Division. This well-designed garment was used by airborne soldiers as it was, without modifications as had been the case with the 'Coat, parachute jumper's.'

The plastic buttons inside the waistband were for attaching suspenders.

4. Individual equipment

KNIFE, POCKET, M2, PARACHUTIST'S

This switchblade knife was located in the small vertical pocket under the collar of the jump coat (➡ page 138). Its purpose was to cut the canopy risers when landing in a difficult spot.

Top
A knife marked 'Presto Pat. Jan 30 40/Made in USA' on one side of the ricasso, and 'Geo. Schrade/Bridgeport/Conn' on the other side.
Bottom.
Another M2 knife, made by Schrade Walden/NY USA.

PARACHUTE FIRST AID PACKET

This waterproof pouch contained a first aid packet in a cardboard container (➡ page 226), a tourniquet and a 1/2 grain of morphine tartrate in an expendable syrette (➡ page 228). The four tie tapes were for affixing the pouch on the helmet, uniform or equipment. This article was also given to first wave ground troops on D-day.

ROPE, PARACHUTIST'S, DIAMETER 3/8", LENGTH 30'

A strong rope used by paratroopers to lower themselves from trees, roofs, or other high places they might have landed in by accident.

Instruction sheet for the camo cream, issued at the ratio of one for every hundred sticks.

LUMINOUS MARKER RADIOACTIVE, TYPE 1

This phosphorescent marker was an Engineer item used for road or path marking at night. It was also used by airborne units for nocturnal moves, tied on clothing or equipment. There was another model fitted on the back with a spring clip. The warning 'Poison inside' can be read on the back.

Another general issue item, this stick of camouflage cream has two compartments closed by a thin metal cap. Three different sticks offered two-tone combinations: Light Green and Loam (Stock No 29-P-800), Light Green and Sand (Stock No 29-P-825) and White and Loam (Stock No 29-P-850).

M-1910 intrenching shovel (➡ page 82) with shortened handle, found after the war near Sainte-Mère-Eglise in Normandy. E-tools were often modified by paratroopers to minimize injury hazards during combat jumps.

COMPASS, WRIST, LIQUID FILLED

Plastic wrist compass with leather adjustable band. The needle point is phosphorescent. This was a general issue item designed by the Corps of Engineers (➡ page 86).

CARBINE, CAL .30, M1A1

This model is identical to the M1 except for the stock: a separate grip is attached to the stock and a folding, skeleton stock-extension is hinged onto the grip. This was introduced in May 1942 for Airborne troops. Original M1A1 carbines were manufactured by the Inland Division of the General Motors Co., which was also committed to provide spare folding stocks to the Ordnance department for repairs and fitting to regular carbines. The weapon shown here is an early make, as demonstrated by the 'L' rear sight and no cut-out on the handguard.

M1A1 carbine with the stock folded.

SCABBARD, CARBINE, CAL .30, M1A1, CANVAS

A special belt holster for carrying the folding stock carbine during the jump. This was padded with felt on the leg side. Adopted in February 1943, it was made of olive drab No 3 canvas, then of greener olive drab No 7 material. The scabbard was held onto the leg by the strap and buckle at the muzzle end.

Another M1A1 carbine scabbard, also made in 1943. The rear view shows the wide belt loop.

HOLSTER, ASSEMBLY, PARACHUTIST'S, RIFLE

This piece of equipment was designed by the Airforce for protecting the M1 rifle as well as the soldier during combat jumps. The M1 rifle was dismantled in two elements. The cover was attached to the parachute harness with the snap hook sewn on the rear side. This particular holster has been lengthened in order to accommodate a Thompson SMG with the Cutts compensator on the muzzle (M-1928A1, ➡ page 96). It is a second pattern holster with a full length zipper closure instead of snaps.

5. Miscellaneous equipment

First pattern demolition bag for paratroopers, made by Boyt in 1942. This was worn as a backpack with two long adjustable webbing straps.

POUCH, MEDICAL, PARACHUTIST

1 & 2. A large first-aid bag for paratroop medics in dark green canvas (od No 7), this was strapped on the chest for the drop. This particular pouch has been made by Johansen in 1945.

Later pattern demolition bag for parachutists, in light then greener olive drab waterproofed material. It was usually slung on the body with its wide adjustable strap. For combat jumps, a movable snap hook on the strap was attached to a chest buckle on the parachute harness. Tie tapes sewn at the base of the bag kept it from flapping around.

6. The T-5 paratrooper's parachute

The T-5 parachute was adopted in June 1941, it had one main pack and one reserve (chest) pack. The T-5 was used in combat until the D-day jump over Normandy. It was thereafter modified by the addition of a quick-release box for the harness straps, which ultimately led to the new T-7 parachute.

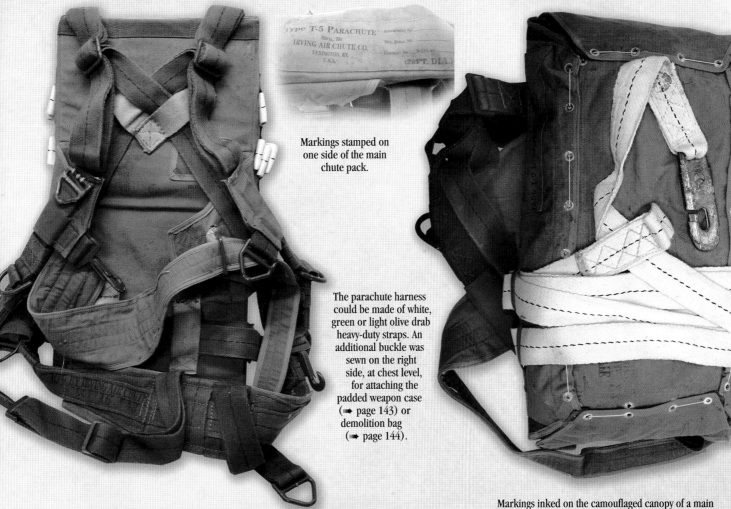

Markings stamped on one side of the main chute pack.

The parachute harness could be made of white, green or light olive drab heavy-duty straps. An additional buckle was sewn on the right side, at chest level, for attaching the padded weapon case (➡ page 143) or demolition bag (➡ page 144).

Markings inked on the camouflaged canopy of a main chute made in 1943.

The reserve chute's 24-gore canopy was made of white silk or nylon. It was packed into the T-5 Chest Pack Assembly or the AN-6513-1A Chest Pack.

Back view of the reserve chute pack, the two sturdy snap hooks connected the pack with the harness, on the stomach.

The parachute log record, usually stored inside a special pocket sewn on the main pack, recorded every jump, repair and overhaul, until the parachute was struck off.

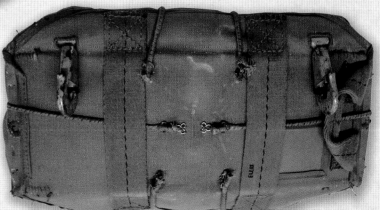

7. Airborne troops signals equipment

For airborne operations, crack pathfinder units were dispatched in advance on the drop zones in order to guide in the troop carrying aircraft of larger units. Pathfinders were outfitted for this purpose with ground radio beacons, made in the United States after a British design.

The aircraft had on board an apparatus code-named 'Rebecca'

sending interrogator waves. On the ground, the pathfinders operated the 'Eureka' responder beacon, on which the lead carrier aircraft homed in. Each beacon was preset on a certain frequency, specific to each Airforce troop carrier unit. At close range, short voice or Morse signals could be exchanged. This secret equipment could under no circumstances be captured, it was therefore spiked with a self-destruction charge. The PPN-1 beacon was used for the Normandy operation, thereafter it was superseded by the PPN-2.

Felt-padded bag for the PPN-1 beacon, in water-resistant canvas. There is an inner compartment for the sectional antenna. The bag was hooked under the reserve parachute, and carried on the back after landing.

AS-73 'Umbrella' antenna for the PPN-2 beacon. About 9,5" high, this had three vertical sections instead of two for the PPN-1. It was plugged vertically on top of the beacon.

Nomenclature plate for a PPN-2 beacon manufactured in 1944.

MX183 bag for the AN/PP-2 beacon, padded inside with felt and made of water-resistant canvas.

PPN-2 BEACON

Characteristics:

– 5 preset VHF wavelengths

– Power supply: a BB-212 2-volt battery

– Range: 15-48 miles.

Between the two large frequency adjustment knobs can be seen the red self-destruction button. An HS-30 earphone headset (➡ page 130) could be plugged in, a push-button enabled Morse transmission.

Second pattern bag for the PPN-1 beacon (Stock No 2 Z 565 1-2), this was made of rubberized canvas.

8. Optical signals

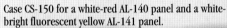

Case CS-150 for a white-red AL-140 panel and a white-bright fluorescent yellow AL-141 panel.

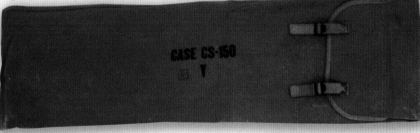

SIGNAL LAMP EQUIPMENT SE-11

Portable flashlight-type signal lamp, to transmit morse code by day or night. This was aimed like a gun when fitted with the M-341 stock. The lamp could also be remote-controlled with the J-51 trigger key when attached to its tripod. At night, flashes were red or white depending on the added filter.

Range without filter: 2,000 yards in daylight, 800 yards at night

Range with filter: 1,000 yards in daylight, 440 yards at night.

The complete SE-11 signal equipment was composed of:
1. 1 BG-131 bag
2. 1 M-227 lamp
3. 1 M-341 detachable stock
4. 1 LG-21 tripod
5. 1 MC-430 filter
6. 1 M-172 night vision goggles
7. 1 CD-701 cord
8. 1 J-51 trigger key
  – 11 LM-61 bulbs (10 as spares)
  – 10 BA-30 batteries (5 as spares)
9. 1 TM-11-392 Technical manual.

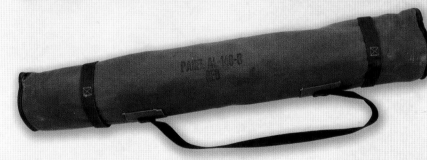

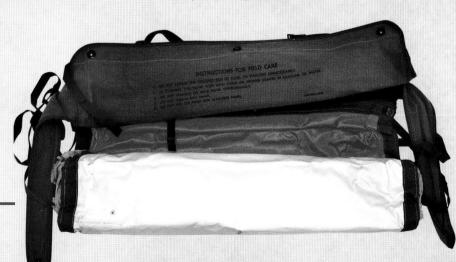

AL-140 signal panel, double-sided, white and red (10" by 2.6"). Several assembled panels were used to spell out symbols for aerial liaison. The panels could be staked to the ground or attached to vehicles with tapes.

9. Aerial delivery containers

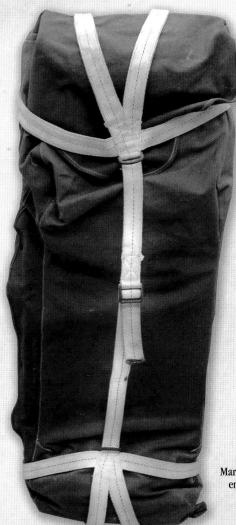

CONTAINER, AERIAL DELIVERY, PARACRATE M1

A strong canvas container. This was attached in special racks under the C-47 troop carrying aircraft's wings and contained one of six elements of the 75-mm Pack Howitzer. This container has been made in 1944 by the Milwaukee Saddlery Co.

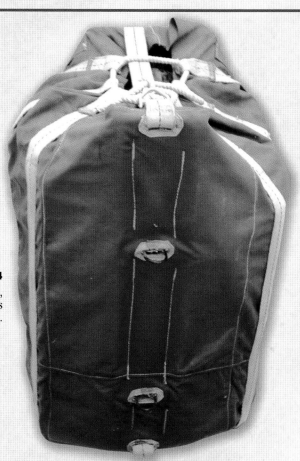

CONTAINER, AERIAL DELIVERY, A-4

Container in heavy-duty green canvas, used for delivery of rations and medical supplies.

Markings on the right end cover of an A-5 ammunition container.

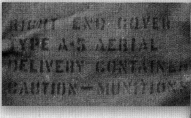

LAMP ASSEMBLY IDENTIFICATION, AERIAL DELIVERY CONTAINER

A lamp that was automatically turned on as the parachute opened, and that assisted with locating cargo containers on the ground during night drops. Different light colors were used depending on the cargo.

CONTAINER, AERIAL DELIVERY, A-5

It was in fact two padded bags and a two-piece outside cover, made with several rifle jump cases (➡ page 145) sewn together. A G-1 cargo parachute was tied to the top and a padded shock absorber attached to its base.

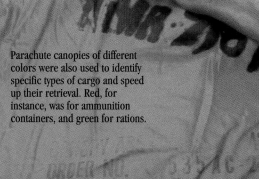

Parachute canopies of different colors were also used to identify specific types of cargo and speed up their retrieval. Red, for instance, was for ammunition containers, and green for rations.

10. Utility hand carts

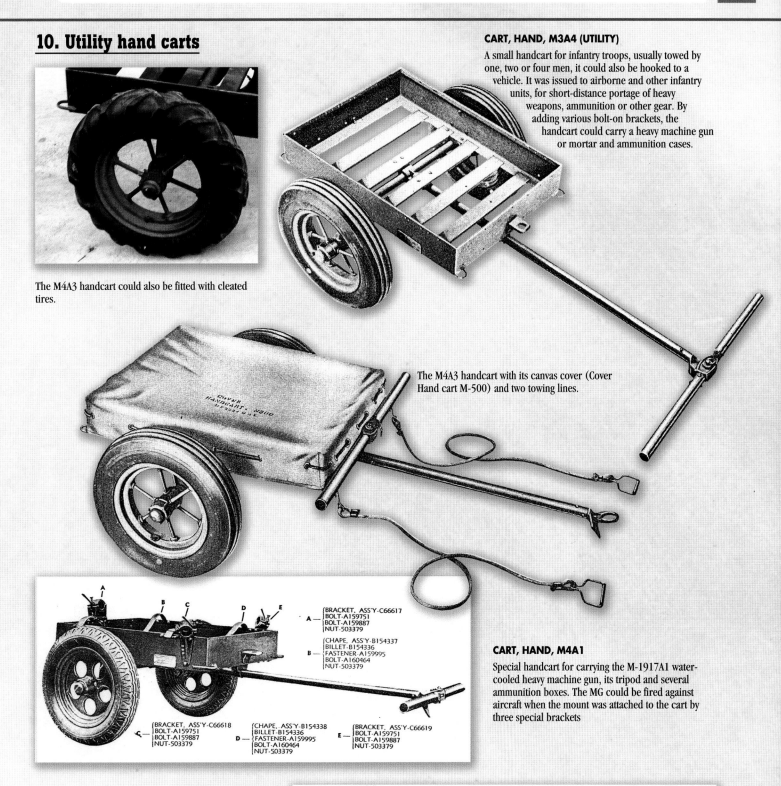

The M4A3 handcart could also be fitted with cleated tires.

CART, HAND, M3A4 (UTILITY)

A small handcart for infantry troops, usually towed by one, two or four men, it could also be hooked to a vehicle. It was issued to airborne and other infantry units, for short-distance portage of heavy weapons, ammunition or other gear. By adding various bolt-on brackets, the handcart could carry a heavy machine gun or mortar and ammunition cases.

The M4A3 handcart with its canvas cover (Cover Hand cart M-500) and two towing lines.

A —
BRACKET, ASS'Y-C66617
BOLT-A159751
BOLT-A159887
NUT-503379

B —
CHAPE, ASS'Y-B154337
BILLET-B154336
FASTENER-A159995
BOLT-A160464
NUT-503379

CART, HAND, M4A1

Special handcart for carrying the M-1917A1 water-cooled heavy machine gun, its tripod and several ammunition boxes. The MG could be fired against aircraft when the mount was attached to the cart by three special brackets

BRACKET, ASS'Y-C66618
BOLT-A159751
BOLT-A159887
NUT-503379

CHAPE, ASS'Y-B154338
BILLET-B154336
FASTENER-A159995
BOLT-A160464
NUT-503379

E —
BRACKET, ASS'Y-C66619
BOLT-A159751
BOLT-A159887
NUT-503379

CART, HAND, M6A1

Hand cart for heavy mortar sections. Quick-release brackets held the 81-mm mortar tube and leather straps secured the shell boxes.

Nomenclature plate for an M4A3 handcart, located on the body front.

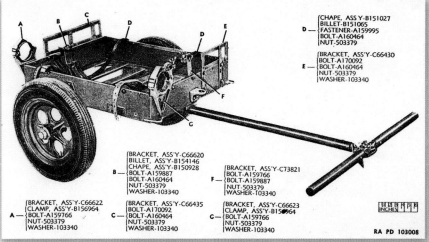

D —
CHAPE, ASS'Y-B151027
BILLET-B151065
FASTENER-A159995
BOLT-A160464
NUT-503379

E —
BRACKET, ASS'Y-C66430
BOLT-A170092
BOLT-A160464
NUT-503379
WASHER-103340

B —
BRACKET, ASS'Y-C66620
BILLET, ASS'Y-B154146
CHAPE, ASS'Y-B150928
BOLT-A159887
BOLT-A160464
NUT-503379
WASHER-103340

F —
BRACKET, ASS'Y-C73821
BOLT-A159766
BOLT-A159887
NUT-503379
WASHER-103340

A —
BRACKET, ASS'Y-C66622
CLAMP, ASS'Y-B156964
BOLT-A159766
NUT-503379
WASHER-103340

C —
BRACKET, ASS'Y-C66435
BOLT-A170092
BOLT-A160464
NUT-503379
WASHER-103340

G —
BRACKET, ASS'Y-C66623
CLAMP, ASS'Y-B156964
BOLT-A159766
NUT-503379
WASHER-103340

RA PD 103008

1. Mountain troops history

A. The 10th Mountain Division

In 1939, the Soviet Army invaded nearby Finland. In the course of this difficult winter campaign, mobile Finnish ski troops managed to defeat two Soviet armored divisions. This success did not go unnoticed to Charles Minot Dole, president of the US National Ski Patrol. Dole was eager to promote mountain and ski troops in the US Army and, in September 1940, managed to sell Chief of Staff General George C. Marshall on this idea. The first such American unit, the 87th (Mountain) Infantry Battalion was activated at Fort Lewis (Wash.) on December 8, 1941. Two additional battalions were created in May and June 1942, the three battalions making up the new 87th Infantry Regiment.

On July 15, 1943, the 10th Light Division (Alpine) was established at Camp Hale (Colorado), led by Brigadier General Lloyd E. Jones. The division's infantry component was made up of the 85th, 86th and 87th Regiments. The unit was renamed 10th Mountain Division on November 6, 1944 on the triangular division pattern of three infantry regiments of 3 battalions with a heavy weapons company each. The division was ultimately shipped to Italy where it started on January 8, 1945 its campaign in the Northern mountain ranges. It would then fight to gain access to the Po valley. In 114 days of combat, the 10th Mountain division defeated five crack German divisions.

B. The First Special Service Force

The concept of an elite unit for mountain warfare originated from Englishman Geoffrey Pike, who was on the Staff of the British 'Combined Operations' command. Due to lack of resources, the idea was passed to General Marshall, who managed to persuade President Roosevelt of its worth. Lieutenant General Robert T. Frederick was picked to form a composite American/Canadian unit, able to perform commando-type as well as airborne missions.

The First Special Service Force was activated on July 20, 1942 at Fort William Henry Harrison (Montana). The FSSF became a fully fledged branch of the Army, and upheld the traditions of the Indian scouts of old. After a brief commitment to the Aleutians in August 1943, the FSSF was shipped to Italy where it would gain fame. It was then part of Operation 'Dragoon' (invasion of Southern France) and fought there until it was disbanded in December 1944.

During Stateside training and later in Europe, the 10th Mountain Division and First Special Service Force were outfitted with specialized equipment, which is described in this chapter.

Shoulder sleeve insignia and smaller size enameled insignia for the 10th Mountain Division

Shoulder sleeve insignia for the First Special Service Force

**SHIRT, KNIT
(STOCK NO 55-S-7500/55-S-7520)**

A light knit shirt with buttoned high neck, issued to jungle and mountain troops. This was worn over the standard flannel shirt (➡ page 32) and under a thicker wool sweater (➡ page 52)
(Photo Militaria Magazine, Coleman collection)

2. Mountain and ski clothing

JACKET, MOUNTAIN
(STOCK NO 55-J-544-25/55-J-545-90)

Rain and wind-resistant poplin jacket in Olive drab No 3 shade. It has two breast pockets, with zipper and flap closure. The two cut-in hip pockets have buttoned flaps. The jacket closes down the front with an almost full-length zipper and a covering band with 3 buttons, plus one under the collar.

A long belt, identical to the issue trouser belt (➡ page 53) is slipped into wide loops around the waist. It is however missing here. The mountain jacket was worn together with a warm undershirt, the standard flannel shirt and several sweaters if needed.

The mountain jacket features a large-capacity cargo pocket across the back, which closes on the left side by a zipper. This pocket was for carrying spare clothing and food when the rucksack could not be taken along. The integral hood could be neatly folded in a hidden pouch between the shoulders.

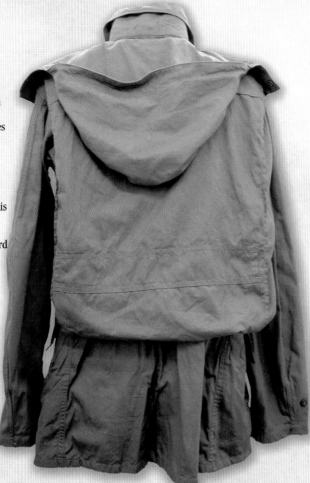

A system of inner suspenders supports the weight of the pockets when these are full.

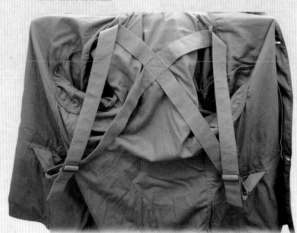

TROUSERS, MOUNTAIN
(STOCK NO 55-T-39820-29/55-T-39832-30)

Matching trousers for the jacket, in cotton sateen material, also adopted in 1942. These tapered-leg trousers have two slanted side pockets closed by a zipper. The two large cargo pockets on the thighs - pleated down the middle - are covered by wide flaps with two buttons. Both hip pockets also feature a buttoned flap. The trousers have a zip fly and two buttons on the waistband. They could be worn with the mountain jacket, a parka (➡ page 152) or later in Europe, the M-1943 jacket (➡ page 38). The special suspenders used with the mountain trousers are shown ➡ page 53.

The leg bottoms have elasticated foot loops to keep them on top of the shoes.

CAP, SKI
(STOCK No 73-C-40000/73-C-40025)

A cotton poplin cap in Olive Drab No 3 shade, according to Spec. No 78 of June 16, 1942. It has a wide ear flap that could be turned down and an adjustable fabric chinstrap. The second type ski cap had no chinstrap, but two metal grommets for ventilation. It formed the basis for the new field cap of the M-1943 outfit (➡ page 62).

PARKA, REVERSIBLE, SKI, FUR TRIMMED
(STOCK No 55-P- 4903/55-P-4909)

Final pattern of reversible (green-white) parka (Spec. No 201 of July 14, 1942). It was made of two ply water-resistant poplin. The hood was trimmed with wolf fur. The cuffs and slanted opening inner front pockets are closed by plastic buttons. A drawstring at the bottom was for gathering the garment round the legs.

This pattern replaced the previous Parka, Reversible, Ski (Spec. No 70A, May 22 1941) without fur trimming, and the Parka Reversible fur trimmed (Spec. No 66 of May 21, 1941) which was a longer garment for arctic regions. This had fur trimmed cuffs and hood.

GAITERS, SKI
(STOCK No 72-G-1000/
72-G-1004)

Gaiters worn with the mountain shoe, these were laced on the side, and held close to the shoe by a leather understrap. Early gaiters such as these were in Olive Drab No 3, changed to a darker green in 1943.

BOOTS, SKI-MOUNTAIN, WITH RUBBER CLEATED SOLE
(STOCK No 72-B-2845-50/72-B-2851-16)

Heavy shoes in greased leather, with rubber cleated sole. Metal plates ('Protectors, Sole, Ski-Boot') were screwed on the leather sole edge against damage caused by the ski bindings. In 1943, the rubber-soled shoe replaced the former leather soled shoe which could be cleated with Tricouni type nails.

TROUSERS, WOOL, SKI (STOCK No 55-T-41210/ 55-T-41339)

Tapered-leg trousers authorized in 1941 (Spec. No 75 of June 23, 1941). These were cut from brown serge material, with two side pockets shut by a zipper, and two hip pockets with buttoned flap. The zipper fly also has 3 buttons on the waistband. Elasticated tape loops are located at the leg bottoms.

GOGGLES, SKI-MOUNTAIN (STOCK No 74-G-79)

Goggles with green tinted glass lenses, issued to mountain troops to prevent snow blindness. The goggles were carried in an artificial leather case, holding two spare lenses. This pattern superseded other mountain goggles which had triangular lenses and a larger case closed by two snap buttons.

TROUSERS, SKI, WHITE (STOCK No 55-T-41005/ 55-T-41070)

Over-trousers, tied at the waist and leg bottom by a drawstring. This was slipped over the mountain or ski trousers, or any type of wool trousers.

BOOTS, MUKLUK (STOCK NO 72-B-1130/72-B-1132)

These boots were made of white canvas for the top part, and buck or suede for the bottom. Copied after an Eskimo pattern, these boots were used in extreme cold weather, for walking in dry snow. Mukluks were worn over several pairs of socks and with felt insoles.

Ski gaiters in white canvas for snow camouflage.

3. Mountain troops equipment

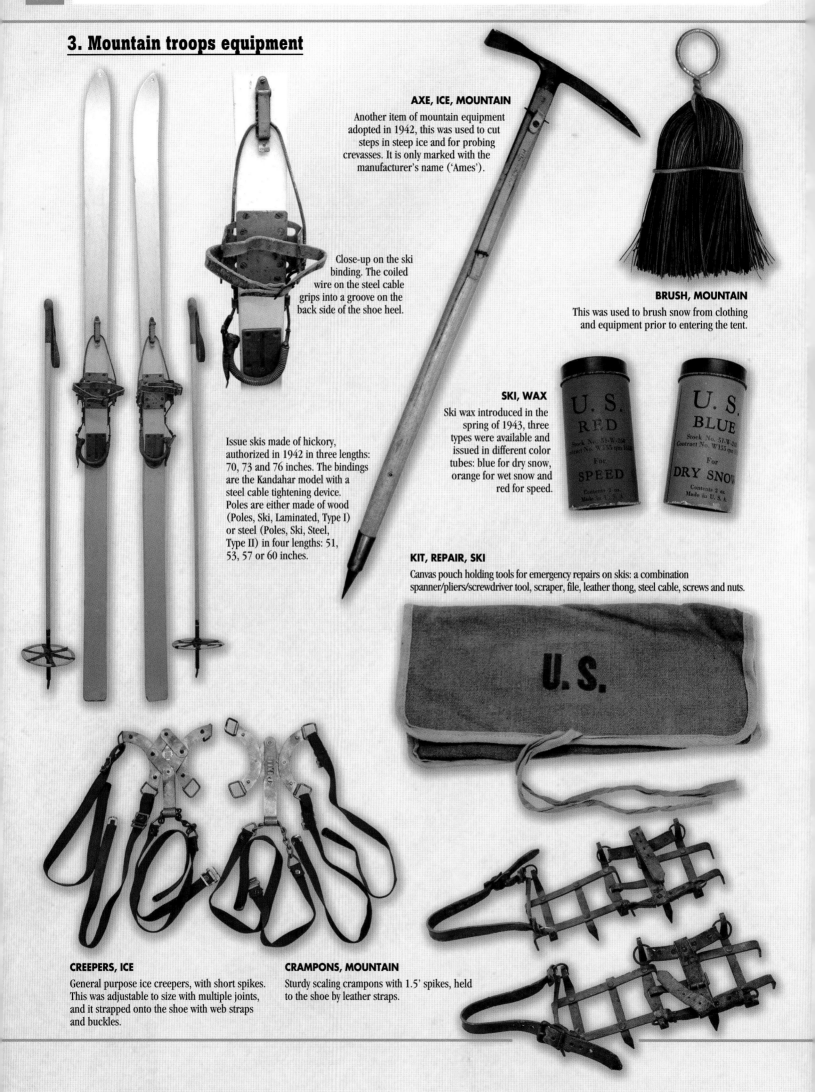

AXE, ICE, MOUNTAIN

Another item of mountain equipment adopted in 1942, this was used to cut steps in steep ice and for probing crevasses. It is only marked with the manufacturer's name ('Ames').

Close-up on the ski binding. The coiled wire on the steel cable grips into a groove on the back side of the shoe heel.

BRUSH, MOUNTAIN

This was used to brush snow from clothing and equipment prior to entering the tent.

SKI, WAX

Ski wax introduced in the spring of 1943, three types were available and issued in different color tubes: blue for dry snow, orange for wet snow and red for speed.

Issue skis made of hickory, authorized in 1942 in three lengths: 70, 73 and 76 inches. The bindings are the Kandahar model with a steel cable tightening device. Poles are either made of wood (Poles, Ski, Laminated, Type I) or steel (Poles, Ski, Steel, Type II) in four lengths: 51, 53, 57 or 60 inches.

KIT, REPAIR, SKI

Canvas pouch holding tools for emergency repairs on skis: a combination spanner/pliers/screwdriver tool, scraper, file, leather thong, steel cable, screws and nuts.

CREEPERS, ICE

General purpose ice creepers, with short spikes. This was adjustable to size with multiple joints, and it strapped onto the shoe with web straps and buckles.

CRAMPONS, MOUNTAIN

Sturdy scaling crampons with 1.5' spikes, held to the shoe by leather straps.

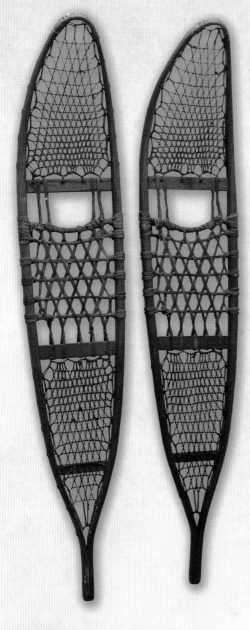

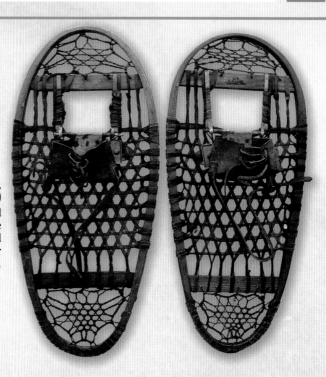

SNOWSHOES, TRAIL (10 X 58 INCHES)

Large size snowshoes used preferably in unobstructed terrain. They are shown here without their bindings. Snowshoes were used with Shoe pacs (➡ page 60), mountain shoes (➡ page 152) or Mukluks (➡ page 153).

SNOWSHOES, BEARPAW, (13 X 28 INCHES)

Snowshoes used in brush or wooded terrain. The boot is attached to the snowshoe by wide laced leather straps and a movable steel plate. The long leather strap is placed on the heel.

SNOWSHOES, EMERGENCY, (10.5 X 20 INCHES)

Smaller snowshoes worn when skis cannot be used, these were carried in the rucksack. The binding comprises two rawhide thongs, 55-in. long ('Binding, Snowshoe, Emergency').

PADS, SNOWSHOE, MOUNTAIN

Rawhide pads placed underneath the steel-cleated mountain shoe when worn with snowshoes.

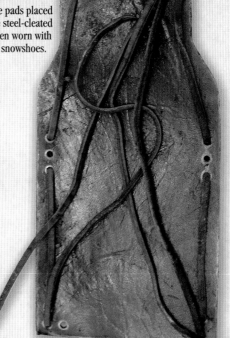

HAMMER, PITON, MOUNTAIN AND PITONS

Special mountain troops hammer. When scaling, used to drive pitons in crevices. Also shown are the type I, II and V (from bottom to top) soft steel pitons.

CLIMBERS, SKI, MOHAIR

These were issued in 3 sizes, according to the ski length.

TENT, MOUNTAIN, 2-MAN, COMPLETE WITH PINS AND POLES

Lightweight tent made of reversible (green-white) airship material. It had an integral floor, a ventilation duct near the top and a windproof entry hole at each end. This model made in 1944 replaced an earlier tent in a lighter green material, with a single entry opening.

The mountain tent was pitched with four three-section poles and six aluminium pins.

KNIFE, MOUNTAIN

A multi-purpose pocket knife, with a spike and cross-headed tip screwdriver for emergency ski repairs.

COOKSET, MOUNTAIN

This was issued to every two men in the mountain troops. The set comprised three aluminium pieces: the two pans fitted one inside the other, and the cover/pan with folding handles. The M-1942 burner (➡ page 181) was designed to fit inside the cookset.

CASE, WATER-REPELLENT, BAG, SLEEPING

Water-repellent case that fit over all mummy-shaped sleeping bags (➡ page 111). The mountain sleeping bag and its case could be carried inside a special bag.
This could be slipped over the bag for added insulation of the feet.

RUCKSACK

Mountain troops rucksack in Olive drab No 3 canvas. This Bergans type sack was strapped onto a lightweight tubular metal frame. Three large pockets are sewn on the outside, to help balance the load. The bayonet or entrenching tool could be hooked to the grommeted tabs on the left side.

In snowy surroundings, a white canvas cover was tightened by a drawstring over the rucksack.

BAG, SLEEPING, MOUNTAIN

Mummy shaped sleeping bag, filled with down and feathers. This is the pattern of 1942, with half-length zipper. It was rolled up after use and tied with straps sewn in at the foot.

HARNESS, MAN, TWO TRACE, APRON TYPE

A piece of equipment designed for mountain troops, this was to ensure human traction of heavy sleds. Other men could assist the man fitted with the harness, by pulling on the toggle end of additional drag ropes.

ROPE, DRAG, WITH SHOULDER STRAP, M-1918

This was used to tow a light artillery piece, cart or sled.

1. Red Cross volunteers

A. A short history of the American Red Cross

The United States accepted the terms of the Geneva Convention in 1881, after active campaigning by Clara Barton, the famous Civil War nurse, who became the first president of the American Red Cross. The organization gained momentum during World War One, with a peak strength of 20 million members. In 1942, the ARC already boasted 14,565,000 members. The Red Cross performed numerous functions to uphold morale in the forces, in the USA and abroad. Its assignments were multiple: rest centers, libraries, mobile canteens, assistance to hospital staffs, compress manufacturing, as well as knitting warm clothing for soldiers. The ARC was staffed by male and female personnel,

we will however deal solely with women volunteers, who contributed widely to the war effort by comforting homesick soldiers the World over.

B. ARC dress

The ARC women volunteers' service uniform was made of blue-gray wool serge: jacket and matching skirt, peaked cap, white blouse and black low shoes. This dress was worn Stateside and as a dress and going-out uniform in the theaters of operations. Various work clothes were worn according to the volunteer's assignment.

The indoor work uniform called for a head-dress and dress made of blue and white striped cotton material.

Above.
Sleeve patch worn on the left arm of the blue-gray jacket.

American Red Cross volunteer work uniform head-dress.

Dark bronze insignia for female volunteers, worn on the blue wool jacket collar.

Insignia of Red Cross volunteers, sewn on the left sleeve of the dress. The red bar (here slightly kinked because of the sleeve crease) is for one year's service; a red chevron would indicate four years.

Enameled insignia for the wool peaked cap.

White buck pumps worn with the summer work uniform.

Short-sleeved summer work dress. This pattern closes down the front with mother-of-pearl buttons. It is gathered at the waist by a self-belt in matching cloth, closed by two buttons. The red cross on a white field is the regulation insignia for indoors work clothing.

2. The Army Nurse Corps

Army Nurse Corps collar insignia.

A. A short history of the ANC

During the war against Spain which begun in 1898, volunteer nurses of the American Red Cross were accepted as hospital staff helpers in the Medical Department, which did not have female nursing personnel. The Surgeon General soon established a permanent female nursing corps, which was officially embodied into the Army Nurse Corps on February 2, 1901. ANC strength would then vary as conflicts erupted and flared out. In 1921, all Army Nurses were granted officer status. During the Second World War, Army nurses were involved on all fronts to care for American and Allied wounded.

B. Army Nurses' going-out dress

CAP, SERVICE, WOOL, OD, NURSE'S
(STOCK NO 73-C-33010/73-C-33035)

Olive drab No 51 wool peaked cap, worn with the ANC dress in matching officer's material or the summer going-out dress jacket (Jacket, Cotton, Seersucker, Nurse's).

DRESS, OFF-DUTY, NURSE'S

Going-out dress in OD shade 51 rayon. The waist is gathered by a self-belt in matching material, closed by a gilt uniform button. Civilian cuff links are necessary for the sleeve closure. This dress was authorized in September 1942 and replaced a similar garment in dark blue which was to be issued until stocks were exhausted, and worn in the United States only.

Manufacturer's label inside a Nurse's off-duty dress.

January, 8, 1944. This official photograph taken in the States depicts the new (left) Army Nurse Corps uniform in Olive drab (➡ page 163), and the old blue uniform (right).
(National Archives)

C. Hospital dress

When working in proper hospital buildings, nurses were outfitted in seersucker clothing, with thin white and brown stripes. Two sorts of dresses were issued: one a long dress and nurse cap, the other calling for a shirt and slacks, which could be also be worn with the summer off-duty jacket described previous page.

SHIRT, COTTON, SEERSUCKER, NURSES' (STOCK NO 55-S-2102/55-S-2111)

A convertible collar shirt with two patch pockets and buttoned flaps.

CAP, SEERSUCKER, NURSE'S (STOCK NO 73-C-29000)

Nurse cap, tied at the back by tapes. This head-dress was worn with the cotton seersucker garments illustrated on this page.

UNIFORM, COTTON, SEERSUCKER, NURSE'S (STOCK NO 55-U-9510/55-U-9546)

Short-sleeved dress, with two small breast pockets and a larger open-topped patch pocket on the right side. The fabric belt is tied at the waist. This dress replaced a World War One pattern in white cotton.

SLACKS, COTTON, SEERSUCKER, NURSE'S (STOCK NO 55-S-38905/55-S-38923)

Slacks, pleated at the waist, and closed on the left side by three buttons, single right-hand side pocket.

D. Female personnel field clothing

Before the inception of the M-1943 field uniform, Army Nurses were given men's field jackets (➡ page 36). This issue was not granted to WACs who had not full military status at the time.

D. Female personnel field clothing

WAIST, WOOL, WOMEN'S (STOCK NO 55-W-1328-25/55-W-1346-32)

A flannel shirt cut to follow feminine curves, authorized mid-1944. It closed on the right side as all women's blouses. It had a semi-stiff collar and breast pockets with a pointed flap. The former pattern had a stiff collar and square pocket flaps. All issue clothing featuring "Women's" in their nomenclature could be issued to both Nurses and WACs.

HBT shirt of later manufacture in the dark green OD No 7 shade. This variant has black metal tack buttons instead of plastic buttons.

SHIRT, HERRINGBONE TWILL, WOMEN'S, SPECIAL (STOCK NO 55-S-7020/55-S-7027)

Early light green color HBT jacket, with the anti-gas flap behind the front fly. Authorized in 1942, the jacket was worn with matching trousers.

TROUSERS, HERRINGBONE TWILL, WOMEN'S, SPECIAL (STOCK NO 55-T-38370/55-T-38377)

Light green HBT work trousers. This pattern has patch pockets on the thighs, shut by a pointed buttoned flap.

SHOES, FIELD, WOMEN'S (STOCK NO 72-S-116-52/72-S-126-28)

Field shoes in the regulation russet shade. These had a rubber heel and sole and were worn together with 'Leggings, Canvas, Women's.'

Late-war pattern HBT trousers: dark green color and squarish pocket flaps.

3. The Women's Army Corps

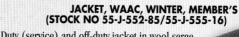

Collar insignia for Women's Army Corps officers.

A. A short history of the Women's Army Corps

Congresswoman Edith Nourse Rogers introduced in May 1941 a bill that would establish a women's auxiliary branch in the Army, distinct from the Army Nurse Corps. After lengthy consultations with interested parties, the Women's Army Auxiliary Corps (WAAC) was created on May 14, 1942. Oveta Culp Hobby (chief of the Women's Interest Section in the War Department's public relations division) was chosen as its 'Director.' Women volunteers did not have military status, but were tasked with assisting the Army in several functions, barring actual combat. Female auxiliaries ('members') were granted full military status in July 1943, when the WAAC evolved into the Women's Army Corps (WAC). At first, WACs were confined to clerical jobs but at war's end, they worked under 250 occupational specialties in the fields of medical care, personnel management, signals, mechanics, photography, meteorology, transportation and supply. In the ETO, the first WAC battalion arrived in London in July 1943 and a year later, WACs disembarked in Normandy. WACs would serve all over the world and as a reward for their distinguished services, the WAC was retained in the post-war army structure.

B. WAC members' service uniform

The 'WAAC' tab was worn under sleeve rank chevrons until July 1943, when women auxiliaries became fully-fledged Army personnel.

**JACKET, WAAC, WINTER, MEMBER'S
(STOCK NO 55-J-552-85/55-J-555-16)**

Duty (service) and off-duty jacket in wool serge. Authorized in 1942, it had an integral belt that was deleted in October of the same year. The buttons bearing the WAC emblem were replaced in July 1943 by standard uniform buttons with the US coat of arms (➡ page 35). The jacket's new nomenclature yet became 'Jacket, WAC, Winter, Member's.'

**CAP, WAAC, WINTER, MEMBER'S
(STOCK NO 73-C-64574-10/73-C-64582)**

Wool serge peaked cap for WAAC enlisted personnel, authorized in 1942 and called the 'Hobby Hat' in honor of the Corps' director. Lacking in comfort and ease of laundering, it was gradually replaced as of 1943 by a men's pattern garrison cap, then by a specific garrison cap in 1944. The cap insignia is for WAACs only: an American eagle with spread wings, head turned to sinister. This design was also embossed on uniform buttons.

**CAP, GARRISON, WOOL, WAC
(STOCK NO 73-C-24019-50/73-C-24024-50)**

Head-dress worn with the duty and off-duty uniform of enlisted WACs. It is piped in the corps' colors of moss green and old gold. The elongated and curved shape is typical of women's garrison caps.

**SKIRT, WAAC, WINTER, MEMBER'S
(STOCK NO 55-S-34075/55-S-34096)**

Six-gore classic skirt in wool serge, its color matching the jacket's. It was renamed in July 1943 'Skirt, WAC, Winter, Enlisted Women's.'

**SHOES, SERVICE, WOMEN'S, LOW
(STOCK NO 72-S-2375-20/72-S-2384-29)**

Oxford low shoes in russet leather, with rubber heel and sole. These were worn with the service uniform by all female personnel.

(Photo Martin Brayley)

C. WAC Officers' Service Uniforms

JACKET, WAAC, OFFICER'S, WINTER

A jacket in Olive drab 51 officer's wool material. The buttons are in the specific women's auxiliaries' design. The jacket has perpendicular shoulder tabs and the Army officers' braid on the sleeves.

JACKET, WOOL, OD, WOMEN'S, OFFICER'S (STOCK NO 55-J-571-500/ 55-J-572-95)

The final pattern of women officers' wool service jacket for both Army Nurses and WAC officers. It has standard Army brass buttons.

SKIRT, WOOL, OD, DARK, WOMEN'S, OFFICER'S (STOCK NO 55-S-37008/55-S-37047)

Matching skirt for the jacket depicted above.

D. Accessories for Women Auxiliaries

Label glued to the paper wrapping of an unissued WAC handbag.

BAG, UTILITY, WAAC

Brown leather handbag, lined with green cotton cloth. The removable strap enabled the bag to be carried as a purse. It has two inside compartments and four smaller pockets, and also contains a separate purse. The bag was slung on the right shoulder and rested on the left side. It became the 'Bag, Utility, WAC' in July 1943.

Patriotic powder compact, with a mirror under the lid, powder and rouge compartments and powder puff.

Private purchase hair net for female military personnel.

KIT, SEWING

One of the many types of sewing kits used by Army personnel. It has different color threads and buttons for each type of issue garment.

4. Field clothing for female personnel

**HOOD, JACKET, FIELD, M-1943, WOMEN'S
(STOCK NO 73-H-66830/73-H-66832)**

Removable hood for the M-1943 Jacket, in matching material. This was introduced at the end of 1944 and identical, albeit smaller, to the men's issue.

**JACKET, FIELD, M-1943, WOMEN'S
(STOCK NO 55-J-193-26/55-J-194-70)**

A green cotton sateen jacket authorized at the end of 1943 for all female personnel. It closes down on the right side, the buttons are visible. There are no breast pockets, however decorative pockets flaps were retained. The garment was worn in cold climates over its specific removable liner (shown below), and over several layers of warm underwear.

**LINER, JACKET, FIELD, M-1943, WOMEN'S
(STOCK NO 55-L-203-20/55-L-203-800)**

Thick wool flannel liner, with knit cuffs and neck, standardized during the summer of 1944. According to the insulation system by successive layers, the liner was worn under the sateen field jacket, and over a wool shirt and sweater.

TROUSERS, WOMEN'S, OUTER COVER (STOCK NO 55-T-62655/ 55-T-62698)

Green cotton sateen trousers with a tapered leg, introduced in the summer of 1943. The side pockets and inside waistband are cut from tan cotton. The trousers feature a closure on the left hip by four buttons and buttoned side tabs for adjustment when worn over a woolen liner. An elasticated understrap is sewn at each leg bottom.

This item was replaced at the end of 1944 by a new straight-leg pattern closed on the left hip by three buttons. This had a white cotton lining, a single side pocket and adjustment tab on the right side.

TROUSERS, WOMEN'S, WOOL, LINER (STOCK NO 55-T-62747/55-T-62788)

Straight-leg trousers in olive drab wool, with a single pocket on the left hip and a button closure on the right side. This was adopted in November 1944 for all Army female personnel to be worn by itself, or under the cotton sateen trousers shown at left. It superseded an older pattern of 1943, which had knit cuffs at the leg bottoms.

BOOTS, SERVICE, COMBAT, WOMEN'S (STOCK NO 72-B-2766-16/72-B-2772-26)

New 'buckle boot' for field wear, adopted in November 1944. Similar the men's issue, its last was however modified for the female foot.

OVERSHOES, ARCTIC, WOMEN'S, 4-BUCKLE, M-1944 (STOCK NO 72-O-737-100/72-O-737-300)

Overshoes with a rubber sole and canvas top, similar to the men's pattern (➡ page 60), but whose last fitted the female foot. These were slipped over the Field shoes (➡ page 161) or the Combat boots (above).

1. Missions and organization of the Military Police

Before the war, military police was only a temporary function undertaken by the units themselves. The Corps of Military Police was established in September 1941 and came under the Army Service Forces in March 1942. Its commander was the Provost Marshal General and its primary duties were:

– training corps personnel

– handling prisoners of war, ensuring their internment and use as labor in the United States

– investigating crimes involving Army personnel

MP Officer's collar insignia

– the protection of military and industrial installations against sabotage.

A Provost Marshal was attached to the staff of each major command (division, corps, army), his missions were to advise the commanding officer on provost matters and to undertake all MP duties in the theater of operations. These were, among others: control of military traffic, police in liberated countries, maintenance of discipline, protection of Army personnel and property, and the handling, identification and detention of Prisoners of War.

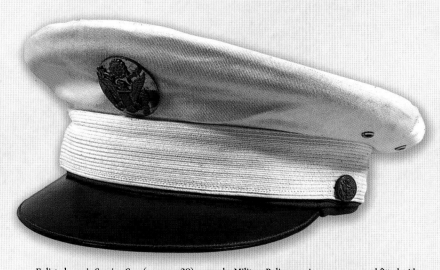

Enlisted man's Service Cap (➡ page 28), worn by Military Policemen in rear areas, and fitted with a removable white cotton top. The cap had been replaced by the garrison cap for most arms and services early in the war, it was however retained by MPs as a distinctive item of duty uniform.
(Coleman collection, photo Militaria Magazine)

Removable white cotton top, most likely a Navy item, used by MPs with the service cap.

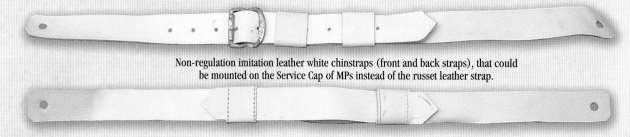

Non-regulation imitation leather white chinstraps (front and back straps), that could be mounted on the Service Cap of MPs instead of the russet leather strap.

THE INFANTRY DIVISION MILITARY POLICE PLATOON (TO & E 19-7, JULY 1943)

• Under the authority of a Major (divisional provost marshal), attached to the divisional staff

• Commanded by a 1st Lieutenant, assisted by a 2d Lieutenant

• 70 enlisted men total

– NCOs: 1 Staff Sergeant, 8 Sergeants, 1 Technician 4th Grade

– 24 Privates First class, 30 Privates

• Armament: 55 carbines, 1 caliber .45 pistol, 17 M-1903 rifles

• Unit transport: 15 jeeps, 3 Weapons carriers.

Note. The MP Platoon has a Traffic section and a Police Section

These MPs take part in an amphibious exercise in Britain prior to D-day. Their helmet markings indicate they are an element of an Engineer Special Brigade. The paratrooper jump boots were a special issue to troops operating on the beach. *(National Archives)*

2. Military Police equipment

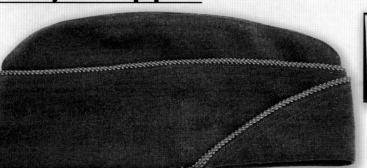

Example of MP helmet markings. No regulation covered the nature, size or color of MP helmet markings during the Second World War. It is however common knowledge that a white band was for independent MP units, and a yellow band for the divisional MP Platoon.

OD wool Garrison Cap (➡ page 29) for the off-duty uniforms of MP enlisted men. The piping is in the distinctive yellow and green.

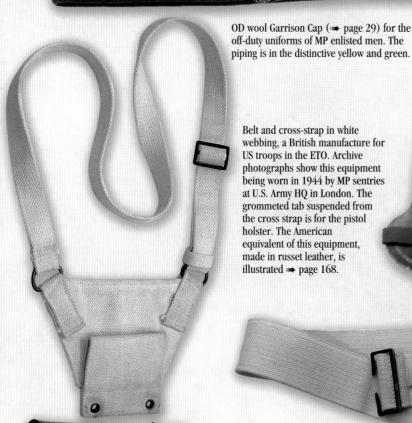

Belt and cross-strap in white webbing, a British manufacture for US troops in the ETO. Archive photographs show this equipment being worn in 1944 by MP sentries at U.S. Army HQ in London. The grommeted tab suspended from the cross strap is for the pistol holster. The American equivalent of this equipment, made in russet leather, is illustrated ➡ page 168.

MP helmet liner markings were varied as well. This example has an overall white finish. The initials MP in black could also be painted on the front, and the unit (division, etc.) insignia was sometimes painted on the front or sides of the helmet liner and shell.

One of the many variations of brass whistles used by MPs, and mostly by small unit leaders (Squad, Platoon, etc.). This one is marked 'Regulation, US Army, Solid Brass.'

Another issue whistle, made in green plastic and marked '*US Army*,' together with the manufacturer and date (1944). MPs carry the whistle on the left side, the chain hook on the left shoulder strap, and the whistle suspended from its ring on the breast pocket button.

STRAP, SHOULDER, MILITARY POLICE

Russet leather cross strap, worn to support the weight of the sidearm. The strap is slung on the left shoulder, the pistol holster resting on the right side. The belt slides into the wide loop above the grommets.

Enlisted man's leather belt ('Garrison belt'). Phased out in March 1941 but retained by the Military Police to be worn with the special leather cross strap.

CLUB, POLICEMAN, M-1944

Issue item authorized in 1944, the leather thong is tied by a knot on a groove at the base of the handle. This replaced the 1943 'Club, Policeman,' a heavier club on which the leather lanyard passed into a hole drilled at the top of the handle.

POUCH, FIRST AID PACKET, LEATHER

The belt loop is also riveted

Issue M-1916 (or M1) pistol holster in russet leather.

POCKET, MAGAZINE, DOUBLE, LEATHER

Pocket for two .45 Caliber pistol magazines. On this 1940-dated example, the belt loop on the back is attached by four brass rivets.

BRASSARD, ARM, MP, NEW TYPE

Regulation Military Police armband, pattern of November 1941, made in dark blue wool felt material, with cut-out white initials in a similar material. Like most regulation brassards, it is 18 by 4 inches. There was no fastening device, therefore the armband was usually held on the left arm by a safety pin.

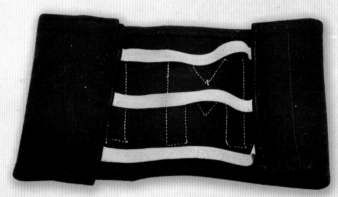

A common modification of the MP brassard, this one has been shortened and fitted with elastic tapes.

Collar disk worn on the service coat or Ike jacket by MP personnel.
(Militaria Magazine photo)

Technical Manual TM 19-250 was a training aid listing all Military Police forms and reports.

A booklet printed in France in 1945, given to all MP personnel returning home.

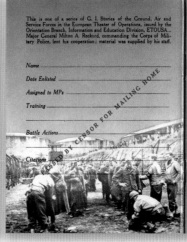

3. The Prisoners of War

Generalleutnant von Schlieben, der Verteidiger von Cherbourg, verlässt seinen Gefechtsstand im Fort du Roule, um sich den Amerikanern zu ergeben. Die Lage war hoffnungslos. Auch Schliebens Tod hätte nichts daran ändern können. Deshalb setzte sich Generalleutnant von Schlieben, zusammen mit 18 000 anderen in der gleichen Lage, über den Führerbefehl hinweg, zu dem sie sich mit ihrer Unterschrift verpflichten mussten.

„dass sie ungeachtet der Lage ihren Platz mit Einsatz ihres Lebens bis zum letzten Mann und zur letzten Patrone zu verteidigen haben."

Generalleutnant von Schlieben und die 18 000 sind jetzt in England. Sie warten auf das Ende des Krieges und auf ein Deutschland, in dem solche erpresserischen Verpflichtungen unmöglich sind.

A leaflet dropped in late June 1944 by the USAAF over German lines on the Normandy front. Under the headline 'Cherbourg has fallen,' a picture shows General von Schlieben, in a muddy uniform, leaving for a POW cage with his staff. The purpose of the leaflet was to weaken the morale of German soldiers and induce them to surrender.

Safe-conduct in both German and English promising fair treatment, food, medical care and evacuation to all German soldiers giving themselves up with this document.

Official US Army postcard provided to German POWs for sending news to their families.

Letter from a German POW interned in the Aliceville (Alabama) camp. This form could also be used by Italian and Japanese prisoners.

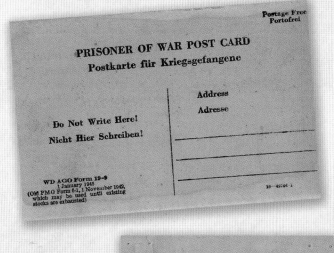

Special baggage tag for the personal belongings of a German prisoner freed from the Fort Jackson (South Carolina) POW camp. POW luggage was shipped through the Red Cross International Committee in Switzerland.

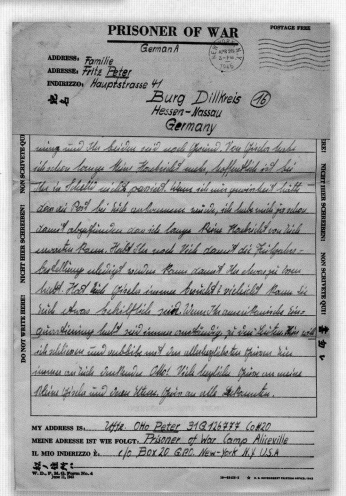

When their original uniforms were worn out, prisoners of war interned in the United States were issued with reclaimed American uniforms. These were however clearly marked with large PW letters.

On this Field Jacket (➡ page 36), the PW letters are painted on the back and each sleeve as well.

Olive drab flannel shirt.

Olive drab wool serge trousers.

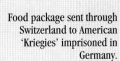

Food package sent through Switzerland to American 'Kriegies' imprisoned in Germany.

This crate for American POWs in German hands contained 1,200 packages of 5 razor blades each.

AMERICAN RED CROSS
PRISONER OF WAR
FOOD PACKAGE
NO. 10
FOR DISTRIBUTION THROUGH
INTERNATIONAL RED CROSS COMMITTEE

AMERICAN RED CROSS
TO INTERNATIONAL RED CROSS COMMITTEE
GENEVA, SWITZERLAND
FOR PRISONERS OF WAR
CONTENTS 1200 PKG. 5 EACH BLADES VEHICLE
CASE # GB 2. 25
GR WT. 37 LBS.   CU 1.3

A ration is defined by Army regulations 30-2210 as: *"The allowance of food for the subsistence of one person for one day."*

Introduction

One of the Quartermaster Corps primary missions was to feed troops wherever they were operating. During the Second World war, this task was successfully undertaken, thanks mostly to breakthroughs in packaging and use of modern means of transportation.

In 1939, the QMC introduced a new classification for Army subsistence and created four types of field rations: A, B, C and D. Nine other field rations were added during the war, especially the K and 10-in-1 rations.

1. Rations A and B

The Field Ration A nearly corresponded with the Garrison ration and was meant for issue in the United States at camps and posts. It was also used overseas where perishables and frozen foods were available. Field ration B was used in operations overseas as well as during training in the States. Its main staples were similar to the A ration's, except that non perishable processed or canned products replaced fresh items. The B ration was usually prepared in field kitchens behind the combat lines.

CAP, BAKER'S AND COOK'S, WHITE

A traditional cap in white cotton, which was usually worn with special work clothing (jacket, trousers, apron) in the same sturdy material.

RANGE, FIELD, M-1937

This gasoline oven and its accessories were part of the M-1937 Field range, which was considered as basic equipment for preparing meals for 50 soldiers in the field.

ROLL, COMMISSARY

An array of cutlery and utensils for weighing and preparing food and ingredients before cooking.

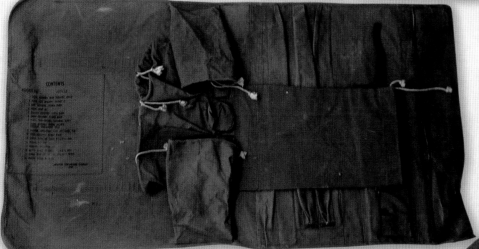

OUTFIT, COOKING, CAVALRY, PACK

A simple assortment of cooking utensils issued to pack units, and carried on mules. This was used together with the M-1937 field range.

OUTFIT, COOKING 20-MAN

A later-war set, this roll of kitchen utensils was issued together with a double-burner M-1942 gasoline stove and four cooksets.

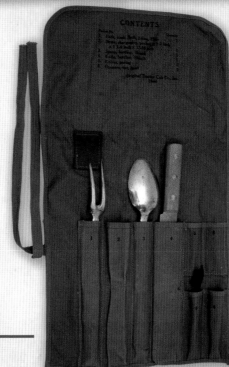

Aluminium milk pitcher with a spring loaded lid.

OUTFIT, OFFICER'S, MESS, M-1941

A wood and fiber trunk containing a complete set of cutlery and enameled plates and dishes for 8 officers.

STOCK N° 83-C-559
U.S.A. TENT SPEC N° 299782041
CONTR N° W431 QM 7047 QI 6055
JEFFERSONVILLE
QM DEPOT-3-2-42
BELBER TRUNK & BAG CO.

CONTAINER, ROUND, INSULATED, M-1941, WITH INSERTS

Food container for carrying and serving hot meals in the field. It could be used with or without its three aluminium airtight inserts.

Two empty glass bottles of beer.

Can of 'Fort Pitt' beer.

COCA-COLA BOTTLES

The green-tinted glass bottle bears the following markings:

– Under the Coca-Cola trade mark: *Trade mark registered --- Min - Contents 6-fl. ozs --- Bottle Pat D-105529*

– On the base: lot number, glassmaker's logo and date (42).

– On the bottom: *Bakersfield --- Calif.*

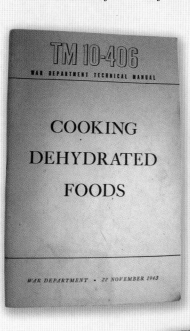

TM 10-406
WAR DEPARTMENT TECHNICAL MANUAL

COOKING

DEHYDRATED

FOODS

WAR DEPARTMENT • 22 NOVEMBER 1943

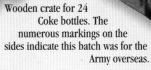

Wooden crate for 24 Coke bottles. The numerous markings on the sides indicate this batch was for the Army overseas.

Galvanized iron measuring ladle.

Large can of 'Ben Hur' Coffee.

2. The Field Ration C

This was developed as of 1938 and tested during the 1940 manoeuvres. This combat ration, providing nourishment for one man for one day, calls for 6 metal cans (three B-units and three M-Units) weighing about 12 oz. each. Salt, cigarettes, matches, chewing gum and toilet paper were also issued with the C-ration. The six cans were carried inside the M-1928 haversack (➡ page 69). A B-unit contained hard biscuit, sweets, sugar and instant coffee. Other ingredients such as cereals and jam were added later in the war so contents were more varied, and six B-unit assortments became available.

The M (meat)-unit was a dish of meat and vegetables, and three different meals were initially issued:
– M1 (Meat and Beans): 40% beef, 10% pork, 20% beans and 30% tomato sauce
– M2 (Meat and Vegetable Hash): 40% beef, 10% pork, 48% potatoes and 2% onions.
M3 (Meat and Vegetable Stew): 50% beef (or 40% beef and 10% pork) 15% potatoes, 15% carrots, 8% beans and 12% tomatoes.

In 1945, a total of 10 different meat and vegetables preparations were provided.

B-Unit packed in September 1941.

Wooden crate for 8 complete C-rations (48 cans).

A complete C-ration of 6 cans. One of the B-units has been opened to reveal its contents. *(National Archives)*

3. The Field Ration D

A carton of 12 D-bars. A larger wooden crate held 12 such cartons (144 rations).

The D-bar became the 'Ration Type D' in February 1944, the ingredients were printed on the side of the box.

Field ration D packed in November 1942. The three bars are sealed in cellophane and packed in waxed cardboard. The ingredients are indicated on the front of the box. Vitamin B2 (Thiamin Hypochloride) also gave the epiderm a measure of insect-repellency against malaria.

Starting in the early summer 1944, a malaria prevention message was printed on the back of the D ration box.

In 1934, the QMC endeavored to replace the First World War vintage emergency 'Armour' ration. The new ration would provide a maximum of calories under all latitudes, in a minimal volume, while still being palatable. The final ration was adopted in 1937: a 40 oz. bar bringing 600 calories. The principal ingredient was chocolate, with sugar, oat flour, skim milk powder, cocoa fat and artificial flavoring.

The complete ration was made of three bars packed in metallized paper, followed by a two-ply waterproofed paper wrapping. The ration became the Field Ration D in 1939 and mass production lasted from 1941 to 1944, with only a few changes in packaging.

This survival ration was only issued in case of emergency when no other kind of field ration was available.

4. The K Ration

The compact K ration was the result of a requirement expressed by Airborne troops in 1941, to replace the heavier C ration cans. The new combat ration was developed under Doctor Ancel Keys, a nutritionist. The ration, dubbed the 'K-ration' in honor of this scientist, was standardized in November 1942 for general issue. A set of 3 boxes, one for each meal, would suffice for one man's subsistence for one day. All the ingredients were packed inside a double package. The inner box, of waxed cardboard, only indicated the meal (Breakfast, Dinner or Supper). The outer brown cardboard box bore the following print: *'US Army Field Ration K'* then *'Ration type K'* as of 1943. Outer boxes printed with a different color and design according to the meal were adopted in 1944. Typical contents of a K ration box would be: a small can of food, biscuits, chewing gum, confectionery, cigarettes and matches, powdered drink.

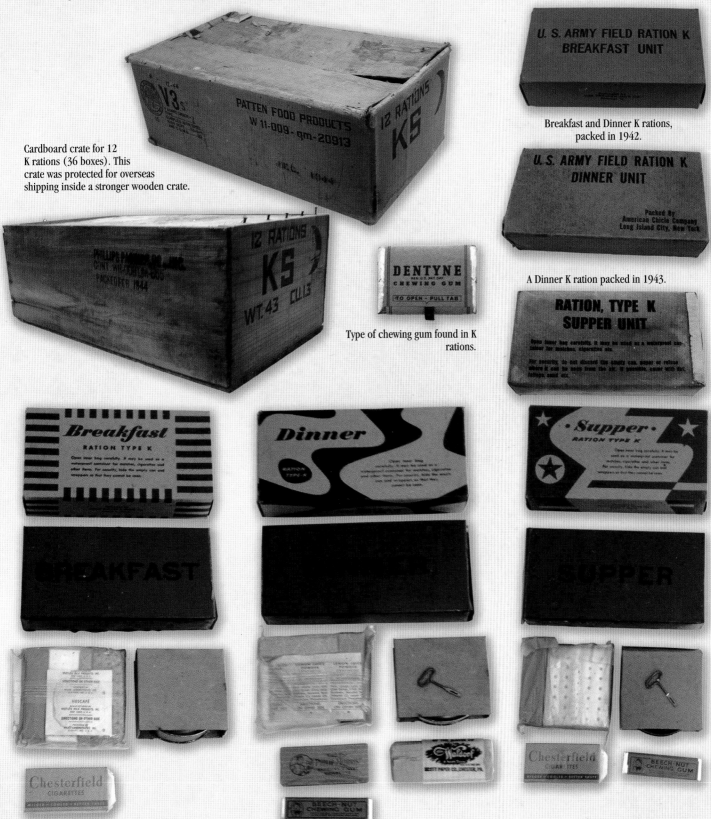

Cardboard crate for 12
K rations (36 boxes). This
crate was protected for overseas
shipping inside a stronger wooden crate.

Breakfast and Dinner K rations,
packed in 1942.

Type of chewing gum found in K
rations.

A Dinner K ration packed in 1943.

A complete set of Ration type K, packed in 1944. To prevent the tin from crushing softer elements, it was slid into a cardboard sleeve, and most of the loose ingredients were sealed in a cellophane envelope.

5. The Ten-in-One ration

This bulkier ration was adopted in June 1943: it consisted of a main crate holding four smaller boxes: two in corrugated cardboard ('First half of 5 rations') and another two in stronger laminated and bituminized cardboard ('Second half of 5 rations'). The idea was copied from the British 'Compo' Ration of 1942, its purpose was to feed ten men for one day. The 10-in-1 ration was issued according to 5 different menus and its main staple were: cereal, jam, coffee, tinned milk, biscuits, various meat and vegetables courses, tinned fruit, confections, etc.

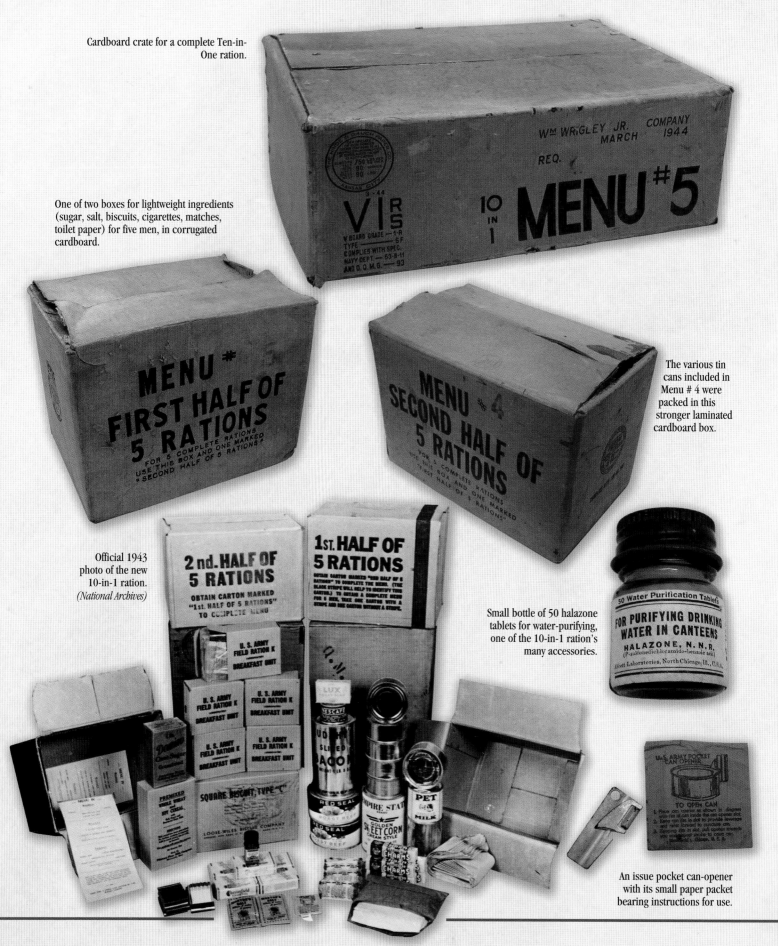

Cardboard crate for a complete Ten-in-One ration.

One of two boxes for lightweight ingredients (sugar, salt, biscuits, cigarettes, matches, toilet paper) for five men, in corrugated cardboard.

The various tin cans included in Menu # 4 were packed in this stronger laminated cardboard box.

Official 1943 photo of the new 10-in-1 ration. *(National Archives)*

Small bottle of 50 halazone tablets for water-purifying, one of the 10-in-1 ration's many accessories.

An issue pocket can-opener with its small paper packet bearing instructions for use.

An assortment of menus for the Partial Dinner units. The tin cans for these menus were packed in the laminated board carton ('Second Half of 5 rations').

The 'Dinner' part of the 10-in-1 ration was either made of a 'Partial Dinner unit' or of a K ration (in a partial package, the tin can being with other cans in the other box).

10-in-1 ration cereal component, made by the Quaker oats Co.

Partial K ration used as the 'Dinner' part of a 10-in-1 ration.

Matchbooks issued with rations. The green matchbook has the malaria prevention slogan added in 1944 at the Medical Department's request.

Large size packet of synthetic lemon juice crystals.

Assorted sweets.

6. Meat cans and cutlery

CAN, MEAT, M-1932

Aluminium mess tin with partitioned stamped metal lid. The cast-metal handle is similar to the handle of WW1 meat cans. Manufacturer is M.A. Co 1942.

CAN, MEAT, M-1910

Mess tin in aluminium, with the convex lid introduced in 1918. One of many WW1 items still issued during WW2. Manufacturer is Landers, Frary & Clark (L. F & C) Co. 1918.

CAN, MEAT, M-1932

Variant of this model, in aluminium, but with a slightly curved handle in stamped metal. Manufacturer is The Vollrath Co. 1942.

CAN, MEAT, M-1942

Mess tin in tin- or zinc-coated steel, made in 1942 to save on aluminium. Manufacturer is the Knapp Monarch Co., 1942.

CAN, MEAT, STAINLESS STEEL

Another pattern authorized in 1943 to save on aluminium. Manufacturer is E.A. Co 1944.

Private purchase pocket knife, made by the Camillus Cutlery Company.

FORK, SPOON AND KNIFE, M-1926

Variation fork and spoon in stainless steel, the knife has a cast aluminium handle.

FORK, SPOON AND KNIFE, M-1926

Tin-plated fork and spoon, and knife with black plastic handle. The fork and knife are fitted with a leather sheath so the edges do not damage the meat can pouch strapped on the M-1928 haversack flap (➡ page 69).

7. Field cooking

An archive photo illustrating a late-war metal 'Stand, Heating, Cup, Canteen' used with chemical fuels described on this page.

Issue candle.

STOVE, COOKING, GASOLINE, M-1941, 1-BURNER

A cooker burning vaporized gasoline, designed initially for mountain troops, and replaced in 1942 by a more compact design in stainless steel. Both types of burner were carried in a straight-sided aluminium pot with an adjustable top.

Wood alcohol cans and fuel tablets for heating the contents of the meat can or canteen cup (➡ page 77).

STOVE, COOKING, GASOLINE, M-1942, 1-BURNER

A lighter stove that could nest inside the mountain cookset (➡ page 156). It was soon adopted for widespread issue to squads and vehicle crews.

Issue matches.

BOX, MATCH, WATERPROOF

Later pattern of waterproof matchbox, in green plastic, with its cardboard storage carton.

'Spitfire' brand lighter, private purchase.

BOX, MATCH, WATERPROOF, WITH COMPASS.

A match striker is glued inside the screw-on top, which also has a small compass for jungle orientation.

8. Tobaccania

Prewar packet of Lucky Strikes with the distinctive green design and a civilian tax label. Early in the war, the design background changed to white to save on color pigments.

Various brands of cigarettes for military issue (Army and Navy), with the yellow 'free of tax' label for armed forces overseas, or based in Alaska and Hawaii.

A carton of 'Camels'.

Berkeley brand lighter, private purchase.

'Zippo' lighter. Starting in 1943, this famous windproof lighter was made in steel and given a black crinkled paint finish. The name and address of the manufacturer (Zippo Mfg Co. Bradford PA) as well as the patent number (2 032 695) were stamped on the unpainted insert. The Zippo patent dated from 1936, the last patent registered in 1944 was 2 366 153.

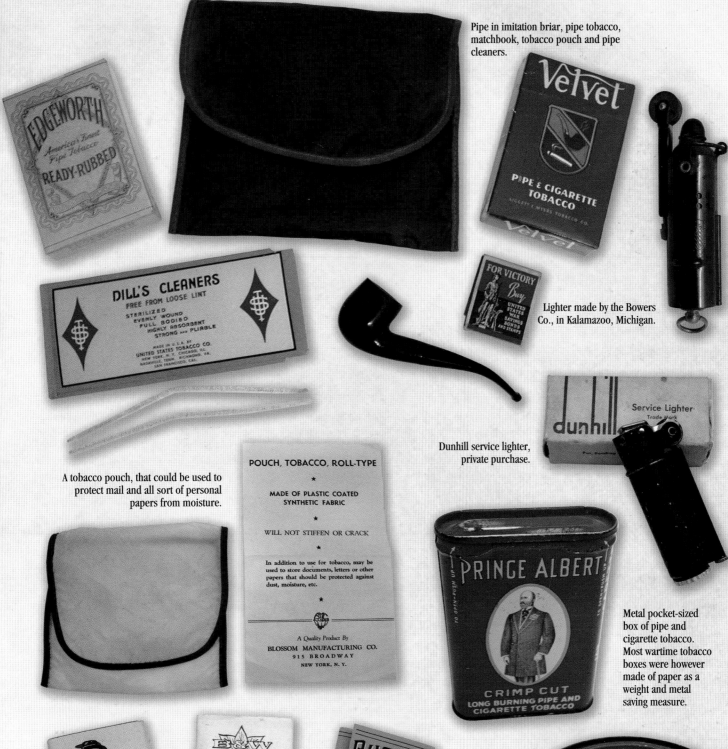

Pipe in imitation briar, pipe tobacco, matchbook, tobacco pouch and pipe cleaners.

Lighter made by the Bowers Co., in Kalamazoo, Michigan.

Dunhill service lighter, private purchase.

A tobacco pouch, that could be used to protect mail and all sort of personal papers from moisture.

POUCH, TOBACCO, ROLL-TYPE

★

MADE OF PLASTIC COATED
SYNTHETIC FABRIC

★

WILL NOT STIFFEN OR CRACK

In addition to use for tobacco, may be used to store documents, letters or other papers that should be protected against dust, moisture, etc.

★

A Quality Product By
BLOSSOM MANUFACTURING CO.
915 BROADWAY
NEW YORK, N. Y.

Metal pocket-sized box of pipe and cigarette tobacco. Most wartime tobacco boxes were however made of paper as a weight and metal saving measure.

Several books of cigarette paper.

Larger counter-top metallic tobacco jar for bulk sales in PXs and post stores.

1. Missions of the Corps of Engineers

Collar insignia for Engineer officers

The Corps of Engineers performs all field construction work needed to enable other combat troops to fight and move, and prepares obstacles to hinder enemy movement. To fulfill these tasks, engineer units are trained to build and repair roads, railways and bridges; to lay or remove mines, camouflage materiel and installations, rehabilitate ports, prepare airstrips and construct gasoline pipelines from the beachheads to the front.

25 July 1944, a bulldozer from a First Army engineer unit works at filling an aerial bomb crater after the operation 'Cobra' raids. *(National Archives)*

METASCOPE TYPE U.S. /F.

Hand carried device for determining the composition and tensile strength of a metallic alloy, by comparing the specter revealed by infrared rays with data on the reference table.

2. Surveying equipment

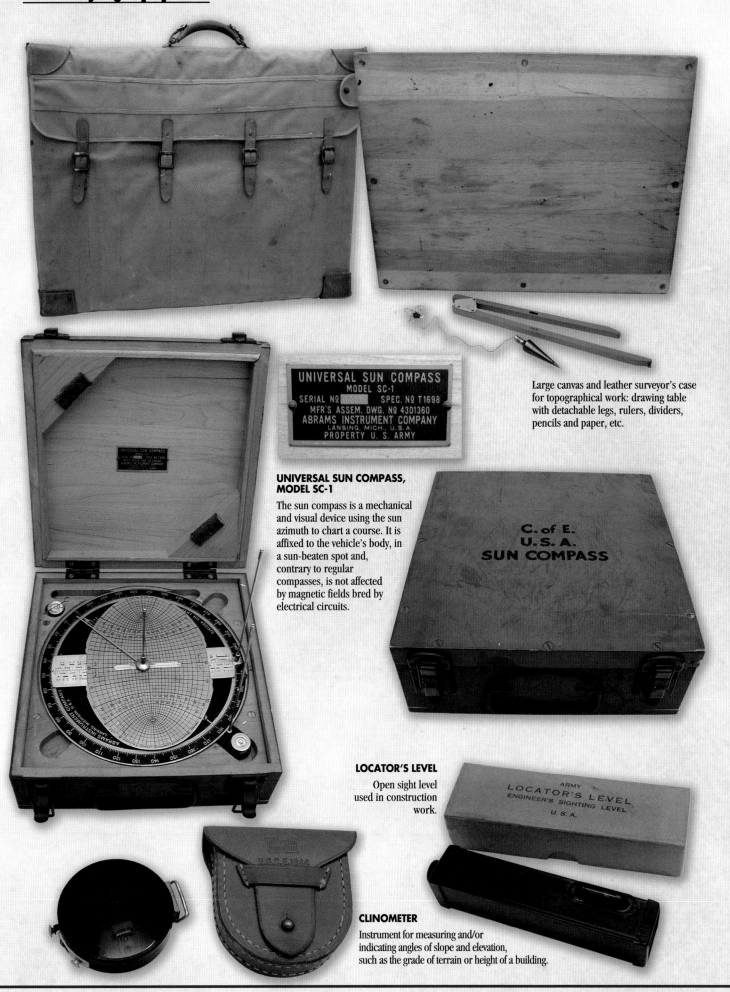

UNIVERSAL SUN COMPASS
MODEL SC-1
SERIAL Nº   SPEC. Nº T1698
MFR'S ASSEM. DWG. Nº 43D1360
ABRAMS INSTRUMENT COMPANY
LANSING, MICH., U.S.A.
PROPERTY U. S. ARMY

Large canvas and leather surveyor's case for topographical work: drawing table with detachable legs, rulers, dividers, pencils and paper, etc.

UNIVERSAL SUN COMPASS, MODEL SC-1

The sun compass is a mechanical and visual device using the sun azimuth to chart a course. It is affixed to the vehicle's body, in a sun-beaten spot and, contrary to regular compasses, is not affected by magnetic fields bred by electrical circuits.

C. of E.
U.S.A.
SUN COMPASS

LOCATOR'S LEVEL

Open sight level used in construction work.

ARMY
LOCATOR'S LEVEL
ENGINEER'S SIGHTING LEVEL
U.S.A.

CLINOMETER

Instrument for measuring and/or indicating angles of slope and elevation, such as the grade of terrain or height of a building.

3. Mine-sweeping equipment

DETECTOR SET SCR-625 (TM 11-1122)

SCR = Set Complete Radio

Introduced in 1942, the SCR-625 detector was used for locating metal cased mines, buried between 6 and 12 inches deep.

The complete set is made of:
- 1 BC-1141 amplifier assembly
- 1 BG-151 bag
- 1 BC-1140 control box
- 1 M-350 exploring rod
- 2 M-356 resonators (one

spare)
- 1 C-446 detector disk
- 1 ST-56 strap
- 2 BA-30 batteries
- 1 BA-38 battery
- 1 CH-156 carrying case.

DON'T LET YOUR SEARCH COIL TOUCH THE GROUND **OR** BE HELD IN THE AIR. KEEP IT ABOUT 10" ABOVE THE GROUND.

Extract from TM-11-1122

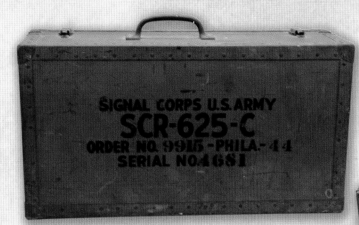

The CH-156-F chest for the dismantled SCR-625 detector set.

The SCR-625 taken down and stored in the special chest.

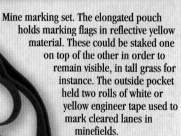

Mine marking set. The elongated pouch holds marking flags in reflective yellow material. These could be staked one on top of the other in order to remain visible, in tall grass for instance. The outside pocket held two rolls of white or yellow engineer tape used to mark cleared lanes in minefields.

The main components of the SCR-625.

Mine probe: metal spike and wooden handle for mechanical mine clearing. A bayonet could also be used for the same purpose.

The CY-91 chest for the AN/PRS-1 detector.

DETECTOR SET AN/PRS-1 (TM 11-1151)

AN stands for Army/Navy, indicating a joint nomenclature of components.

The AN/PRS-1, adopted in January 1944, was also sensitive to difference in densities and therefore able to detect non-metallic mines, such as the German wooden of glass case mines.

The complete AN/PRS-1 was made up of:
- 1 AM-32 amplifier assembly
- 1 CY-90 bag
- 1 DT-5 detector head
- 2 MX-125 exploring rod extensions
- 1 M-256 resonator
- 1HS-30 headset
- 1 CX- 122 cord
- 1 CX-123 cord
- Antenna protective horns
- 1 CY-91 carrying case.

Extract from TM 11-1151 showing the main components of the detector.

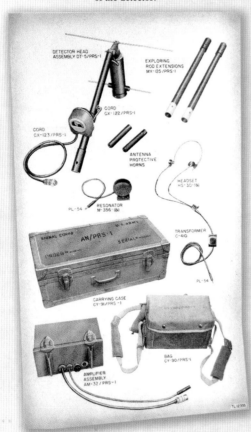

The AN/PRS-1 detector taken down and stored in the special chest.

Another picture from TM 11-1151 illustrating the detector in use.

Painted metal sign posted by engineers to indicate partial mine clearing work.

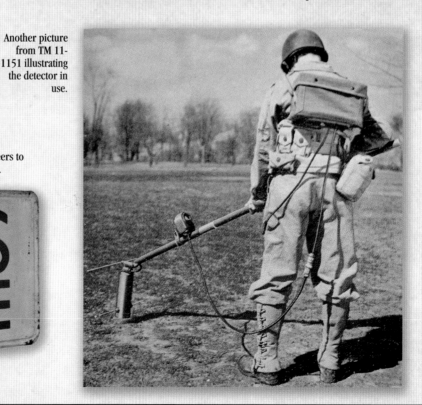

4. Demolition equipment

BLASTING MACHINE (10-CAP)

Mechanical exploder used to set off a chain of ten linked blasting caps, detonators and main charges.

SATCHEL CHARGE

Canvas bag for eight M3 blocks of C-2 explosive. Two of these pre-packed charges were stored in a special wooden crate.

Reel of engineer wire, sheathed in red plastic to tell it apart from signal wire, and used for the electrical firing of explosive charges.

SPECIAL FRICTION TAPE

Tape used to make up explosive charges, attaching and waterproofing fuzes, etc.

BLASTING GALVANOMETER

Special tool used to test the electrical circuit linking electrical blasting caps

Standard half-pound block of TNT explosive used in most engineer demolition charges.

HIGH EXPLOSIVE TNT ½ POUND NET CORPS OF ENGINEERS, U. S. A. DANGEROUS

1 Pound block of TNT high explosive.

M2 multi-purpose pliers and crimper: one handle ends as a screwdriver blade, the other is a spike for boring a small hole in the TNT block and inserting a fuze. The crimping claws are for attaching a blasting cap or length of detonating cord to the fuze.

Large-size wire cutters, with insulated rubber handles.

TOOL EQUIPMENT TE-33

A tool pouch designed and issued by the Signal Corps, and used by engineers for splicing electrical wire. The leather CS-34 belt case holds a pair of TL-13 pliers and a TL-29 electrician's pocket knife. The latter has two blades, one regular knife blade, and a screwdriver blade that locks open.

Demolitions kit: one large satchel with TNT blocks, and a smaller bag with miscellaneous engineer accessories: fuzes, pull- or traction-release igniters, special connecting clips for Primacord (detonating cord), friction tape, pocket knife, M2 crimpers, etc.

Small metal shock-proof containers for six or ten non-electrical fuzes.

This metal box, placed in the smaller demolitions bag, was for carrying various devices necessary to prepare explosive charges.

ELECTRIC BLASTING CAP 12-ft. WIRES Danger

Electric blasting cap and its 12-feet electric wire.

FUZE, LIGHTER M1

Pull-type fuze lighters in their red cardboard tube.
(J. Gawne collection)

INSTRUCTIONS FOR USE
ADHESIVE, PASTE, FOR DEMOLITION CHARGES ½ LB. M-1

USE: To stick explosive blocks to vertical, horizontal, sloping, or overhead surfaces. This can contains enough adhesive for fifteen ½-pound TNT blocks or equivalent.
(See bottom of can.)

ADHESIVE PASTE M1

Special paste to stick up to 15 TNT blocks, on any surface, in any position.

DELAY TYPE FIRING DEVICES M1, ASSORTED

Chemically-activated firing devices. A printed table gives precise indications on how to set the delay according to the ambient temperature and the color of the safety pin.

Flat metal box for 5 American-made delay type firing devices.

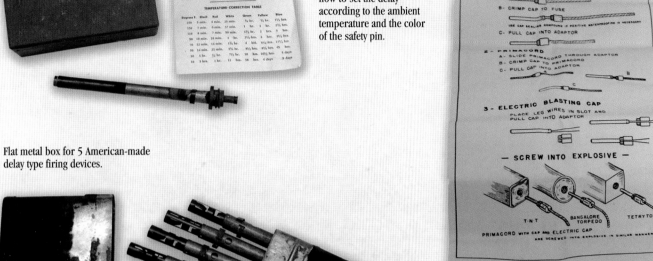

PRIMING ADAPTORS M1A3

These were used to screw the blasting cap or Primacord into the well on one end of the TNT blocks.

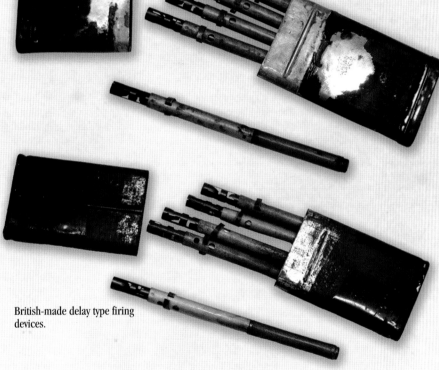

British-made delay type firing devices.

DETONATING CLIP M1

These clips were used to link several lengths of Primacord prior to setting off the detonating chain.

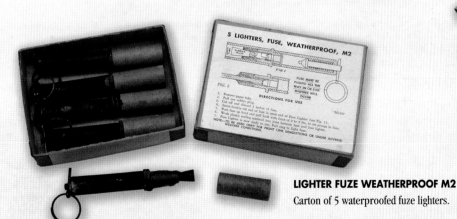

LIGHTER FUZE WEATHERPROOF M2

Carton of 5 waterproofed fuze lighters.

1. Structure and assignments

The essential task of the Signal Corps was to ensure communication between units. Different means were employed, such as telephone, telegraph, radios and mes-

Signal Corps officers' tunic lapel insignia

sengers. The Signal Corps was also responsible for all army photo and cinema work (training films). In the field, the Signal Corps committed various formations, such as pigeon, signals operation, intelligence, repair and depot units.

LOUDSPEAKER LS-6

This was part of the PA-4 public address equipment used when speaking to large bodies of assembled troops or civilian population.

The PA-4 (TM 11-435) equipment was composed of: LS-6 loudspeaker, ST-39 strap, M-230 tripod, BC-641 amplifier and T-36 microphone.

MESSAGE BAG BG-21

A padded and weighted bag, for dropping messages from a plane. It has a long yellow rayon streamer and a TL-124 electrical light.

MEGAPHONE M-64

Fiber megaphone with green canvas carrying strap.

ORGANIZATION AND PERSONNEL OF SIGNAL CORPS UNITS IN THE THEATERS OF OPERATIONS

Unit	Off	WO	EM	Remarks
1. Signal Construction Battalion	23	1	571	1 per field army and TO: line construction
2. Signal photographic Company	17	1	170	1 per field army: still and motion pictures
3. Signal Pigeon Co.	10		168	1 per field army
4. Signal radio Intelligence Co	7	1	251	1 per field army and TO: monitoring of enemy signals, radio goniometry
5. Signal Photo lab Mobile unit	3		45	
6. Signal Operations Battalion	28	3	631	1 per field army
7. Signal Operations Co.	9	1	287	Incorporated into a battalion, or separate
8. Signal depot Co.	5	4	182	1 at least per TO, 1 per field army
9. Signal Repair Co.	6	1	181	1 per field army, 1 as general reserve
10. Signal Installation Co.	6		100	Builds permanent telephone exchanges
11. HQ Signal Service Army	16		50	1 per field army HQ, command echelon of all subordinate signal units (1, 6, 8, 2, 3, 4, 9)

2. Optical signals

BX-22 power unit and J-45 Morse key.

SIGNAL CORPS   U. S. ARMY
BOX BX-22
DESIGNED AT SIGNAL CORPS LABORATORIES
FORT MONMOUTH   NEW JERSEY
SERIAL NO.   ORDER NO. 1247-PHILA 43
MADE BY
J. A. MAURER, INC.
NEW YORK   NEW YORK

SIGNAL LAMP EQUIPMENT EE-84 (TM 11-391)

Equipment used by artillery and signal units for line of sight communication. It sent Morse code signals in white or red flashes.

Main components of EE-84: BG-72 & BG-73 bags, M-132 signal lamp, 3 LM-22 bulbs (2 spares), FT-159 lamp mounting, tripod and mount assembly, BX-22 supply box, 16 BA-30 batteries (8 spares), CD-332 & MC-189 cords, M-172 goggles.

Range: 5,000 yds without filter in clear weather, and many times that figure at night. Adding a colored filter divided actual range in half. (➡ page 147 for other visual signals gear).

The EE-84's wooden tripod.

An extract from TM 11-391 showing the various components of the EE-84 signal lamp.

BAG BG-73
BOX BX-22
SIGNAL LAMP M-132 & LAMP MOUNTING FT-159
BAG BG-72
TRIPOD
BATTERIES: BA-30
GOGGLES M-172
FILTER MC-189
MOUNT ASSEMBLY
KEY J-46
CORD CD-332
LAMPS LM-22
SCL-975

BG-72 & BG-73 bags for the EE-84 signal lamp.

3. Carrier pigeon equipment

SIGNAL CORPS
CONTAINER PG-102/CB

CONTAINER PG-102/CB
Folding wooden cage for two carrier pigeons.

CONTAINER PG-107/PB
Collapsible fiber cage for two carrier pigeons.

FROM HIPWELL MANUFACTURING CO., INC.
YONKERS, NEW YORK
STOCK NO. 9A-1856
PARTIAL NO. 45
B/L   WO. J5a86981
TO: SSO
        PHILA. SIGNAL DEPOT
        ANNEX NO. 1
        22ND & LEHIGH AVE
        PHILA., PA.
1 EACH PIGEON EQUIPMENT PG-60
MADE UP IN CONTAINER PG-51 ON
ORDER NO. 7591-PHILA.-43
SERIAL NO.   WEIGHT 14 LBS.

Delivery cardboard crate for the
Pigeon Equipment PG-60

The complete PG-60 called for:
a PG-51 cage, a M-210 message
book, 24 PG-67 message holders,
2 books of transparent map
overlays and 2 pencils.

CONTAINER PG-51
Portable 2-cage pigeon loft for
four carrier pigeons. The
perforated clear plastic
windows protected the birds
from exposure.

SIGNAL CORPS   U.S. ARMY
CONTAINER PG-51
DESIGNED AT SIGNAL CORPS LABORATORIES
FORT MONMOUTH,   NEW JERSEY
SERIAL NO. 2892   ORDER NO.7591-PHILA-43
SUPPLIED BY
HIPWELL MFG. COMPANY, INC.
YONKERS,   NEW YORK

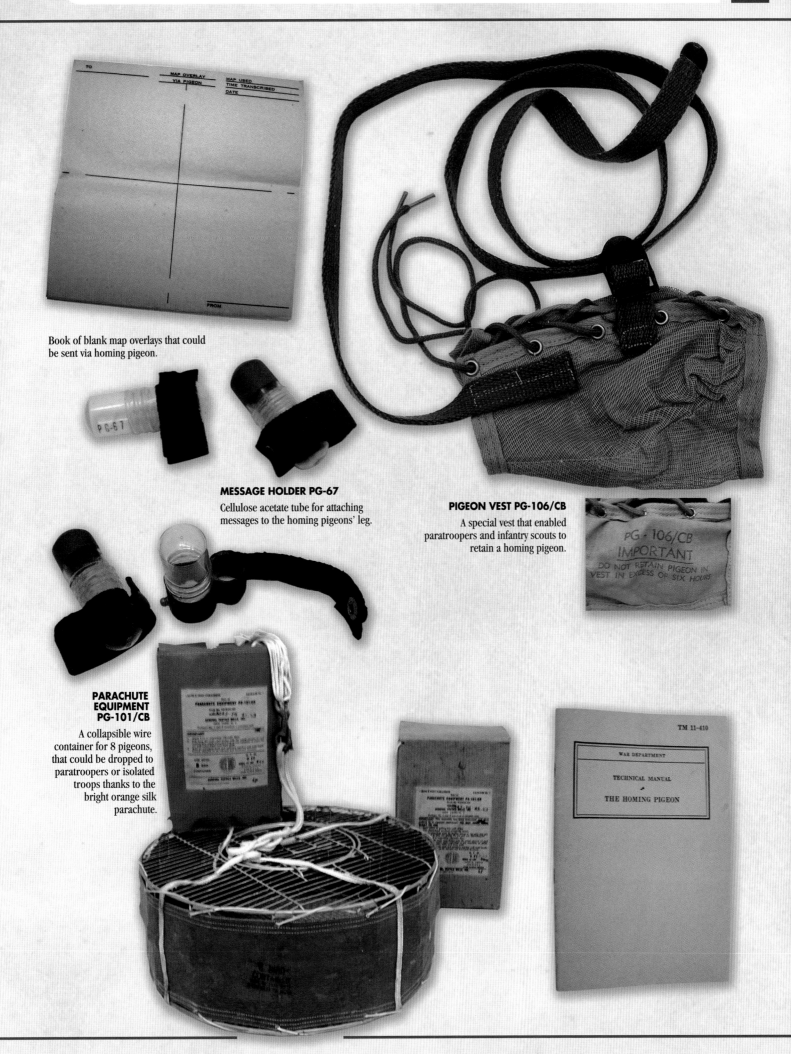

Book of blank map overlays that could be sent via homing pigeon.

MESSAGE HOLDER PG-67
Cellulose acetate tube for attaching messages to the homing pigeons' leg.

PIGEON VEST PG-106/CB
A special vest that enabled paratroopers and infantry scouts to retain a homing pigeon.

PARACHUTE EQUIPMENT PG-101/CB

A collapsible wire container for 8 pigeons, that could be dropped to paratroopers or isolated troops thanks to the bright orange silk parachute.

4. Telephone open wire construction equipment

BAG BG-44

A heavy-duty canvas bag for all tools and equipment required by open wire telephone linemen, including the TE-21 Lineman's set:

- LC-23 belt with safety strap
- LC-5 climbers and straps
- LC-24 twisting pliers
- HM-1 hammer
- TL-107 cutting pliers
- TL-106 screwdriver
- LC-25A screw spike wrench
- TL-83 friction tape rolls and
- TL-192 rubber tape rolls.

BELT LC-23

Adjustable lineman's belt and its safety strap fitted with strong snap hooks. Most tools were suspended from the belt, rolls of friction tape hung from the leather thong on the left side.

1. TL-107 pliers/cutters, carried on the lineman's belt in their leather pouch.

2. LC-25 wrench for spike screws, and LC-24 pliers for twisting and splicing open wire

CLIMBERS LC-5

Metal climbers strapped under the foot and on the inside calf. The sharp spike helped with climbing trees or wooden telephone poles.

BUCKET LC-57

White canvas bag with leather-covered bottom, for various line construction items. This could be suspended from the belt when working on a tree or pole.

LC-10 GLOVES

Strong leather gloves with cuffs.

REEL EQUIPMENT CE-11 (TM 11-250)

Equipment for manually laying W-130 light telephone wire (assault wire) on short distances. The equipment was strapped on the chest and operated by one man.

The CE-11 called for:
– 1 reel RL-39 with its two ST-34 & 35 support straps
– 1 DR-8 wire spool with a M-221 connector, and 1/4 mile of twisted W-130 assault cable
– 1 TS-10 handset with ST-33 strap. This sound-powered (magnetic) phone could, without an electrical supply, enable voice communication at a range between 3 and 5 miles.

Manufacturer paper tag on a spool of telephone wire.

STRAP ST-19A

Among other purposes, it was used to hand-carry the RL-31 reel unit.

In rugged terrain, telephone wire spools could be carried on a packboard (➡ page 75)

REEL UNIT RL-31 (TM 11-362)

Larger reel and cradle for laying field wire from a 1,800 yard capacity DR-5 reel, or two DR-4 reels. The RL-31 could be operated stretcher-style by two men, with two ST-19 straps, or as a wheelbarrow pushed by one man. The RL-31 was also commonly attached to the rear body of a jeep or truck.

RL-31 components were: RL-311 cradle, RL-31 axle, GC-4 crank, GC-10 brake, 2 ST-19A straps, and various attachment plates.

Manufacturer and nomenclature plate of an RL-31.

5. Telephone switchboards

SWITCHBOARD BD-71

Portable 6-line telephone switchboard, with crank-activated generator for ringing. It was housed in a plywood case with two handles on the sides and four collapsible metal legs. This type of switchboard could be found at the message center of every small unit's command post.

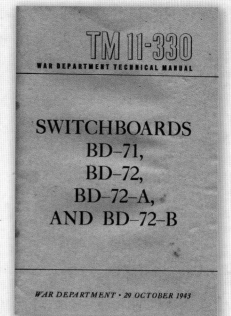

TM 11-330
WAR DEPARTMENT TECHNICAL MANUAL

SWITCHBOARDS
BD–71,
BD–72,
BD–72–A,
AND BD–72–B

WAR DEPARTMENT · 29 OCTOBER 1943

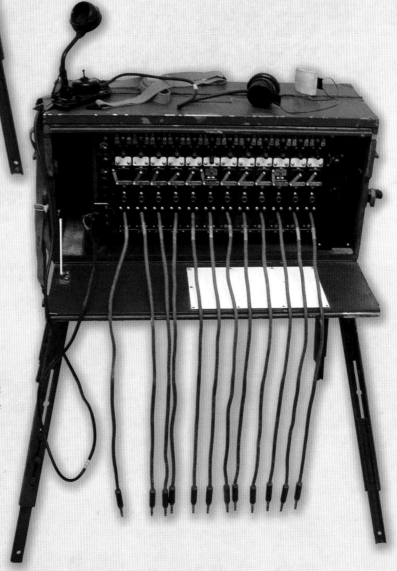

SWITCHBOARD BD-72

12-line capacity field switchboard. Four lines could be dedicated to telegraphs, against two for the BD-71.

TELEPHONE CENTRAL OFFICE SET TC-12 (TM 11-336)

A lightweight telephone exchange, using a BD-91 switchboard of 20-line capacity.

TC-12 components were: BD-91 switchboard, M-222 converter, Telering, HS-19 chest set, cords CD-452 & CO-258, 4 batteries BA-23 (2 spare), 12 batteries BA-30 (6 spare) and Maintenance equipment ME-30.

TELEPHONE REPEATER SET TC-29 A (TM 11-348)

A portable repeater for four-wire operation, used with the W-110, W-110 B, W-143 or W-548 telephone wires. TC-29 components were: EE-99 repeater, PE-204 power supply, field telephone EE-8, grounding pole MX-148 G, bracket TM-106, 2 battery clips and 25 feet of wire W-108 A.

CONVERTER M-222

This device draws direct current from low-voltage batteries and converts it into high voltage for calling.

TELEPHONE REPEATER EE-99

On a W-110 wire telephone line, the repeater set was inserted at each end and every 10 miles in order to boost the range to 28 miles or a maximum of 60 miles with constant upkeep.

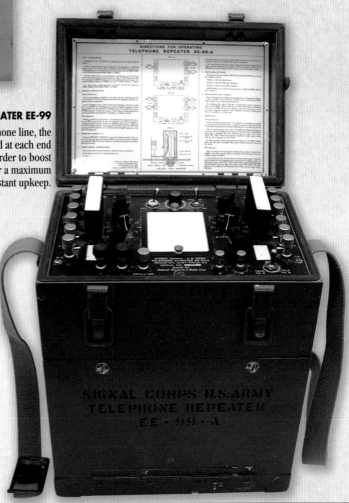

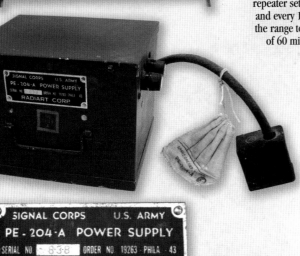

POWER SUPPLY PE-204

This was used with the EE-99 and was composed of the PE-204 vibrator plugged into a 12-volt battery or coupled 6-volt batteries.

SWITCHBOARD BD-57 B

This was one of the components for the Code Practice Equipment EE-81: a classroom Morse code practice set for training up to 20 operators under an instructor.

CODE, TRAINING, SET, AN/GSC-T1 (TM 11-437)

A visual and audible Morse code practice set.

KEY J-38

This Morse key was an element of the EE-81 code practice set.

CHEST SET TD-3

This chest set variation was developed for use with a gas mask, the transmitter being a lip microphone T-45 (➡ page 210) or the throat microphone T-30 (➡ page 130).

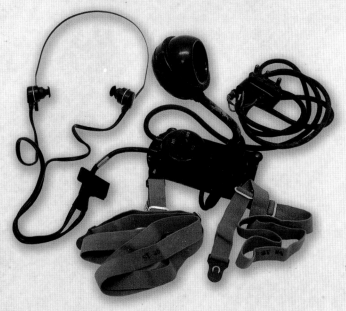

CHEST SET TD-1 and HEAD SET HS-30

Set attached to the operator's chest by two straps (ST-24 & ST-25), with press-to-talk switch on the chest plate, used with all signal equipment featuring the JK-37 jack. The headphones, usually of the HS-30 type, were connected to the top of the switch box. The HS-30 could be worn under the steel helmet.

6. Field telephone and desk telephones

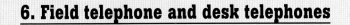

TELEPHONE TP-9 (TM 11-2059)

A portable set including the generator and ringing components of the EE-8 plus a vacuum-tube amplifier which extended the talking range of the wire line.

TELEPHONE EE-8 A (TM 11-333)

Field telephone used as a local or central set. Carried in a leather case, the aluminium frame holds batteries and ringing equipment. The handset was a TS-9.

TELEPHONE TP-6

Desk telephone, off-the-shelf commercial pattern. This could be fitted with a dial for connection with an automatic exchange. The TP-6 was made by 5 different manufacturers and variants can be encountered. The TP-6 was stored by tens inside the wooden CS-74 chest.

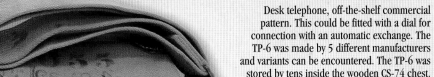

7. Telegraph TG-5

TELEGRAPH SET TG-5 B (TM 11-351)

A portable six-pound field set or buzzer for manual keying and receiving. The headset HS-20 has a single earphone (R-3). The telegraph was carried in the CS-49 case of canvas and leather with adjustable strap.

8. Telephone line and equipment maintenance

TEST SET EE-65 F (TM 11-361)

Telephone line test equipment used in the field or permanent installations. Housed in a wooden portable chest, it allowed for voice communication, and locating groundings and mix-ups, through loop and insulation resistance measures.

TEST SET TS-27/TSM (TM 11-2057)

Portable test set for telephone lines, used for locating breaks, loops, and groundings by measuring insulation resistance.

TEST SET I-51 A (TM 11-379)

Large test set contained in wooden chest, for locating breaks in cables.

MAINTENANCE EQUIPMENT ME-30

Special repairman's case, furnished with tools, various meters and spare parts for the TC-12 telephone exchange (→ page 199).

TEST SET TS-67 B (TM 11-2046)
Small circuit tester used for the repair of various telephone sets.

TM 11-2046

INSTRUCTIONS
67B AND 67B (SPL) TEST SETS
PER D-173231
TEST RECEIVER WITH EXTERNAL RESISTANCE

Manufactured by
WESTERN ELECTRIC COMPANY
NEW YORK, N. Y.

RESTRICTED

OFFICE OF THE CHIEF SIGNAL OFFICER
ARMY COMMUNICATIONS SERVICE
PLANT ENGINEERING AGENCY
U. S. ARMY

STOCK No. 3C1084F-3
ONE EACH
COIL COARSE "X"
ORDER No. 4764
PHILA-44
ITEM 4
CARRON MFG. CO.
CHICAGO, ILL.

Various spare parts for telephone exchanges.

SIGNAL CORPS, U. S. ARMY
ONE EACH JACK JK-37
STOCK No. 2Z5537
ORDER No. 26973 - PHILA-43
Made by
UNIVERSAL MICROPHONE CO., Ltd.
Inglewood, California

INSULATOR IN-15
Glass single groove insulator.

WIDTH ¾ IN.   LENGTH 15 FT.
ONE ROLL
TAPE TL-192
A. T. & T. Co., SPEC. No. 6863
FILE No. 13470 - PHILA - 43

MANUFACTURED BY
VAN CLEEF BROS.
CHICAGO, U. S. A.
DUTCH BRAND

STAPLE IW-6
Box of 100 insulated staples for line construction.

TOOL EQUIPMENT TE-5
Leather wallet for linemen. Its contents were: electrician knife TL-29, scissors, cutting pliers, tweezers, file, screwdriver and folding ruler.

100 ea STAPLE I W 6
Stock No. 6L31006
SUPERIOR INSULATED STAPLE
Order No. 12403-Phila-43
Graybar Electric Co., Inc

TAPE TL-192
Rubber-coated tape used with the TL-83 friction tape in insulating wire splices.

9. Army radios

A. The SCR-511 (TM 11-245)

Portable tactical radio in voice only communication, developed for the cavalry and standardized in Feb. 1942. It was also frequently used early in the war by the infantry (company-to-company, and company-to-battalion communication). The 5-mile range could be reduced by natural obstacles. The 511 was replaced by the SCR-300 as of late 1943.

SCR-511 components: 1 BC-745 receiver and transmitter, 1 chest unit T-39, 2 BC-746 Tuning units, 1 battery BA-49, 1 Power supply unit PE-157, 1 cord CD-3, 1 CS-131 wooden chest for spare parts.

CHEST UNIT T-39

Chest unit with dual purpose horn (mike-earphone), also containing the BA-49 battery and an alternate tuning unit (BC-746).

Chest Unit T-39-
Cord CD-571-
Press talk switch
Radio Receiver and Transmitter BC-745-
Cord CD-571-
Cord CD-3
Case - CS- 131-
Power supply unit PE-157

RADIO RECEIVER AND TRANSMITTER BC-745

Radio component, activated by pulling out the telescopic antenna. The round window on the front showed the channel. The radio could be slung thanks to the ST-43 strap.

SIGNAL CORPS   U.S. ARMY
TUNING UNIT BC-746-B
CHAN.
6312 :CGG 7 10156-PHILA-44
FREQUENCY KC-3245.0

This picture from TM 11-245 shows how the SCR-511 was used with the T-39 chest unit and PE-157 power unit.

TUNING UNIT BC-746

Preset tuning unit inserted in the BC-745. The 13 different tuning units were identified by the white figure on the manufacturer's plate, as well as the same number of dots in relief to allow for ready identification in the dark by touch.

SIGNAL CORPS   U.S. ARMY
POWER SUPPLY UNIT
PE-157-A
SERIAL NO. 1356 ORDER NO. 26378-PHILA-43
MADE BY
GALVIN MFG. CORPORATION
CHICAGO   ILLINOIS

POWER SUPPLY UNIT PE-157

Alternate power source, fed by a BB-54 wet battery. When the T-39 chest unit was not used, a T-17 microphone and HS-30 headset could be plugged into the power unit.

SIGNAL CORPS U.S. ARMY
RADIO RECEIVER AND
TRANSMITTER BC-745-B
SERIAL NO.   ORDER NO.
2036 MADE 31816-PHILA-43
BY
GALVIN MFG. CORPORATION
CHICAGO   ILLINOIS

B. The SCR-536 'Handie-talkie'

The first actual handie-talkie radio, that could be operated with one hand. Developed at the same time as the 511 for the Infantry, it offered a short range (1.2 mi.) voice communication capability to small units (company, squad).

The SCR-536 main component is the BC-611 transmitter and receiver, with preset channels, powered by BA-37 and 38 dry batteries. Pulling out the telescoped antenna turned the radio on.

BOX BX-49

Containers for spare tubes, crystals and coils necessary for presetting channels on the BC-611.

CASE CS-156
Zippered canvas carrying case for the handie-talkie.

HOMING MODIFICATION KIT, MC-619

Simple goniometry device for homing on a similar radio: frame-type antenna AN-190, coupling unit BC-1387, case CS-157, headset HS-30, cord CD-605 and modified base cover.

Detail of the modified base cover, with a socket for the HS-30 headset used when homing.

C. The SCR-300 (TM 11-242)

The '300' was the first actual walkie-talkie backpack radio, allowing for voice only communication on 41 alternate channels. Range was 3 to 5 miles with the AN-131 long antenna, and 2.5 miles with the short 'whip' AN-130 antenna.

The SCR-300 replaced, depending on availability, the SCR-511 and SCR-194-195 starting March 1943. The 300 was used within the infantry battalion net and by forward artillery observers.

SCR-300 components: transmitter and receiver BC-1000, sectional antenna AN-131, short antenna AN-130, battery case CS-128, battery BA-70, handset TS-15, headset HS-30, belt ST-55, harness ST-54, pad M-391; strap ST-50; accessories bag BG-150.

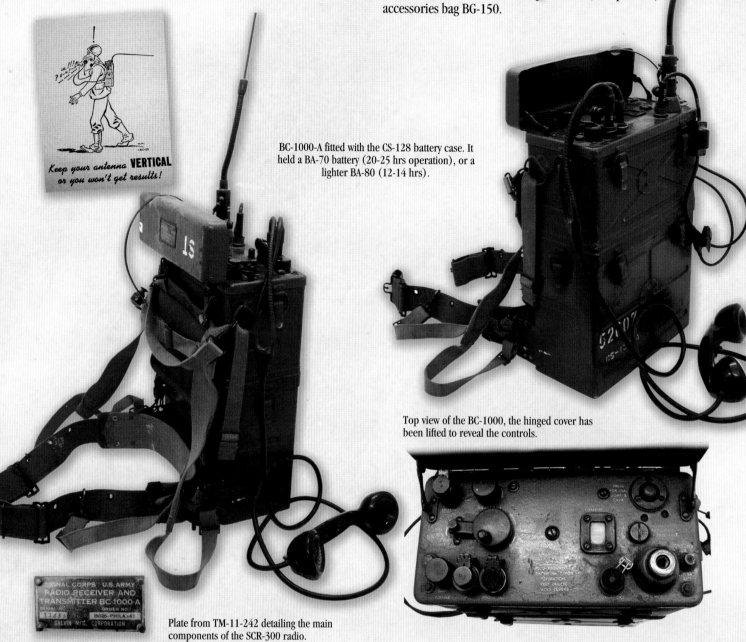

Keep your antenna VERTICAL or you won't get results!

BC-1000-A fitted with the CS-128 battery case. It held a BA-70 battery (20-25 hrs operation), or a lighter BA-80 (12-14 hrs).

Top view of the BC-1000, the hinged cover has been lifted to reveal the controls.

Plate from TM-11-242 detailing the main components of the SCR-300 radio.

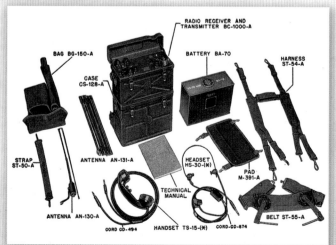

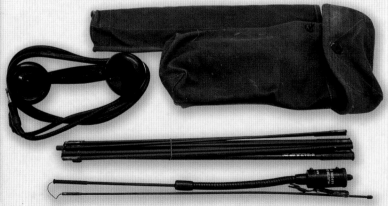

The BG-150 bag was fitted with two belt loops and held a TS-15 handset, the AN-131 sectional antenna, the AN-130 whip antenna and an HS-30 headset.

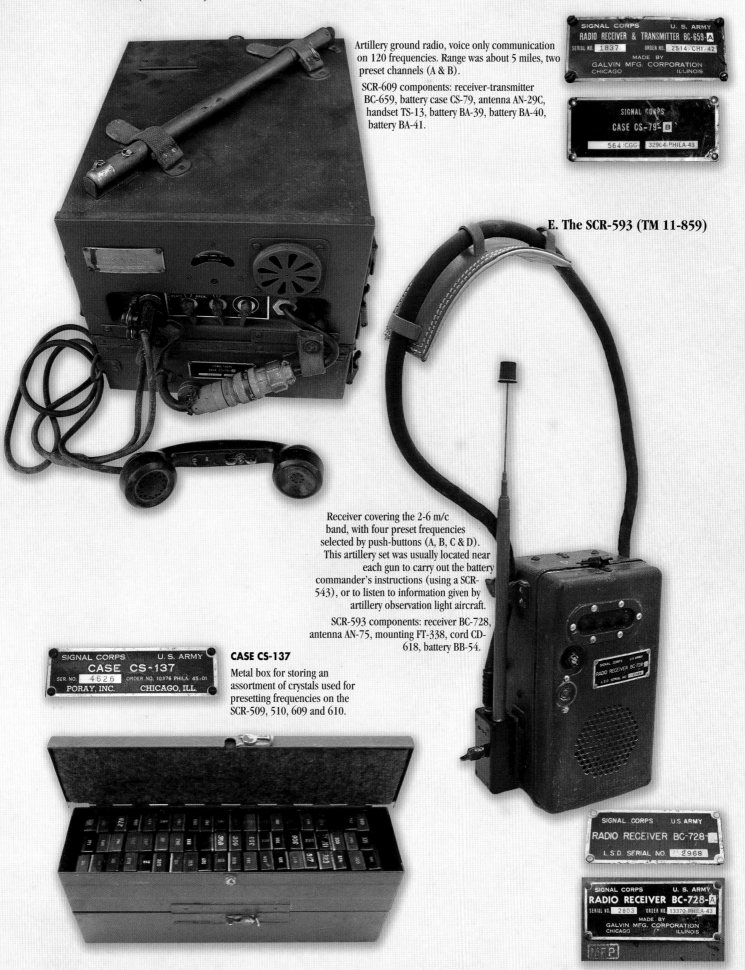

D. The SCR-609 (TM 11-615)

Artillery ground radio, voice only communication on 120 frequencies. Range was about 5 miles, two preset channels (A & B).

SCR-609 components: receiver-transmitter BC-659, battery case CS-79, antenna AN-29C, handset TS-13, battery BA-39, battery BA-40, battery BA-41.

SIGNAL CORPS U.S. ARMY
RADIO RECEIVER & TRANSMITTER BC-659-A
SERIAL NO. 1837 ORDER NO. 2514-CHI-42
MADE BY
GALVIN MFG. CORPORATION
CHICAGO ILLINOIS

SIGNAL CORPS
CASE CS-79-B
564 :CGG 32904-PHILA-43

E. The SCR-593 (TM 11-859)

Receiver covering the 2-6 m/c band, with four preset frequencies selected by push-buttons (A, B, C & D). This artillery set was usually located near each gun to carry out the battery commander's instructions (using a SCR-543), or to listen to information given by artillery observation light aircraft.

SCR-593 components: receiver BC-728, antenna AN-75, mounting FT-338, cord CD-618, battery BB-54.

CASE CS-137

Metal box for storing an assortment of crystals used for presetting frequencies on the SCR-509, 510, 609 and 610.

SIGNAL CORPS U.S. ARMY
CASE CS-137
SER. NO. 4626 ORDER NO. 10376 PHILA. 45-01
PORAY, INC. CHICAGO, ILL.

SIGNAL CORPS U.S. ARMY
RADIO RECEIVER BC-728-
L.S.D. SERIAL NO. 2968

SIGNAL CORPS U.S. ARMY
RADIO RECEIVER BC-728-A
SERIAL NO. 2803 ORDER NO. 13370-PHILA-43
MADE BY
GALVIN MFG. CORPORATION
CHICAGO ILLINOIS

F. The SCR-284 (TM 11-275)

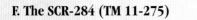
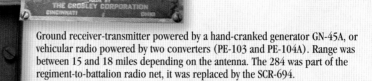

Ground receiver-transmitter powered by a hand-cranked generator GN-45A, or vehicular radio powered by two converters (PE-103 and PE-104A). Range was between 15 and 18 miles depending on the antenna. The 284 was part of the regiment-to-battalion radio net, it was replaced by the SCR-694.

Ground radio components: receiver-transmitter BC-654 A, generator GN-45 A and its accessories, 8-section antenna (MS-49 to MS-56), antenna insulator IN-106 A.

Vehicular radio: receiver-transmitter BC-654 A, converters PE-103 A and PE-104 A, shock-absorber mounting FM-41 A, 5-section whip antenna (MS-49 to MS-53).

GENERATOR GN-45 A

Hand-cranked generator for the ground operation of the SCR-284. Components: 2 legs LG-3, 1 leg with seat LG-2, 1 cord CD-50, 2 cranks GC-7.

G. The SCR-694 (TM 11-230)

Ground portable radio powered by the GN-58 generator, or vehicular radio powered by a PE-237 vibrator. Divided into four loads weighing less than 30 pounds, carried in special canvas bags, the SCR-694 was easier to move than the 284. It was used among others by airborne and mountain troops.

Ground radio components: receiver and transmitter BC-1306, case BG-173, generator GN-58, bag BG-75, accessories set (antenna, morse key, headset and microphone).

Vehicle-mounted radio: receiver and transmitter BC-1306, bag BG-173, mount FT-482, vibrator PE-237, accessories set (antenna, morse key, headset and microphone).

H. Radio remote-control devices

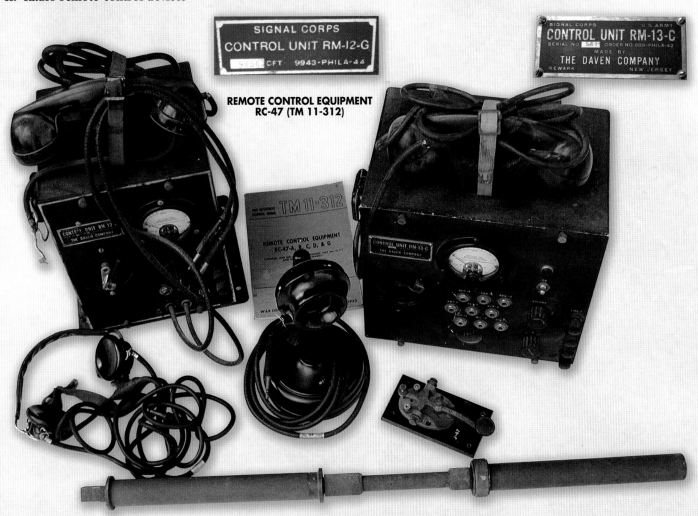

**REMOTE CONTROL EQUIPMENT
RC-47 (TM 11-312)**

Used with the SCR-187-188-287 series ground-to-air long range radios. The RM-12 was linked to the RM-13 located near the BC-191 transmitter by a telephone line carried by W-110B wire, at a maximum range of about 10 miles.

RC-47 components: remote-control units RM-12 and RM-13, chests CH-54 and CH-55, axle for reel RL-27, accessories set (cords, morse key, headset and microphone).

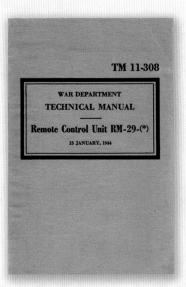

REMOTE CONTROL UNIT RM-29 (TM 11-308)

Remote-control unit for connecting a radio to a telephone net, and reporting observation data from a safe distance. The radio itself was hidden a few hundred yards from the observation post in order to avoid locating by goniometry. The RM-29 was placed near the radio and hooked up to an EE-8 field telephone. The RM-29 was used with the SCR-284, 608, 609, 610, 628 radios.

Components: remote-control unit RM-29 and bag CS-76 C.

10. Radio equipment accessories

A-27 PHANTOM ANTENNA

This antenna was used for tuning the medium-range SCR-506 while avoiding monitoring by the enemy.

PHONE P-18

Earphones comprising a HB-4 headband, two R-2A earphones, a ST-20 strap and a cord fitted with the PL-55 plug. This was issued with the RC-47 remote-control unit, and other radio equipment.

LOUDSPEAKER LS-3

Electro-dynamic loudspeaker protected in a metal case. This was used mostly with the BC-312, 314, 342 and 344 receivers.

MICROPHONE T-17

The T-17, in plastic or in a light metal alloy, was the most common hand-held microphone.

MICROPHONE T-45

The T-45, or 'lip' microphone had a special device for reducing loud ambient noise and was therefore used by tank crews, for instance. The T-45 was also part of the AN-VRC-3 radio, when the SCR-300 was mounted in a tank or motor vehicle.

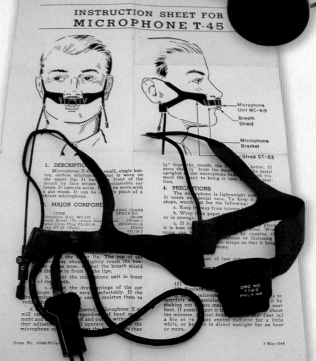

LOUDSPEAKER LS-7

This was connected to the SCR-284 radio and many others.

11. Message center equipment

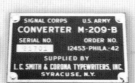

The converter's Signal Corps nomenclature plate.

CONVERTER, M-209

The 'Haglin' converter, a small, portable, hand-operated machine, converting letter by letter into or from a cipher equivalent. This was used for en- or de-ciphering radio messages in tactical units. The code was changed each day by selecting a different setting for the rotors. The originator typed the message with the knob at left, and this was slowly printed on ticker-tape. The encoded message was then sent by radio and the addressee, using the day's setting then deciphered the message.

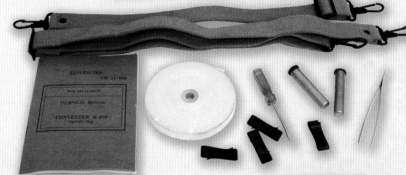

The M-209 converter's accessories: its bag and strap, technical manual, ticker tape roll, screwdriver, tweezers, message clips, oil and ink containers.

MESSAGE ENVELOPE M-40

MESSAGE BOOKS M-210 AND M-210 B

25 forms allowing for triplicates.

Canvas bag for the M-209 converter. The removable strap could be used to keep the machine on the operator's knee in the field or when working in a moving vehicle.

HOLDER M-167 A

1. Special board used by radio operators for writing or logging messages. This particular board has been used by an infantry battalion's radio section.

2. Metallic variant of the M-167A, bearing the stenciled mark of an HQ unit.

3. This holder has been neatly painted with its owner's serial number (D-7731), as well as a reminder of the radio SOPs of the 34th and 36th Infantry divisions.

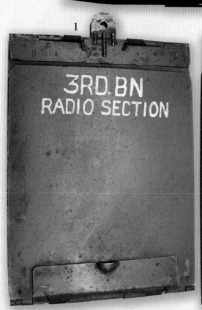

12. Tuning and maintenance of radio material

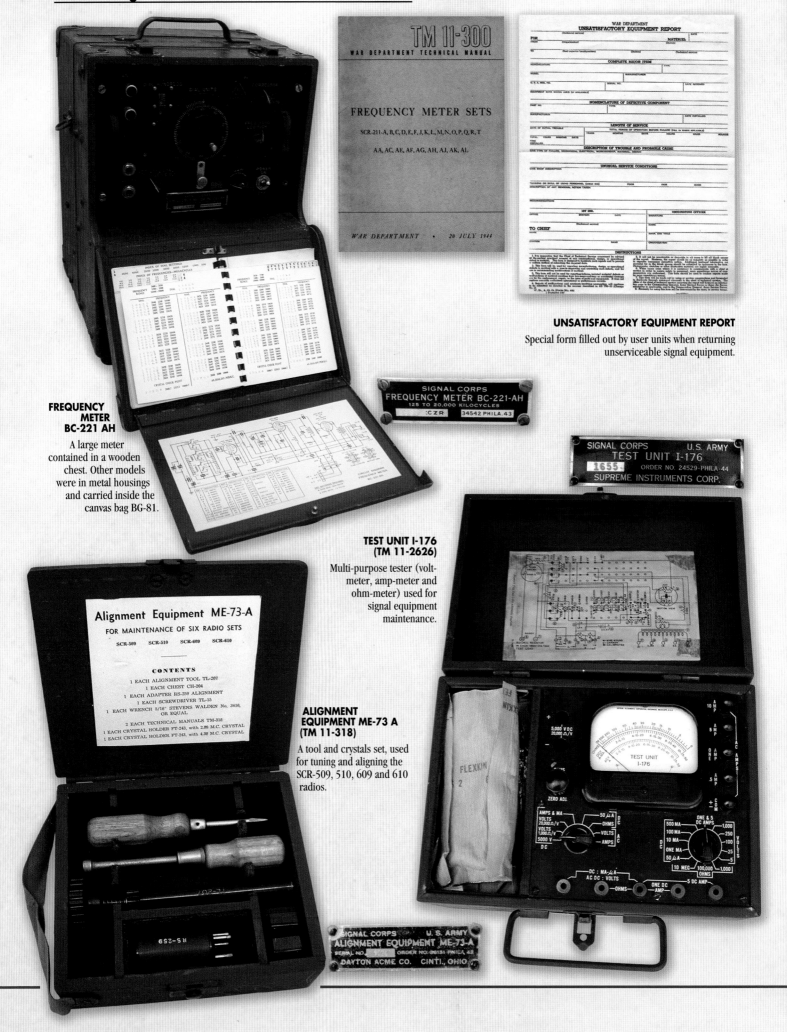

TM 11-300
WAR DEPARTMENT TECHNICAL MANUAL

FREQUENCY METER SETS

SCR-211-A, B, C, D, E, F, J, K, L, M, N, O, P, Q, R, T

AA, AC, AE, AF, AG, AH, AJ, AK, AL

WAR DEPARTMENT • 20 JULY 1944

UNSATISFACTORY EQUIPMENT REPORT
Special form filled out by user units when returning unserviceable signal equipment.

FREQUENCY METER BC-221 AH

A large meter contained in a wooden chest. Other models were in metal housings and carried inside the canvas bag BG-81.

SIGNAL CORPS
FREQUENCY METER BC-221-AH
125 TO 20,000 KILOCYCLES
CZR 34542 PHILA. 43

SIGNAL CORPS   U.S. ARMY
TEST UNIT I-176
1655 ORDER NO. 24529-PHILA-44
SUPREME INSTRUMENTS CORP.

TEST UNIT I-176 (TM 11-2626)
Multi-purpose tester (voltmeter, amp-meter and ohm-meter) used for signal equipment maintenance.

Alignment Equipment ME-73-A
FOR MAINTENANCE OF SIX RADIO SETS

SCR-509   SCR-510   SCR-609   SCR-610

CONTENTS
1 EACH ALIGNMENT TOOL TL-207
1 EACH CHEST CH-204
1 EACH ADAPTER RS-259 ALIGNMENT
1 EACH SCREWDRIVER TL-15
1 EACH WRENCH 5/16" STEVENS WALDEN No. 3410, OR EQUAL
2 EACH TECHNICAL MANUALS TM-318
1 EACH CRYSTAL HOLDER FT-243, with 2.80 M.C. CRYSTAL
1 EACH CRYSTAL HOLDER FT-243, with 4.30 M.C. CRYSTAL

ALIGNMENT EQUIPMENT ME-73 A (TM 11-318)
A tool and crystals set, used for tuning and aligning the SCR-509, 510, 609 and 610 radios.

SIGNAL CORPS   U.S. ARMY
ALIGNMENT EQUIPMENT ME-73-A
SERIAL NO.   ORDER NO. 36131-PHILA. 43
DAYTON ACME CO.   CINTI. OHIO

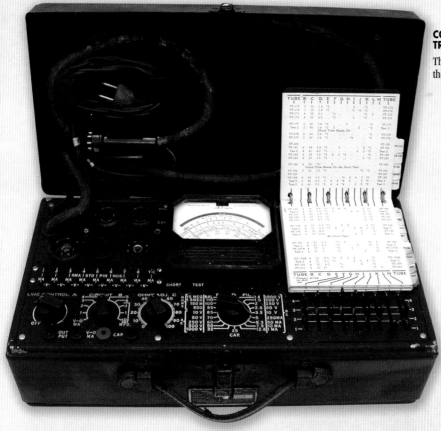

COMBINATION TESTER TRIPLETT MODEL 1183 C

This tube tester was part of the I-56 Test set.

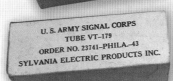

Several types of Signal Corps radio tubes.

A box of 50 VT-49 vacuum tubes. The many labels on the sides are proof of delivery to the Dayton (Ohio) Signal Corps Depot.

BATTERY BA-27

Multiple-unit battery with an 1.5, 3 and 4.5-volt output. It was used for instance with the RM-29 remote-control unit.

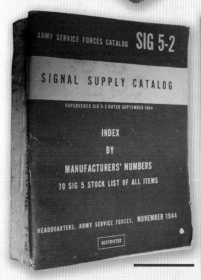

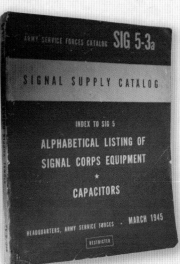

BATTERY BA-28

4.5-volt flat cell.

SIGNAL SUPPLY CATALOGS

Official military catalogs listing all signal equipment stocked and issued by the Signal Corps, by manufacturer (SIG 5-2) or by item (SIG 5-3a).

13. Miscellaneous signal tools

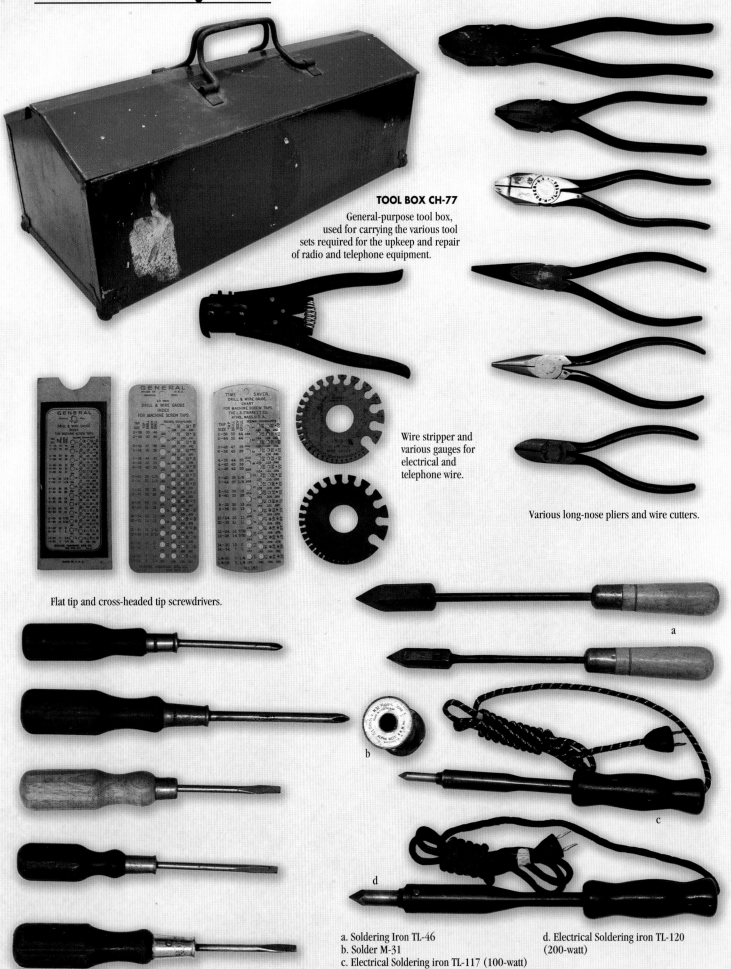

TOOL BOX CH-77
General-purpose tool box, used for carrying the various tool sets required for the upkeep and repair of radio and telephone equipment.

Wire stripper and various gauges for electrical and telephone wire.

Various long-nose pliers and wire cutters.

Flat tip and cross-headed tip screwdrivers.

a. Soldering Iron TL-46
b. Solder M-31
c. Electrical Soldering iron TL-117 (100-watt)
d. Electrical Soldering iron TL-120 (200-watt)

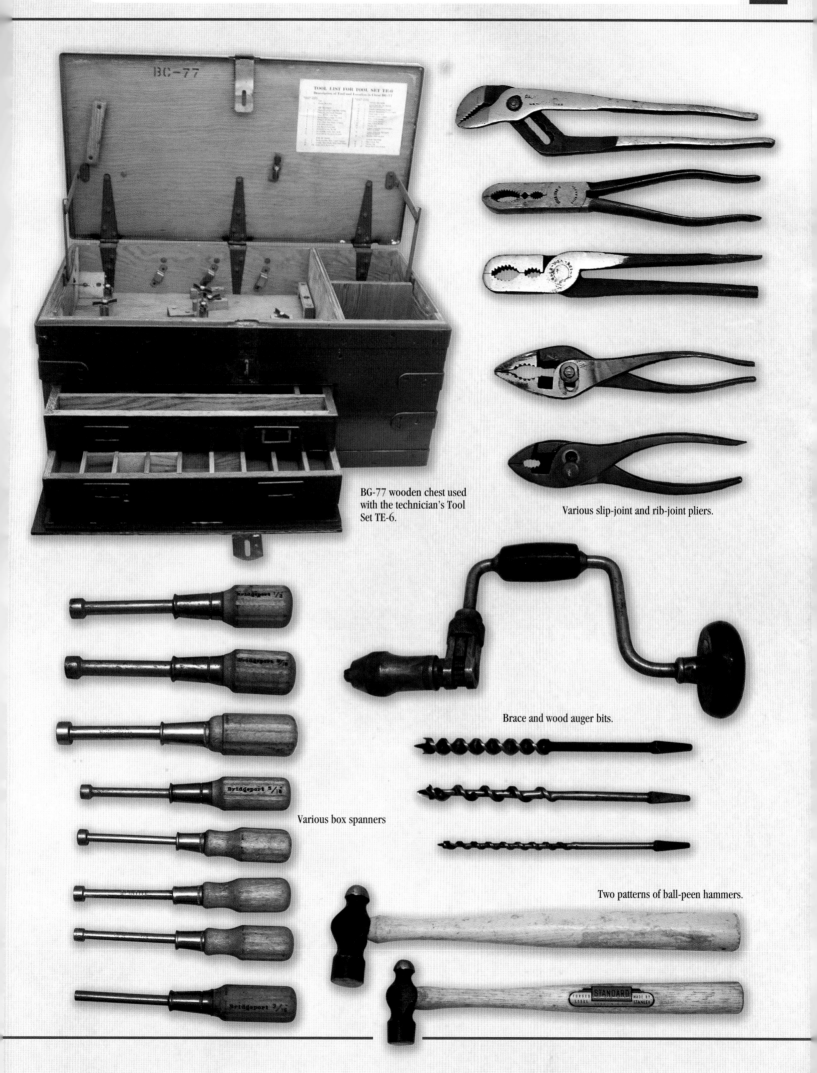

BG-77 wooden chest used with the technician's Tool Set TE-6.

Various slip-joint and rib-joint pliers.

Various box spanners

Brace and wood auger bits.

Two patterns of ball-peen hammers.

1. The Chemical Warfare Service

Lapel insignia for Chemical Warfare Service officers

The CWS developed chemical agents, weapons and munitions (gas, smoke and incendiary). It also designed gas protection equipment and trained specialists in the decontamination of soldiers, equipment and gassed areas.

Chemical Mortar Battalions had been established to spread smoke screens or disseminate poison gases on the battlefield. But, as poi-

Lapel insignia for Chemical Warfare Service officers

sonous agents were not used in battle during the war, these battalions mostly fired 4.2-inch high-explosive ammunition in support of combat units. The 2nd, 3rd, 81st, 83rd, 84th, 86th, 87th, 89th, 90th, 91st, 92nd, 93rd, 94th, 95th, 96th, 97th, 99th and 100th Chemical Mortar Battalions fought in Europe.

19 March 1945, at Rollandseck (Germany), an M2 smoke generator hides a treadway bridge on the Rhine with artificial fog. *(National Archives)*

Shoulder patches for the 93rd and 96th Chemical Mortar Battalions, non-regulation shoulder tabs for the 84th and 91st.

Various Chemical Warfare Service field and technical manuals

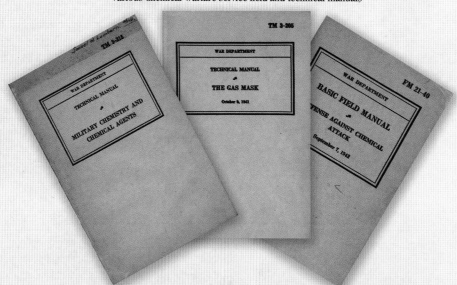

2. Army gas masks

THE SERVICE GAS MASK

By 1941, the issue gas mask was the M1A2 with a cloth-covered rubber face piece. The M2, introduced in July 1941, featured a face piece that was fully molded in rubber. The M2A1 had an M5 exhaust valve in plastic and rubber. The MIXA1 canister was connected to the face piece by a long corrugated rubber tube. The last variant of the Service Gas mask, the M2A2 of 1942, had an M8 round-shaped exhaust valve in plastic. The M2A2 was replaced as of the summer of 1943 by the M3 Lightweight Service Gas Mask.

SERVICE GAS MASK M2A2 - IXA1 - IVA1

Army Gas masks were identified by a series of initials and figures, for each of their main components (face piece, canister and carrier). Masks adopted after September 1940 had only Arabic numerals in their designation.

TRAINING GAS MASK MIA1

Introduced in 1940 as the MI, it changed names to MIA1 when the exhaust valve was improved. These were redesignated M2 and M2A1 in 1941 and production ceased in 1942. The MI cylindrical canister was screwed on the rubber face piece. Due to a shortage of Service gas masks, the Training mask was issued for operations in North Africa and Italy, especially to Airborne units as it was lighter and less bulky.

DIAPHRAGM GAS MASK M3 A1 - IX A1 - IV A1

Developed initially for Armored troops, this was a gas mask enabling speech transmission (radio-telephone). The early M3 mask had a gas-proof acetate diaphragm located in front of the mouth. The canister was that of the regular Service gas mask. The new M3A1 of 1943 had an M8 plastic exhaust valve that incorporated the diaphragm feature. The diaphragm gas mask, which was also issued to officers, was declared limited standard in June 1943.

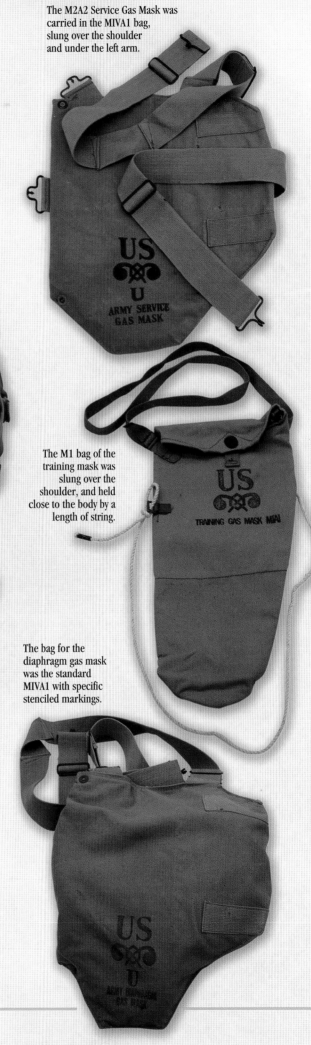

The M2A2 Service Gas Mask was carried in the MIVA1 bag, slung over the shoulder and under the left arm.

The M1 bag of the training mask was slung over the shoulder, and held close to the body by a length of string.

The bag for the diaphragm gas mask was the standard MIVA1 with specific stenciled markings.

Early M6 carrier in Olive drab No 5 material. Later bags were dark green. The bag also contained the anti-dimming, two protective covers and a tube of protective ointment (➡ pages 219-221).

LIGHTWEIGHT SERVICE GAS MASK M3 - 10 A1 - 6

Production started on this lighter mask in January 1943, to replace the Service Gas Mask in front-line units. The M3 face piece was identical to the M2A2, but with an added inner nose cup to reduce fogging of the eyepieces. The cylindrical M10A1 canister was connected to the face piece by a shorter tube. Owing to a shortage of crude rubber, the M3 was also made in black neoprene late in 1943. Production stopped in April 1944. The M4 variant (➡ volume 2 page 175), whose manufacture started early in 1944, was made on the basis of a reworked M2A2 face piece.

ASSAULT GAS MASK M5 - 11 - 7

This light gas mask was made between February and August 1944. The M5 face piece has the M11 canister screwed on the left cheek.

Waterproof M7 carrier for the M5 assault gas mask. Made in neoprene-covered canvas and closed on top by a rolled sleeve and metal snaps, this could be strapped on the hip, chest or thigh.

OPTICAL GAS MASK M1A1 - 10 - 6

Special mask for personnel operating sighting or fire direction equipment, developed in 1939 and made until 1941. The early MI optical mask had round eyepieces ground from optical glass, a diaphragm for voice transmission and an M1 canister strapped behind the head. The bag was an M5 and this mask was very similar to the Navy issue gas mask. Production of optical masks was resumed in 1944: the M1A1 mask was an M3 Lightweight mask fitted with optical glass visors and a diaphragm.

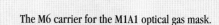

The M6 carrier for the M1A1 optical gas mask.

3. Care and maintenance of protective equipment

Anti-dimming sets were carried in the bottom of the gas mask bag. This early type of anti-dimming calls for a special soap stick and a flannel rag to rub it on the inner side of the eyepieces.

Another type of antidim, the special compound is a tube of 'Fogpruf paste.'

Last type of anti-dimming, the round metal box contains a soft cloth impregnated with the anti-dimming compound.

GAS MASK WATERPROOFING KIT, M1

This was also carried in the gas mask bag. Issued for amphibious operations, the kit held square patches and tapes of adhesive plaster and two metal clamps for waterproofing the canister and rubber hose, as well as an instruction sheet.

UNIVERSAL GAS MASK REPAIR KIT M8

A 1943 canvas roll holding an array of tools necessary for the most simple repair operations of gas masks by user units.

4. Detection of chemical agents on the battlefield

CHEMICAL AGENT DETECTOR KIT M9

A special device for sampling and testing ambient air for gases. A hand-held pump would inject the air samples inside several tubes holding a reactive solution that would reveal the exact nature of the agent.

SLEEVE, GAS, DETECTOR

British-made gas detection armband, a few millions were bought by the US Army. This was made of light brown paper coated with reactive paint. When in contact with vesicant spray, the paper would turn pink in spots. The cloth loop was for attaching the detector to the field jacket shoulder strap. On most period photographs, it appears the detector was placed on the right arm.

PAINT, LIQUID VESICANT DETECTOR M5 (TYPE 2)

This was applied on motor vehicles, especially on the hood, where the ground-to-air recognition star was painted. The brown or green paint would turn red when vesicants were encountered.

5. Protection against vesicant gases

EYESHIELD, M1 (CHEMICAL SPRAY)

Expendable acetate eyeshields worn against vesicant spray. The clear shield was stapled between a visor of impregnated material and a narrow strip of felt where it touched the brow. The cardboard envelope held 4 unfolded shields: 2 clear shields and two dark tinted shields. The shield was held on the face by adjustable elasticated straps.

Late-war metal box with the newer M5 ointment and a tube of British Anti-Lewisite (BAL) eye ointment.

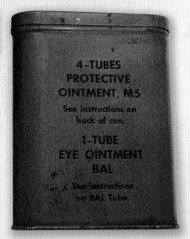

PROTECTIVE OINTMENT M4

Cardboard box holding a large tube of special ointment and cotton waste for cleansing vesicants from the skin. This was carried inside the gas mask bag.

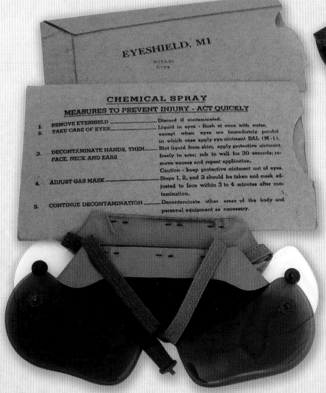

IMPREGNITE, SHOE, M1

A special dubbing for treating leather shoes against vesicants.

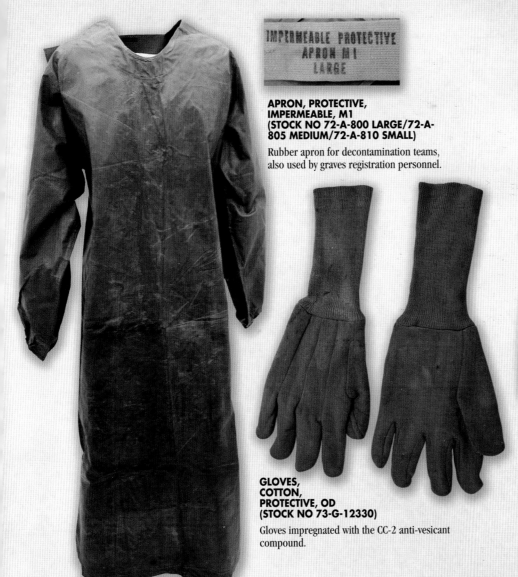

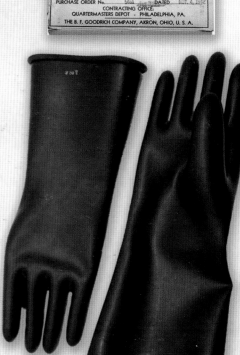

APRON, PROTECTIVE, IMPERMEABLE, M1
(STOCK NO 72-A-800 LARGE/72-A-805 MEDIUM/72-A-810 SMALL)

Rubber apron for decontamination teams, also used by graves registration personnel.

GLOVES, COTTON, PROTECTIVE, OD
(STOCK NO 73-G-12330)

Gloves impregnated with the CC-2 anti-vesicant compound.

GLOVES, PROTECTIVE, IMPERMEABLE
(STOCK NO 73-G-19660/73-G-19690)

Rubber gloves for vesicant decontamination teams, or for handling chemical weapons.

HOOD, WOOL, OD, PROTECTIVE
(STOCK NO 73-H-67020/73-H-67050)

Woolen hood for protection against vesicant gases, worn together with the gas mask. A short tab with two buttonholes at the back were for attaching the hood to the shirt, the HBT jacket or coveralls. The protective hood was also issued as a cold-weather cover during the winter of 1944-45.

COVER, PROTECTIVE, INDIVIDUAL

Anti-vesicant cover in clear and dark green plastic. After unfolding, this completely protected the soldier, together with his weapon and equipment. It was also convenient as an overhead cover in a foxhole, or to line its bottom.

COVER, PROTECTIVE, INDIVIDUAL, COLD CLIMATE

As very low temperatures would cause the plastic cover to crack, a sturdier model was introduced in 1944.

1. Missions of the Medical Department

Medical Department officer's lapel insignia.

Its main missions were the collecting, treatment, triage, evacuation then hospital care and convalescence of the sick and wounded. It was also tasked with defining and enforcing rules of personal and collective hygiene, as well as treat- ing and preventing venereal diseases. The Medical Dept. also ordered, stored and issued medical supplies.

FIELD EVACUATION OF WOUNDED *(Militaria Magazine)*

Normandy, 24 July 1944. In the 30th division sector, aidmen and stretcher bearers are preparing wounded personnel for evacuation to the nearest aid station.
(National Archives)

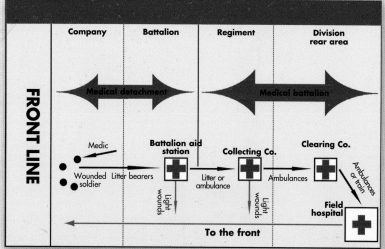

THE MEDICAL BATTALION

(Extract from the Battle for Brest, 1944, *by Jonathan Gawne. With the author's permission)*

HQ and HQ Detachment
7 Off., 2 WO, 33 EM, 1 Chaplain
x 5
x 3
x 2

Collecting Company

Company Headquarters
1 Off., 22 EM

Aid Station Platoon
2 Off., 9 EM
x 3
x 2

Litter bearer Platoon
1 Off., 43 EM

Ambulance Platoon
1 Off., 24 EM
x 10

Clearing Company
12 Off., 100 EM

Company Headquarters
2 Off., 26 EM
x 2
x 2

Clearing Platoon
5 Off., 37 EM
x 3
x 2

CAPTION
2 1/2 ton truck
3/4 ton truck
3/4 ton Command and Recon.
3/4 ton Ambulance
1/4 ton truck
Water trailer
1 ton cargo trailer
1/4 ton trailer

2. Identification of medical personnel in the field

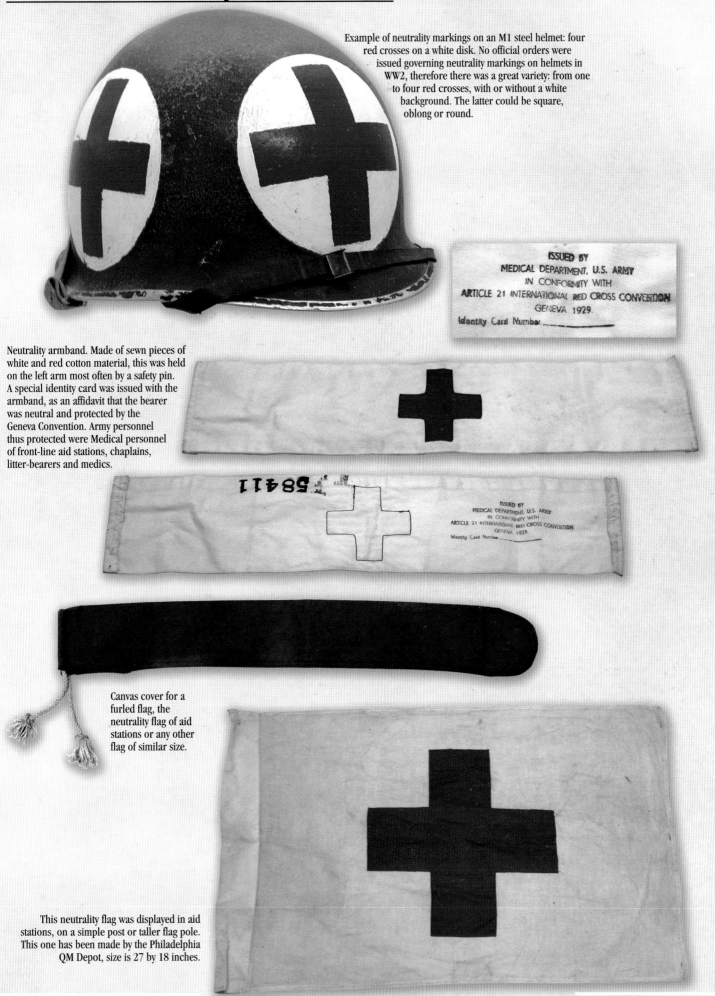

Example of neutrality markings on an M1 steel helmet: four red crosses on a white disk. No official orders were issued governing neutrality markings on helmets in WW2, therefore there was a great variety: from one to four red crosses, with or without a white background. The latter could be square, oblong or round.

Neutrality armband. Made of sewn pieces of white and red cotton material, this was held on the left arm most often by a safety pin. A special identity card was issued with the armband, as an affidavit that the bearer was neutral and protected by the Geneva Convention. Army personnel thus protected were Medical personnel of front-line aid stations, chaplains, litter-bearers and medics.

Canvas cover for a furled flag, the neutrality flag of aid stations or any other flag of similar size.

This neutrality flag was displayed in aid stations, on a simple post or taller flag pole. This one has been made by the Philadelphia QM Depot, size is 27 by 18 inches.

3. Equipment for front-line medical troops

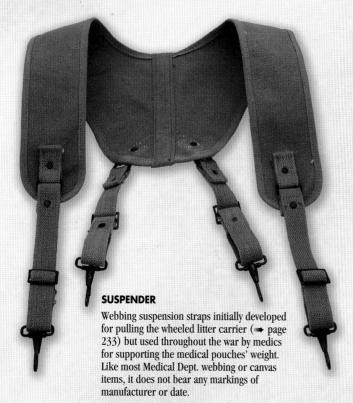

CANTLE, RING, STRAP

Short adjustable webbing strap used to connect the medical bags across the waist, front and back. It was also used as a handle for the pouches when they were not supported by the suspenders.

SUSPENDER

Webbing suspension straps initially developed for pulling the wheeled litter carrier (➡ page 233) but used throughout the war by medics for supporting the medical pouches' weight. Like most Medical Dept. webbing or canvas items, it does not bear any markings of manufacturer or date.

POUCH

Olive drab canvas medic pouch, worn with the suspenders and filled with various first-aid supplies: dressings, bandages, tourniquet, scissors, safety pins, etc. The contents depended upon assignment: Kit Medical officer's/Non-Commissioned Officer's/Private's; Kit Dental Officer's/Private's; Kit Parachutist's; Kit Veterinary Officer's; Non-Commissioned Officer's/Private's. The pouch could be carried by itself or in pairs, slung from a strap or hung from the special suspenders or the pistol belt (➡ page 68).

Two canvas strips with grommets on each face of the pouch could be laced together to make the pouch smaller.

LITTER, STRAP

A long adjustable webbing strap that could be used to support the weight of a litter, or to carry a medical pouch.

INSERT, TYPE I

Multi-pocketed insert, that could be laced inside the top of the pouch. This was part of the enlisted medics equipment.
(Martin Brayley collection and photo)

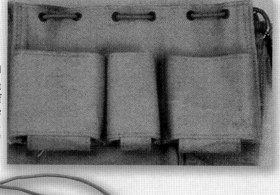

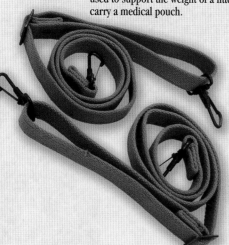

INSERT, TYPE II

Another type of insert, issued to officers and NCOs assigned to aid stations. The loops were for holding plastic tubes of various tablets.

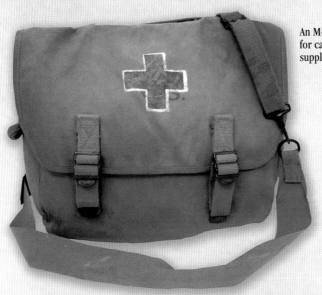

An M-1936 bag used for carrying medical supplies.

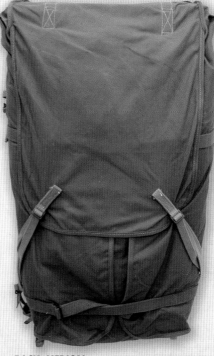

PACK, MEDICAL

This large bag, which could strapped to a Packboard (➡ page 75), was useful in rough terrain for hauling medical supplies. There were other types of packs, whose inner pockets varied with the specialized contents.

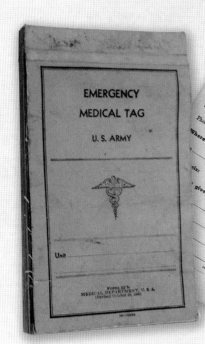

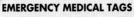

EMERGENCY MEDICAL TAGS

A book of strong paper tags filled by medical personnel with information on the wounded or sick soldier. The tag was tied before evacuation to the man's uniform by a string or thin wire.

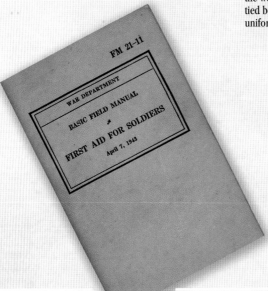

FM 21-11 was general issue to recruits for training in first-aid techniques.

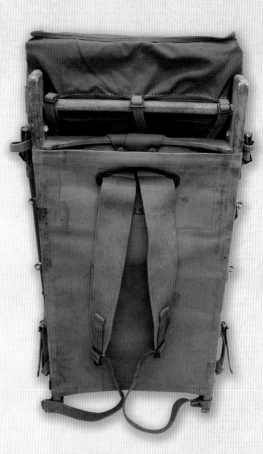

Note on Medical Department Item numbers

Until August 1944, most Medical Dept. equipment and supplies bore a 5-digit 'Item number' (for instance Item No 92040). After this date, a new 7-digit nomenclature was introduced: the first 5 figures remained identical for the item type, the last two indicated a variant (Item No 9204000 or 9608808). US Navy medical items were identified by a 'Stock Number' of two series separated by a dash (Stock No 2-1304 or Stock No 1-885). After 1947 and the unification of Army and Navy supply procedures, all medical items bore a 7-digit stock number in 3 series (for instance: Stock No 9-597-500).

Various types of bandages.

Standard Carlisle individual first-aid dressings (➡ page 80), in the cardboard packages included in various medical kits, like the parachutist's kit (➡ page 142).

Large first-aid dressings in cardboard boxes. The bottom two have been dipped in wax to make them moisture- and gas-proof.

Box of 10 Carlisle first-aid packets. The bright red coat of paint means that a packet of sulfa powder is included in each dressing.

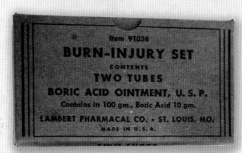

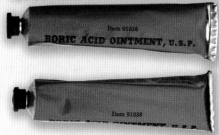

Burn injury set in a brown cardboard package: two tubes of boric acid ointment and a small wooden spatula.

Various kinds of cotton pads for dressing wounds. The absorbent cotton box has been impregnated with wax.

Safety pins. The larger pins were for securing blankets around the wounded on litters.

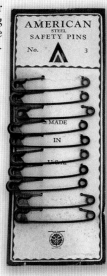

12 'shaker' packages of sulfanilamide crystals for use in aid stations.

'Wound tablets' of sulfadiazine, manufactured by the Upjohn Co. of Kalamazoo (Michigan). These were packaged in a clear plastic box with sliding top, sealed within a laminated envelope. These tablets were carried by every soldier in the first-aid packet pouch (➡ page 81)

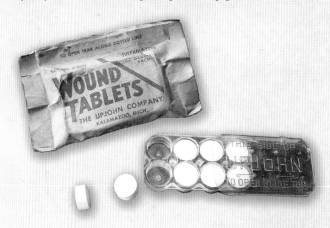

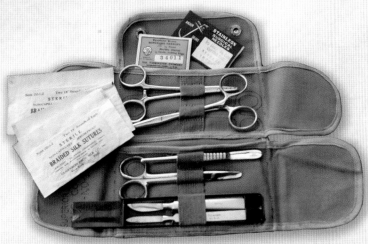

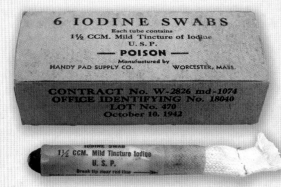

Glass re-usable syringe.

CASE, INSTRUMENT, MEDICAL, OFFICER'S

This was carried by officers in aid stations for initial treatment. Contents were: metal instruments box, lancet, operating knife, artery clamp, hemostatic pincers, suture silk and needles.

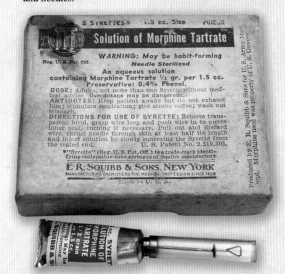

Box of six iodine swabs for disinfecting superficial wounds.

Metal box for 12 iodine swabs.

Storage box of 5 expendable syrettes of a 1/2 grain of morphine tartrate. A syrette, which was also carried inside the *Kit First Aid Parachutist's* (➡ page 142), was made of a soft metal tube fitted with a sterilized needle.

Glass bottle with rubber stopper used for plasma or whole blood transfusion.

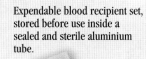

Expendable blood recipient set, stored before use inside a sealed and sterile aluminium tube.

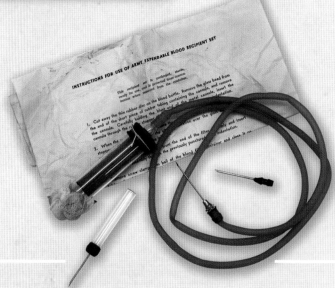

Bottle of Sodium citrate, used as an anticoagulant with freshly donated blood.

4. Evacuation of wounded

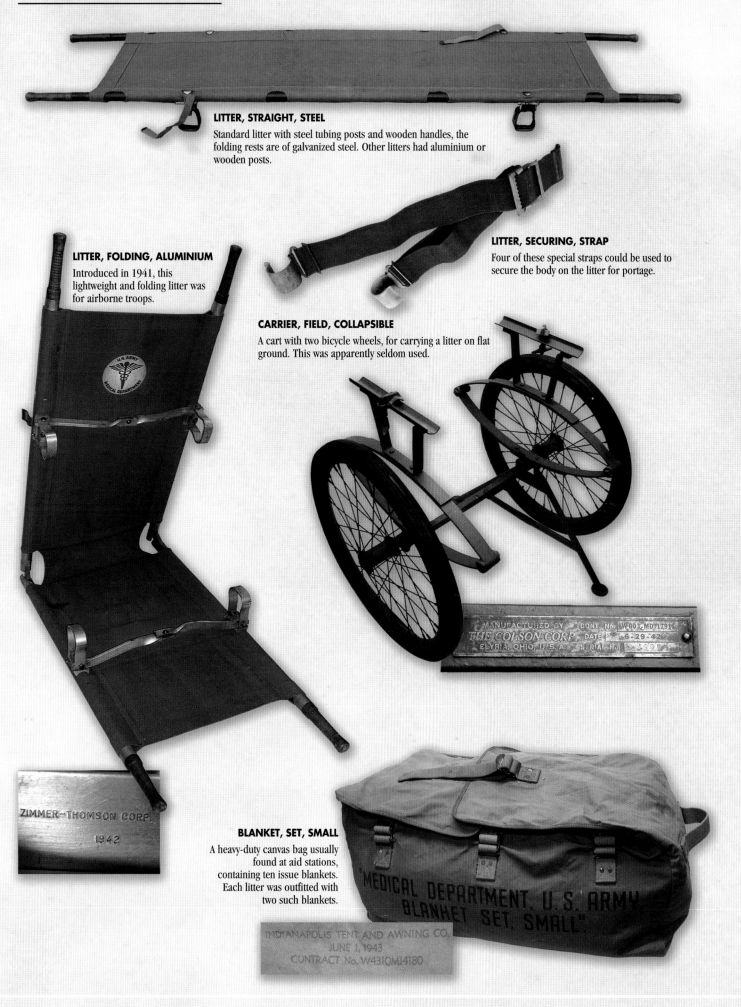

LITTER, STRAIGHT, STEEL
Standard litter with steel tubing posts and wooden handles, the folding rests are of galvanized steel. Other litters had aluminium or wooden posts.

LITTER, FOLDING, ALUMINIUM
Introduced in 1941, this lightweight and folding litter was for airborne troops.

LITTER, SECURING, STRAP
Four of these special straps could be used to secure the body on the litter for portage.

CARRIER, FIELD, COLLAPSIBLE
A cart with two bicycle wheels, for carrying a litter on flat ground. This was apparently seldom used.

ZIMMER-THOMSON CORP.
1942

MANUFACTURED BY CONT. No. W-803-MD-1791
THE COLSON CORP DATE 6-29-42
ELYRIA, OHIO, U.S.A. SERIAL No.

BLANKET, SET, SMALL
A heavy-duty canvas bag usually found at aid stations, containing ten issue blankets. Each litter was outfitted with two such blankets.

"MEDICAL DEPARTMENT, U.S. ARMY BLANKET SET, SMALL"

INDIANAPOLIS TENT AND AWNING CO.
JUNE 1, 1943
CONTRACT No. W4310M14180

5. Convalescence

THE
NITE KRAFT CORP.
Cont. W-669-QM-24232
Dated December 14, 1942
Spec. No. DDD-P-76
Stock No, 71640-05
Phila. Q. M. Depot

INSPECTOR

COAT, PAJAMA, WINTER, HOSPITAL
Flannel pajama top given to the sick and
wounded in hospitals.

TROUSERS, PAJAMA,
HOSPITAL
LUBIN-WEEKER CO., Inc.
Cont. W-669-qm-24234
Dated Dec. 14, 1942
LARGE
Type 2
Medical Dept. Item
No. 71660-05
FED. SPEC. No. DDD-P-76
Dated 12/17/36
Phila. Q. M. Depot

Inspector

**TROUSERS, PAJAMA,
WINTER, HOSPITAL**
The Federal spec., indicating
this was an Army/civil
service item, dates back to
1936.

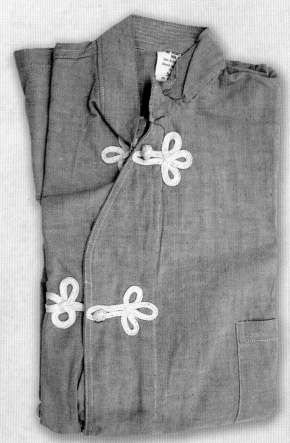

Gray oxford cloth
summer pajama top,
an item defined in
1936.

THE STUART KEITH
MFG. CO.
Cont. W-669-qm-17416
Dated April 13, 1942
Type 1
SMALL
FED. SPEC. No. DDD-P-76
Dated 12/17/36
Phila. Q. M. Depot

Inspector

Enameled hospital ward urinal.

TROUSERS, SUITS, CONVALESCENT

A pair of cotton trousers, identical in
construction to the khaki cotton trousers
(➡ page 34), but in a reddish color.

Hospital robe in corduroy. This
was also issued in dark blue cloth
for variety.

A stainless steel mess tray, this has the MD marking and the
date 1943.

This other pattern of MD mess tray is in bakelite,
1944-dated.

6. Miscellaneous medical equipment

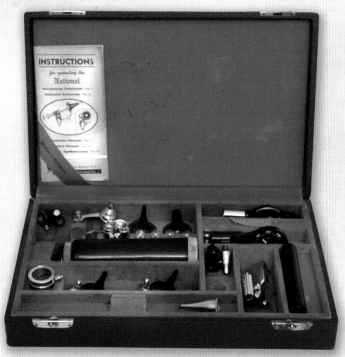

A chest of medical instruments for ear-and-throat doctors. The hinged lid bears the painted markings: 'National 30770 - Medical Dept. U.S. Army'.

Item 93510 was a complete set of anesthesia equipment.

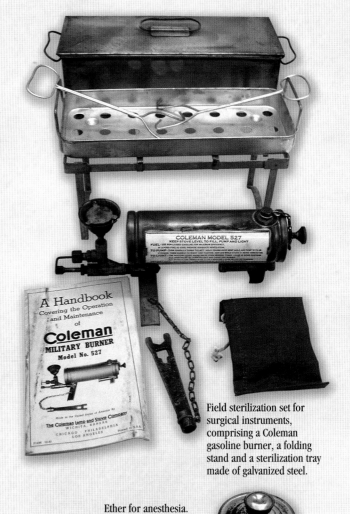

Field sterilization set for surgical instruments, comprising a Coleman gasoline burner, a folding stand and a sterilization tray made of galvanized steel.

Ether for anesthesia.

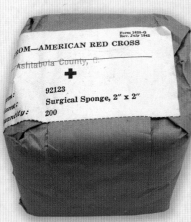

Package of 200 surgical sponges, made and donated by the American Red Cross.

CASE, WARD, COMPLETE

Complete set of medical instruments used in operating wards for dressing wounds.

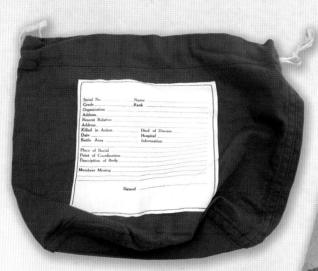

ADDRESSOGRAPH MODEL 70

A simple hand-held printing device used to readily transfer information from a soldier's identification tag (➡ page 259) to any medical form.

A small linen bag with drawstring closure for the personal belongings of soldiers who died in action or of disease. These were later forwarded to the soldier's next of kin.

Package of 50 'Combination pads' made and donated by the American Red Cross. These were used at the completion of a surgical operation.

7. Venereal diseases prevention

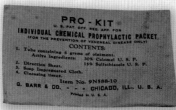

PRO-KIT

The 'Individual Chemical Prophylactic Packet' was issued and administered at Pro Stations if it was suspected the soldier had become infected.

Two brands of rubber contraceptives.

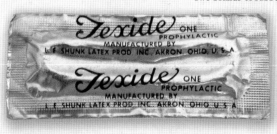

Introduction

Lapel insignia for Christian (left), and Jewish chaplains.

At the front and in garrison, the chaplains shared the life of American soldiers. Like civilian clergymen, they were entrusted with promoting their morality and religion by celebrating mass, administering the last rites and helping with graves registration. Volunteers put forth by each religion and accepted by the Army came under the Chief of Chaplains. After enlisting, the chaplain candidate underwent five weeks' training at the Chaplains school where he studied basic military subjects. As there were never enough volunteers, every Army chaplain had to learn some of the other denominations' rites. After graduation, the chaplain was commissioned as a second lieutenant and usually assigned first to a Stateside unit, then to an overseas command a few months later. As staff officers, two Protestant and one Catholic chaplain were attached to every regiment's HQ. Every division had a single Jewish chaplain.

6 October 1944, at Jarny, France, chaplain Earl C. Whitsitt conducts a religious service for men of the 26th Quartermaster Battalion (3rd Army). *(National Archives)*

A chaplain's overseas cap in Olive drab No 51 wool elastique. As of 1940 all officers except generals wore the same black and gold piping. Some chaplains however retained the distinctive black piping introduced in 1918.

ORGAN, FOLDING, CHAPLAIN'S

A portable field harmonium, the wooden frame was covered in canvas. This instrument has been made by the Estey Organ Corporation of Brattleboro (Vermont) and bears the serial number 464926. The organ was part of the 'Outfit chaplain's,' together with 150 hymnals and prayer books in a wooden chest, a chaplain's flag, a field desk and a typewriter. Chaplains in line units were entitled to a jeep and trailer, together with a driver, who doubled as the chaplain's assistant.

Officer's wool service coat for a 5th Army catholic chaplain, as indicated by the silver crosses on the lapels.

When folded, the organ was just a large wooden chest with a carrying handle.

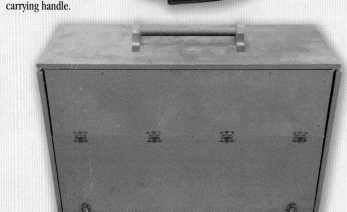

Portable altar. A large suitcase with side panels which folded in the lid or unfolded to form the altar. The liturgical set items, here for the Catholic worship, all bear the initials US, the Army property mark.

The liturgical set was stored in the bottom part of the portable altar.

This portable altar, which once belonged to chaplain George J. Dewitt, bears this officer's serial number and Transport Quartermaster markings (colored bars) for oversea movement.

a - Issue New Testament for Catholic soldiers.

b - Issue New Testament for Protestant soldiers.

c - Holy scriptures for Jewish soldiers.

d - Pocket missal given away by a Catholic congregation.

e - Spiritual and patriotic booklet given by the same.

f - Church manual donated by a Boston religious community.

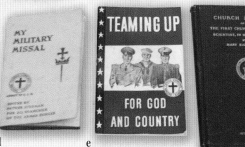

a - Army-issue Hymnal.

b - Army-issue Song and Service book. 150 of these were part of the 'Outfit, chaplain's.'

c - Religious picture.

Kit of religious materials for a Jewish serviceman, containing various scriptures for praying.

On 18 July 1944 in France, a soldier of the 4th Armored Division learns a few words in the Army French language guide. *(National Archives)*

Various Army-issue language guides and phrase books.

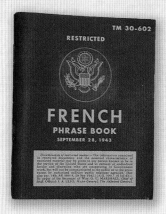

1. Technical manuals

Technical Manuals (TMs) described Army materiel (weapons, vehicles, machines, radios…) and contained instructions for its care and operation.

These were also technical reference books for certain administrative methods, and some provided general information on specific topics as aids for instructors.

17-ARMY PUBLICATIONS

2. Field Manuals (FMs)

Field Manuals contained the basic doctrines of training, tactics and technique.

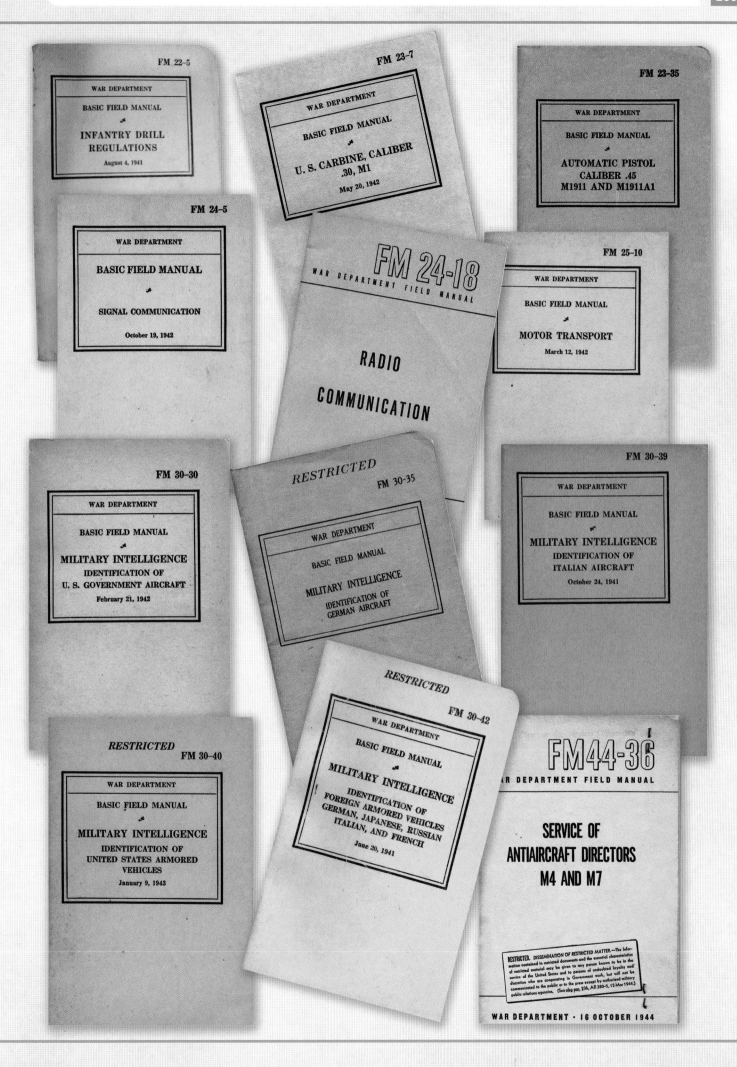

FM 22-5

WAR DEPARTMENT
BASIC FIELD MANUAL
INFANTRY DRILL
REGULATIONS
August 4, 1941

FM 23-7

WAR DEPARTMENT
BASIC FIELD MANUAL
U. S. CARBINE, CALIBER
.30, M1
May 20, 1942

FM 23-35

WAR DEPARTMENT
BASIC FIELD MANUAL
AUTOMATIC PISTOL
CALIBER .45
M1911 AND M1911A1

FM 24-5

WAR DEPARTMENT
BASIC FIELD MANUAL
SIGNAL COMMUNICATION
October 19, 1942

FM 24-18
WAR DEPARTMENT FIELD MANUAL
RADIO
COMMUNICATION

FM 25-10

WAR DEPARTMENT
BASIC FIELD MANUAL
MOTOR TRANSPORT
March 12, 1942

FM 30-30

WAR DEPARTMENT
BASIC FIELD MANUAL
MILITARY INTELLIGENCE
IDENTIFICATION OF
U. S. GOVERNMENT AIRCRAFT
February 21, 1942

RESTRICTED
FM 30-35

WAR DEPARTMENT
BASIC FIELD MANUAL
MILITARY INTELLIGENCE
IDENTIFICATION OF
GERMAN AIRCRAFT

FM 30-39

WAR DEPARTMENT
BASIC FIELD MANUAL
MILITARY INTELLIGENCE
IDENTIFICATION OF
ITALIAN AIRCRAFT
October 24, 1941

RESTRICTED
FM 30-40

WAR DEPARTMENT
BASIC FIELD MANUAL
MILITARY INTELLIGENCE
IDENTIFICATION OF
UNITED STATES ARMORED
VEHICLES
January 9, 1943

RESTRICTED
FM 30-42

WAR DEPARTMENT
BASIC FIELD MANUAL
MILITARY INTELLIGENCE
IDENTIFICATION OF
FOREIGN ARMORED VEHICLES
GERMAN, JAPANESE, RUSSIAN
ITALIAN, AND FRENCH
June 20, 1941

FM44-36
WAR DEPARTMENT FIELD MANUAL
SERVICE OF
ANTIAIRCRAFT DIRECTORS
M4 AND M7

RESTRICTED. DISSEMINATION OF RESTRICTED MATTER.—The information contained in restricted documents and the essential characteristics of restricted materiel may be given to any person known to be in the service of the United States and to persons of undoubted loyalty and discretion who are cooperating in Government work, but will not be communicated to the public or to the press except by authorized military public relations agencies. (See also par. 23b, AR 380-5, 15 Mar 1944.)

WAR DEPARTMENT · 16 OCTOBER 1944

3. Army educational books

These were published and studied in the various Army Service schools, as well as within schools of the US Army Forces Institute (USAFI), established to further the education of soldiers waiting for their discharge at war's end.

4. Miscellaneous publications

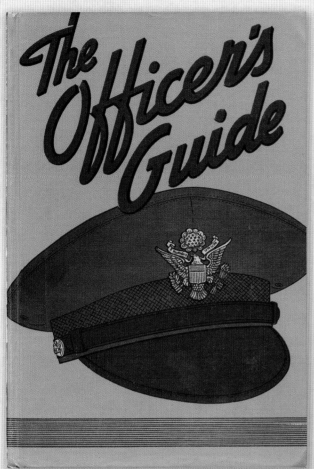

The wartime edition of the *Officer's guide*, a private purchase source book, contained basic information for newly-commissioned officers.

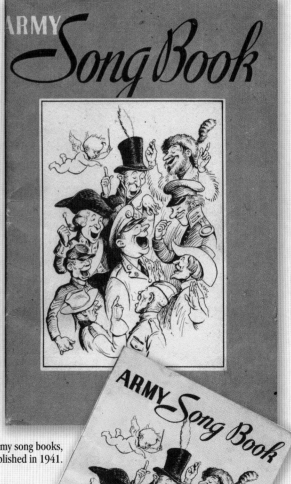

Pocket size book published for the civilian market.

Official Army song books, published in 1941.

Guides and pamphlets

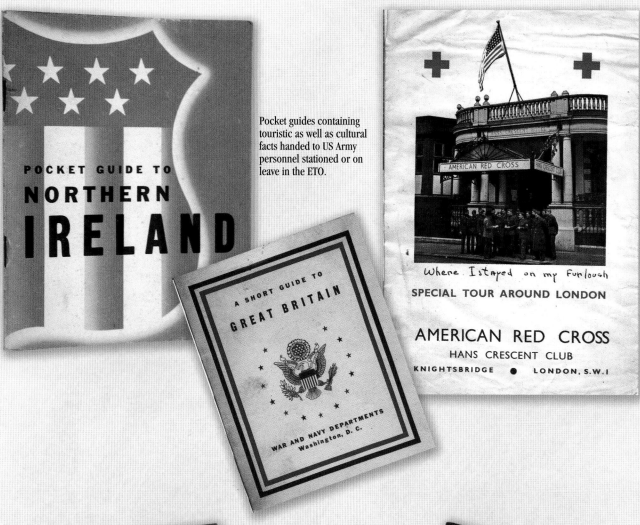

Pocket guides containing touristic as well as cultural facts handed to US Army personnel stationed or on leave in the ETO.

Official Army pocket guides handed to personnel on leave.

A short guide published and sold in France.

Army-issue pocket guides to France.

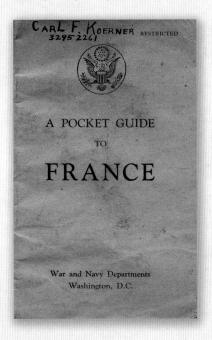

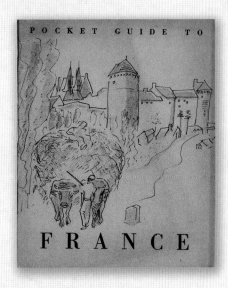

Map of Paris and its underground, given by the American Red Cross.

Information leaflet given to discharged soldiers, listing theirs rights and benefits in civilian life.

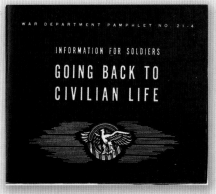

Guide for troops on leave in Paris.

Discharge insignia, worn on the right breast of the shirt, blouse, jacket or overcoat of enlisted men who had been honorably mustered out of the service.

5. Army papers

Stars and Stripes, the semi-official newspaper of the US Army in Europe, was first published in Northern Ireland in April 1942. It became a daily paper in November in London. The staff then followed the advancing armies on the Continent, until the end of the war. The Mediterranean edition had its bureau at one time in Algiers, Tunis, Naples, Rome, Nice or Marseilles. The staff for the Continental edition was based at Sainte-Mère-Eglise in Normandy, Rennes (Brittany), Paris, Liège (Belgium) and finally in Pfungstadt, Germany.

Unit paper of the 29th Infantry Regiment.

6. Army magazines

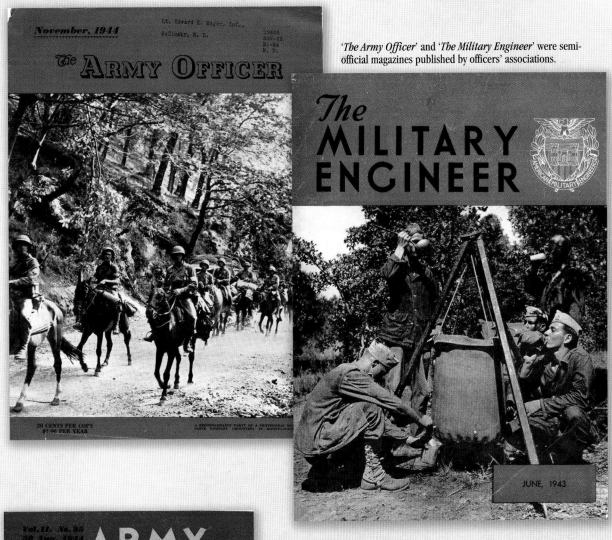

'The Army Officer' and 'The Military Engineer' were semi-official magazines published by officers' associations.

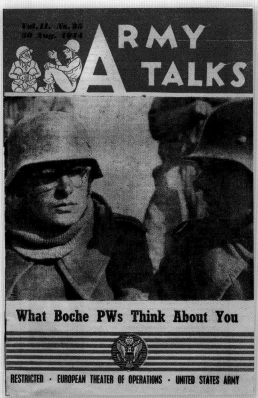

'Army Talks' was a series of brochures published by the ETO HQ and intended to stimulate the readers' thinking.

'Army Motors' was dedicated to Transportation Corps personnel.

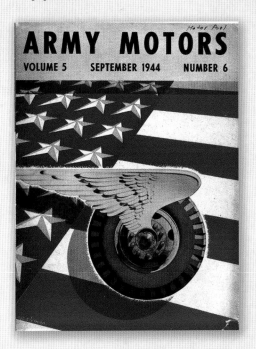

6. Magazines

Yank was the official Army weekly magazine, published in several editions (Continental, British, European) and issued free to military personnel or available by subscription for civilians.

The *Infantry Journal* was one of many semi-official service journals published for soldiers of a specific arm or service.

Life magazine featured military topics, whether in its contents or cover, in most issues during the war.

Another large format photo magazine, this special overseas edition of *Pic* was issued free through the Army service Forces.

The famous '*National Geographic Magazine*' featured numerous photo reports in black and white and color on the World War.

In order to save on weight and shipping space, some magazines such as *Newsweek* or *Time* published smaller size ('Pony' or 'Battle baby') editions for servicemen overseas.

Magazines

Collier's and *Look* were also well-known news and photo magazines, with numerous patriotic reports in color.

Among the many artists commissioned by *Esquire*, A. Varga was most famous for his distinctive pin up girls.

Esquire, the Magazine for Men, had some of its pages graced with pin-up girls, and contained photo reports as well as novels by popular writers.

Coronet was a small format magazine filled with short stories and condensed articles or novels.

7. Period comic books

Comic pulp paper printed in France at the end of the war on behalf of the Special Services Division, Army Service Forces.

8. Pocket books

Civilian humor paperbacks.

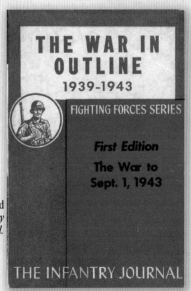

Pocketbook published by the *Infantry Journal*.

The Armed Services Editions

These paperbacks were published as of 1943 by a non-profit organization, the Armed Services Editions. They were given to service personnel only, shipped overseas and given away in hospitals and barracks. The serial-number of each book (at top left, here O-27) is a clue to the year of publication. The A-series was for the first batch of books in September 1943, O indicated an edition of November 1944 and W was for the last series of September 1945. The first page bore a reproduction of the civilian market edition's cover, the book itself was made free of rights for this specific program intended to sustain morale.

9. Leaflets and propaganda

L'Amérique en Guerre was a 2- or 4-page weekly leaflet dropped by aircraft over France, from November 1942 to mid-August 1944. These leaflets were published by the American Office of War Information (OWI) established in June 1942 to oversee domestic and foreign propaganda. Starting at the end of 1942, the OWI circulated leaflets for French civilians (code USF), then the Belgians (USB) in 1943, and finally for the Dutch (code USMH) in 1944.

This leaflet code-named ZF4 was dropped over France on June 6 and 7, 1944. It had been printed by the Army Psychological Warfare Division, established in London in 1943 by SHAEF. As opposed to the OWI, the PWD was tasked to produce exclusively military-oriented propaganda. It would publish several leaflets intended to warn local civilians, or to entice enemy soldiers into giving themselves up. This one warns the local population living near major crossroads to leave the area at once for a few days and stay off the roads.

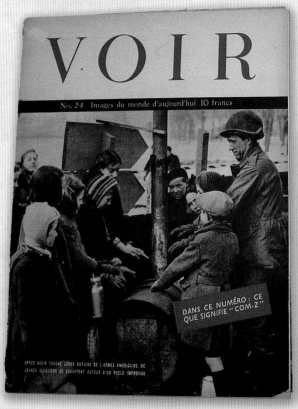

Voir ('to see' in French) was a French language magazine published every two weeks by the OWI as of June 1944. As stated in the contents page, 'Its sole purpose is to present images of the World today to the French people while it is liberated by the Allies, and until a free French press is able to fulfill this

task itself.' The first 10 issues, in smaller format, were given as leaflets. From issue 11 (Aug. 1944), Voir became a large size photo magazine sold in liberated areas. Its last issue was No 36 of September, 15, 1944.

VICTORY, VOLUME 2 NO 2

Victory was published for the French-speaking populations by the OWI, in partnership with the Cromwell-Collier syndicate. An 80-page magazine published every two months, it gave information on the World War as well as an 'idealized' view of America. The six numbers of volume 1 were circulated in North Africa from Algiers. The six numbers of volume 2 and the single issue of vol. 3 were sold in France between July 1944 and July 1945. Beginning with No 5 of volume 2, *Victory* became *Victoire*.

Folding leaflet in color offered to French civilians as a recognition guide to American military personnel.

USA was a propaganda brochure in French, published by the OWI in two formats.

Com Z was another OWI brochure in French, describing the role of Communication zone soldiers, whom local civilians encountered most often in daily life.

Within the US Army, the Army Service Forces Special Services Division provided recreation and entertainment activities for soldiers operating far from the front, in rest areas, or convalescing in hospitals. It also issued magazines and books, as well as games and sports equipment. The Special Services division produced live entertainment shows, motion pictures, comedy and novelty acts with American professional performers.

PROJECTOR PH-222 A
Signal Corps slide projector, used mostly as a training aid.

'Caravan' brand deck of cards. One of the cards bears an advertisement for US savings bonds.

SOLDIER SHOWS

STAGING AREA AND TRANSPORT ENTERTAINMENT GUIDE
COMPRISING

Blackouts, Sketches, Quizzes, Parodies, and Games

HEADQUARTERS, ARMY SERVICE FORCES
WASHINGTON 25, D. C.

SOLDIER SHOWS

TM 21-220

WAR DEPARTMENT

TECHNICAL MANUAL

SPORTS AND GAMES
May 12, 1942

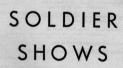

This baseball bat has been made by Hillerich & Brasdsby of Louisville (Kentucky) for the Special Services Division, and bears its engraved mark.

This 78-rpm wind-up phonograph was provided by the Special Services Division to play the soldiers' favorite tunes.

V DISC

A 78-rpm record pressed for the 'Music Section- Entertainment and Recreation Branch, Special Service Division, Army Service Forces.' It was reserved for the Armed Forces and could not be broadcast on civilian stations. The first V discs were shipped overseas in October 1943 and the V disc program carried on until May 1949.

A rendition of '*Lili Marlene*' by Marlene Dietrich, recorded for the American Forces Network in the ETO.

This waxed cardboard 'Recordio,' after recording the serviceman's message, was mailed to his family in a sealed paper sleeve.

FIELD TRANSCRIPTION PLAYER

This machine, which could be found in rest areas or in American Red Cross centers for instance, enabled a soldier to record a short message on a waxed disc for his folks at home. The recorder could also be used to play regular records.

1. Misc. personal items

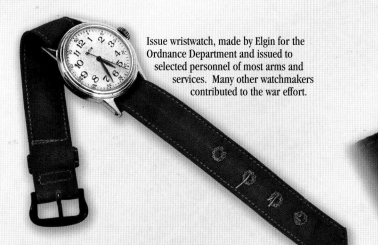

Issue wristwatch, made by Elgin for the Ordnance Department and issued to selected personnel of most arms and services. Many other watchmakers contributed to the war effort.

Close-up on the watch case markings.

Military Payment Certificates issued as military pay in France, and printed by the Forbes Lithograph Corporation, of Chelsea (Massachusetts). The first series bears the French tricolor on the reverse, for notes of 2, 5, 10, 50, 100, 500, 1,000 and 5,000 Francs. The second series, bearing the word 'France' was issued when all French notes of more than 50 Francs held by American personnel were compulsorily exchanged in June 1945.

A Paris 'Métro' (underground) ticket sold at a special rate for American soldiers.

Notes in Italian Lire and in German Marks were also used by American troops garrisoned in these countries.

MONEY BELT

This olive drab cloth money belt was used to carry bank notes around the waist and under the shirt for safekeeping. This was a commercial item and many variants were available.

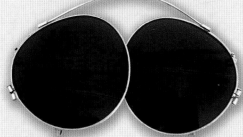

Issue clip-on sunglasses, worn over the issue prescription spectacles. Before use, they were folded into the green imitation leather case.

2. Identification tags

Each soldier was issued, soon after entering the service, with a pair of tags ('dogtags') worn around the neck with a necklace. If he died at war, one tag was buried with the body for further identification by the Graves Registration Service. The other tag was collected for the unit commander and administrative purposes. The oblong tag issued during the Second World War was a 1940 pattern. It had a hole for the chain and a V-notch for securing it on a wood block when embossing the soldier's particulars (➡ page 114). The tag was first made in rust-proof monel, then in brass and stainless steel.

Changes in the information embossed on the tag:

From Nov. 1941 to July 1943

1st Line: first name, middle name initial, last name

2d Line: Army Service Number/T- followed by the year of the anti-tetanus shot and booster injection/blood group (A, B, AB, O)

3rd Line: next-of-kin

4th and 5th Line: next-of-kin's address/Religion (optional): C(atholic), P(rotestant), H(ebrew).

July 1943: the name and address of the next-of-kin were deleted from the tag.

After March 1944, the soldier's last name was inscribed first, before the first name and middle name initial.

Army Serial Numbers

The ASN's first digit indicates the soldier's enlistment status: 1 if he was a Regular Army (professional) soldier, 2 if he came from the National Guard, and 3 or 4 for draftees (Army of the United States). Serial numbers for officers started with an 'O' prefix. The W prefix was for Warrant Officers, N for Nurses, L for WAC officers, V for WAC Warrant officers and finally A for WAC members.

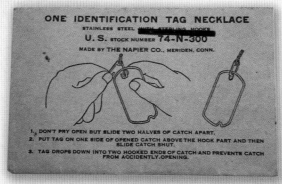

The regulation necklace was issued in a paper envelope with printed instructions.

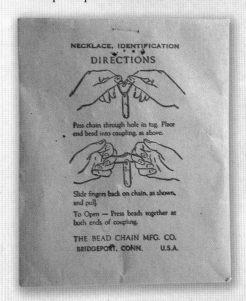

Paper package for a dogtag beaded necklace.

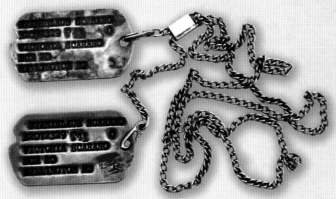

Early type dog tags for an enlisted man, with the next-of-kin's name and address. These are fitted with the issue necklace.

Dogs tags for a draftee called up between July 1943 and March 1944 (no next-of-kin and first name still precedes the last). The small chain is private purchase, with thinner links.

Dogtags for a draftee who entered the service in the Second Corps Area (New Jersey, Delaware, New York), as indicated by the ASN second digit. After inducting more than a million men, the Second Corps area used the figure '4' as the first digit of its new series of ASNs. The stainless steel beaded chain, sold in PXs, became the regulation item after the war.

3. Personal documents

Selective Service notice sent in August 1943 to James W. Cartlidge before his induction.

Photographs of James W. Cartlidge during basic training in the US.

OFFICER'S IDENTIFICATION CARD
Form No 65-1, issued in March 1943 to a Field Artillery (FA) 2nd Lieutenant.

SOLDIER'S INDIVIDUAL PAY RECORD

Form No 28, opened on 31 May 1943 for Private First Class Joseph J. Makara
(➡ page 258).

IMMUNIZATION REGISTER

Immunization Register (Form No 81) of Private Louis Wuycik.

ENLISTED MAN'S TEMPORARY PASS (FORM NO 7)

Pass given to Private First Class Joseph J Makara, serving with the 795th AAA Auto Weapons Bn, for visiting Wilmington (North Carolina).

ENLISTED MAN'S TEMPORARY PASS

CLASS B PASS

Pass issued on 11 April 1944 to Private First Class RA Ghedine, of the 254th Engineer Combat Battalion/1st Army (➡ page 265).

Pass book (Form No 3) used in the ETO for passes not over 48-hours long.

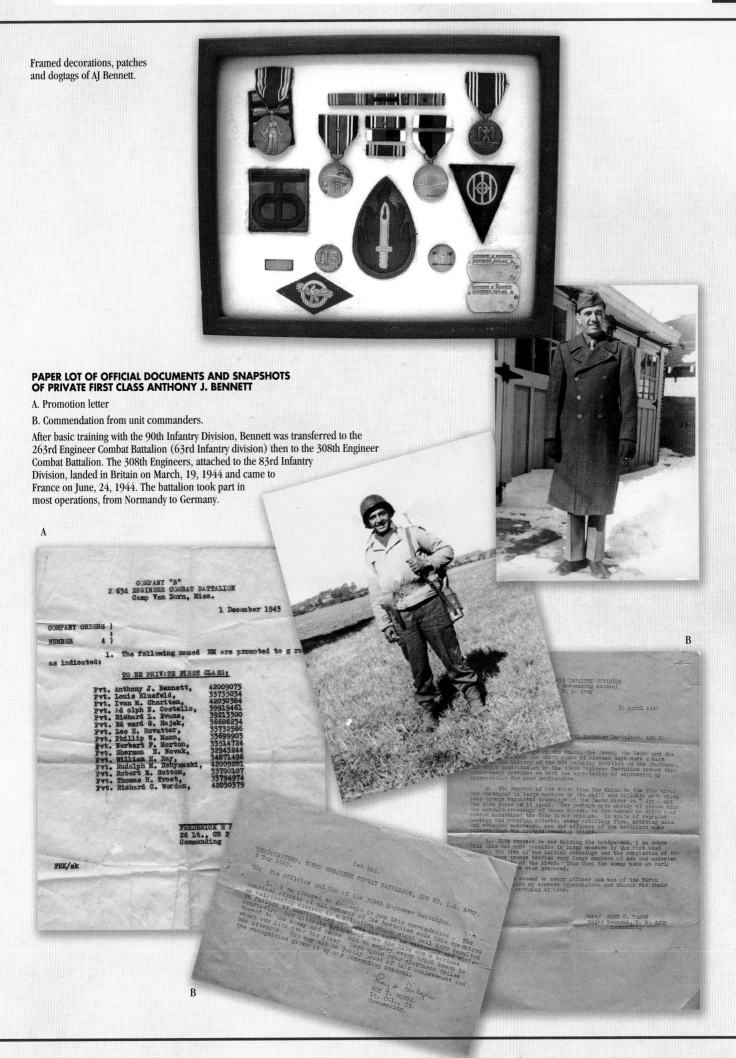

Framed decorations, patches and dogtags of AJ Bennett.

PAPER LOT OF OFFICIAL DOCUMENTS AND SNAPSHOTS OF PRIVATE FIRST CLASS ANTHONY J. BENNETT

A. Promotion letter

B. Commendation from unit commanders.

After basic training with the 90th Infantry Division, Bennett was transferred to the 263rd Engineer Combat Battalion (63rd Infantry division) then to the 308th Engineer Combat Battalion. The 308th Engineers, attached to the 83rd Infantry Division, landed in Britain on March, 19, 1944 and came to France on June, 24, 1944. The battalion took part in most operations, from Normandy to Germany.

A

COMPANY "B"
2 63d ENGINEER COMBAT BATTALION
Camp Van Dorn, Miss.

1 December 1943

COMPANY ORDERS)
                 :
NUMBER   4)

1. The following named EM are promoted to g ra
as indicated:

TO BE PRIVATE FIRST CLASS:

Pvt. Anthony J. Bennett,   42009075
Pvt. Louis Bluefeld,   33733034
Pvt. Ivan M. Chariten   42030384
Pvt. Ad olph N. Costello,   39919461
Pvt. Richard L. Evans,   39213300
Pvt. Ed ward G. Hajek,   36686234
Pvt. Leo H. Hovatter,   33732566
Pvt. Phillip W. Mann,   33699903
Pvt. Norbert F. Morton,   33514724
Pvt. Sherman E. Novak,   52943244
Pvt. William H. Ray,   54871496
Pvt. Rudolph M. Rehyanski,   42009261
Pvt. Robert B. Sutton,   33700107
Pvt. Thomas H. Trost,   33794974
Pvt. Richard C. Worden,   42030379

FREDERICK H
2d Lt., CE 2
Commanding

FHK/ak

B

On this double-page spread are reproduced documents, pictures and personal papers of Technician 3rd Grade William Krantz, who was assigned to the 5th Army Corps HQ. We can follow his steps from his arrival in Great Britain, to Germany, through France and Belgium.

CALLING CARD AND ARMY PAPERS OF LIEUTENANT ZOLTON W. KUTI

This officer was called up from civilian life and served for 21 months in the European Theater of Operations with the 713th Engineer Depot Company.
A. Certificate of proficiency for Mess officers, given at Fort George Meade, Maryland, in July 1943.
B. Commendation letter from president Harry Truman to discharged personnel.
C. Separation qualification record given to ZW Kuti when he was mustered out of the service in April 1946.

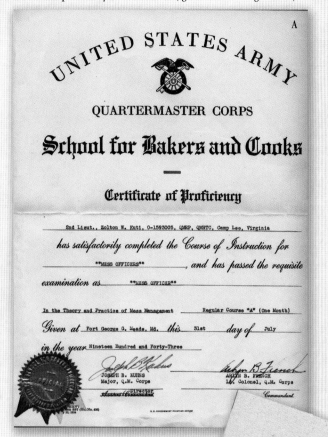

A

UNITED STATES ARMY

QUARTERMASTER CORPS

School for Bakers and Cooks

—

Certificate of Proficiency

2nd Lieut., Zolton W. Kuti, 0-1593005, QMRP, QMRTC, Camp Lee, Virginia

has satisfactorily completed the *Course of Instruction for*

MESS OFFICERS, and has passed the requisite

examination as **MESS OFFICER**

In the Theory and Practice of Mess Management   Regular Course "A" (One Month)

Given at Fort George G. Meade, Md. this 31st day of July

in the year Nineteen Hundred and Forty-Three

JOSEPH B. KUEHS
Major, Q.M. Corps
Director

ARTHUR B. FRENCH
Lt. Colonel, Q.M. Corps
Commandant

B

To you who answered the call of your country and served in its Armed Forces to bring about the total defeat of the enemy, I extend the heartfelt thanks of a grateful Nation. As one of the Nation's finest, you undertook the most severe task one can be called upon to perform. Because you demonstrated the fortitude, resourcefulness and calm judgment necessary to carry out that task, we now look to you for leadership and example in further exalting our country in peace.

ZOLTON W KUTI

Harry Truman

THE WHITE HOUSE

Zolton W. Kuti

Lieutenant
Army of the United States

C

Army of the United States

SEPARATION QUALIFICATION RECORD

SAVE THIS FORM. IT WILL NOT BE REPLACED IF LOST

This record of job assignments and special training received in the Army is furnished to the soldier when he leaves the service. In its preparation, information is taken from available Army records and supplemented by personal interview. The information about civilian education and work experience is based on the individual's own statements. The veteran may present this document to former employers, prospective employers, representatives of schools or colleges, or use it in any other way that may prove beneficial to him.

1. LAST NAME—FIRST NAME—MIDDLE INITIAL

KUTI, ZOLTON W.

2. ARMY SERIAL NO.	3. GRADE	4. SOCIAL SECURITY NO.
O-1593005	1st Lt	225-16-9507

5. PERMANENT MAILING ADDRESS (Street, City, County, State)
17 Hardenbergh St.
New Brunswick, Middlesex County, N.J.

6. DATE OF ENTRY INTO ACTIVE SERVICE	7. DATE OF SEPARATION	8. DATE OF BIRTH
18 Jun 1943	26 Apr 1946	1 Jan 1917

9. PLACE OF SEPARATION
Separation Center, Fort Dix, N.J.

MILITARY OCCUPATIONAL ASSIGNMENTS

10. MONTHS	11. GRADE	12. MILITARY OCCUPATIONAL SPECIALTY
5	1st Lt	Engineer Supply Officer 4470
16	1st Lt	General Service Engineer Unit Commander 1328
3	1st Lt	Real Estate Officer 4312

SUMMARY OF MILITARY OCCUPATIONS

13. TITLE—DESCRIPTION—RELATED CIVILIAN OCCUPATION

ENGINEER SUPPLY OFFICER: Was in charge of receiving and shipping of supplies and equipment in an army engineer depot.
Served in the European Theater of Operations with the 713th Engineer Depot Company for 21 months.

Awarded: European Campaign Medal, American Campaign Medal, American Defense Medal, World War II Victory Medal.

WD AGO FORM
1 JUL 1945 100   This form supersedes WD AGO Form 100, 15 July 1944, which will not be used.

C

MILITARY EDUCATION

...c Course - Fort Belvoir, Va., 1944 8 weeks

CIVILIAN EDUCATION

15. HIGHEST GRADE COMPLETED	16. DEGREES OR DIPLOMAS	17. YEAR LEFT SCHOOL	OTHER TRAINING OR SCHOOLING
4 yrs. H.S.	Diploma	1935	

18. NAME AND ADDRESS OF LAST SCHOOL ATTENDED
New Brunswick High
New Brunswick, N.J.

19. MAJOR COURSES OF STUDY
Academic

CIVILIAN OCCUPATIONS

22. TITLE—NAME AND ADDRESS OF EMPLOYER—INCLUSIVE DATES—DESCRIPTION

APPRENTICE MACHINIST: Operated drills, grinders, drill presses. Served one year apprenticeship with International Motor Corporation, New Brunswick, N.J. Was foreman in charge of shift workers operating paper pulp cutting machines for Johnson and Johnson, New Brunswick, N.J. for two years.

ADDITIONAL INFORMATION

23. REMARKS
Served in the Regular Army from 1935-1938.
Recalled to service in January 1941 as enlisted man.

24. SIGNATURE OF PERSON BEING SEPARATED   25. SIGNATURE OF SEPARATION CLASSIFICATION OFFICER   26. NAME OF OFFICER (Typed or Stamped)
Zolton W. Kuti   W. Von Schlichten   VON SCHLICHTEN MAJ. AGD

PERSONAL PAPERS AND PHOTOGRAPHS PERTAINING TO THE WAR SERVICE OF FIRST SERGEANT LESTER G. DURRIE

of the 44th Signal Company (44th Infantry Division).

A. 1934 discharge papers from the New Jersey National Guard.

B. Souvenir certificate handed out by the New York port of embarkation in July 1945, mentioning that Sgt. Durrie returned home aboard the *HMT Queen Elizabeth*.

A

B

German handguns, knives, headgear and flags were among the most popular war souvenirs brought home by GIs.

Chiseled copper tray presented to Colonel JA Crothers in 1945. This officer served with the Engineers in France in 1917-1918 and became a port officer in Britain during WW2. He participated afterwards in the Normandy beachhead operations before becoming the Army harbor master of Cherbourg.

Wooden decorated tray brought back from Germany by a veteran of the 142d Infantry (36th Infantry Division).

Pillow cover bought by a soldier in the Fort Leavenworth (Kansas) PX, as a gift to his wife.

Photo album put together by Private First Class RA Ghedine of the 254th Engineer Combat Battalion (➡ page 258).

ABBREVIATIONS

AA	Antiaircraft	ETO	European Theater of Operations	PH	Photographic Articles
AAA	Antiaircraft Artillery	FA	Field Artillery	Plat	Platoon
AAF	Army Air Forces	FM	Field Manual	Pvt	Private
AC	Air Corps	G-1	Assistant Chief of Staff for Personnel	PW	Prisoners of War
AEF	American Expeditionary Forces	G-2	Assistant Chief of Staff for Military Intelligence	PX	Post Exchange
AG	Adjutant General	G-3	Assistant Chief of Staff for Operations and Training	QMC	Quartermaster Corps
AGO	Adjutant General's Office	G-4	Assistant Chief of Staff for Supply	Regt	Regiment
ANC	Army Nurse Corps	GI	Government Issue	RL	Reel Equipment
APO	Army Post Office	GN	Generator	ROTC	Reserve Officer's Training Corps
AR	Army Regulations	GPO	Government Printing Office	RTC	Replacement Training Center
ARC	American Red Cross	HBT	Herringbone Twill	SCR	Signal Corps Radio
AT	Antitank	HE	High Explosive	SE	Signal Equipment
BAR	Browning Automatic Rifle	Hosp	Hospital	Sec	Section
BG	Bag	How	Howitzer	Sgt	Sergeant
Bn	Battalion	Hq	Headquarters	SHAEF	Supreme Headquarters Allied Expeditionary Force
BX	Box	HS	Headset	Sig C	Signal Corps
Cal	Caliber	Inf	Infantry	SMG	Submachine Gun
Capt	Captain	LS	Loudspeaker	Sqd	Squad
Cav	Cavalry	Lt	Lieutenant	ST	Strap
CD	Cord	M	Model	SW	Switch
CE	Corps of Engineers	Maj	Major	TD	Tank Destroyer
Ch	Chaplain	MC	Medical Corps (officers)	TE	Tool Equipment
CH	Chest	MD	Medical Department	TG	Telegraph
Co	Company	ME	Maintenance Equipment	TL	Tool
Col	Colonel	Mecz	Mechanized	TM	Technical Manual
Com Z	Communication Zone	MG	Machine Gun	TP	Telephone
Comdt	Commandant	MI	Military Intelligence	USAAF	United States Army Air Forces
Cpl	Corporal	MP	Military Police	USN	United States Navy
CS	Case	Mtn	Mountain	V-E (day)	Victory in Europe (8 May 1945)
CWS	Chemical Warfare Service	Mtd	Mounted	WAAC	Women's Army Auxiliary Corps
Dept	Department	MTO	Mediterranean Theater of Operations	WAC	Women's Army Corps (July 1943)
Div	Division	Mtz	Motorized	WD	War Department
EM	Enlisted Men	NCO	Non-commissioned Officer	WO	Warrant Officer
		Ord	Ordnance	WW1	World War One
		PA	Public Address	WW2	World War Two
		PG	Pigeon Articles		

INDEX

A

Addressograph, Model 70 — 233
Aiming Circle, M1 — 108
Airborne troops — 136-159
    Combat uniforms — 138-141
Alignment Equipment, ME-73 A — 212
Altar, portable — 235
American Red Cross volunteers — 158
Antenna A-27 — 210
Armbands — 6, 169, 223
Artillery (laying equipment) — 108, 109
Assault vest — 42
Axe, Ice, Mountain — 154
Axe, Intrenching, M-1910 — 83

B

Badges — 20, 137
Bag, Ammunition, M2 — 71
Bag, Assembly — 30
Bag, Barrack, M-1929 — 115
Bag, Barrack, od — 115
Bag, Canvas, Field, od, M-1936 — 70
Bag, Canvas, Mail — 124
Bag, Canvas, Valuables — 118
Bag, Canvas, Water, Sterilizing — 112
Bag, Carrying, Ammunition — 71
Bag, Carrying, Grenade — 101
Bag, Carrying, Rocket, M-6 — 104
Bag, Clothing, Waterproof — 72
Bag, Delousing — 115
Bag, Demolition — 144
Bag, Duffel — 115
Bag, mail — 124
Bag, Message, BG-21 — 192
Bag, Sleeping, M-1940 — 111
Bag, Sleeping, Mountain — 157

Bag, Sleeping, Wool — 111
Bag, Utility, WAC — 163
Bag, Waterproof, BG-159 — 74
Bag, Waterproof, BG-169 — 74
Bag, Waterproof, General Purpose — 74
Bandoleer (ammunition) — 94
Banknotes (invasion) — 254
Barometer — 121
Basin, canvas — 116, 119
Batteries — 213
Bayonet, M1 — 94
Bayonet, M-1905 — 93
Bayonet, M-1905 E1 — 94
Bayonet, M-1917 — 93
Bayonet, M-1942 — 94
Beacon, AN PPN-2 — 146
Beacon, PPN-1 — 146
Beer — 175
Belt, Blue, Dress — 26
Belt, Cartridge, Cal .30, M-1917, Dismounted — 93
Belt, Cartridge, Cal .30, M-1918, Mounted — 93
Belt, Cartridge, Cal .30, M-1923, Dismounted — 94
Belt, Leather, Enlisted Men's — 28, 168
Belt, Magazine, BAR, M-1937 — 97
Belt, Money — 254
Belt, Pistol or Revolver, M-1936 — 68
Belt, Web, Waist, EM, M-1937 — 53
Binoculars, type EE & M3 — 86
Blanket, Set, Small — 229
Blanket, Wool, od, M-1934 — 110
Blasting cap, Electric, — 190
Blasting galvanometer — 188
Blasting machine — 188
Blowtorch — 114
Booby traps — 102
Boots, Blucher, High Top — 60
Boots, Jumper, Parachute — 139
Boots, Knee, Wader — 43
Boots, Leather, Laced, EM — 127
Boots, Leather, Laced, Legging Top — 127

Boots, Mukluk 153
Boots, Rubber, Knee 43
Boots, Service, Combat 58
Boots, Service, Combat, Women's 165
Boots, Ski, Mountain 152
Box, Match, Waterproof 181
Breeches 127
Browning Auto Rifle (BAR), Cal .30, M-1918 A2 97
Browning machine gun, Cal .30, M-1919 A4 98
Browning machine gun, Cal .50, M2 HB 99
Brush, Mountain 154
Bucket, Canvas, Water 112
Bucket, LC-57 196
Burners, gasoline 181

C

Candle 181
Can, Meat, M-1932 180
Can, Meat, Stainless Steel 180
Can opener 174, 178
Canteen, Collapsible, Two Quart 77
Canteen, M-1942 76
Canteen, Plastic 76
Canteen, Stainless Steel 76
Cap, Baker's and Cook's 172
Cap, Blue, Dress 26
Cap, Field, Cotton, od, With Visor 62
Cap, Field, Pile, od 63
Cap, Garrison, Khaki 29
Cap, Garrison, od 29
Cap, Garrison, Officer's, od, Dark Elastique 31
Cap, Garrison, Wool, Elastique drab, Officer's 33
Cap, Garrison, Wool, WAC 162
Cap, HBT 128
Cap, Mechanic's, Winter, A-4 141
Cap, Seersucker, Nurse's 160
Cap, Service, EM 28
Cap, Service, Officer's and Warrant Officer's 30, 32
Cap, Service, Wool, od, Nurse's 159
Cap, Ski 152
Cap, WAAC, Winter, Member's 162
Cap, Winter, od 63
Cap, Wool, Knit, M-1941 62
Carbine, Cal .30, M1 92
Carbine, Cal .30, M1A1 143
Carrier, Field, Collapsible, litter 229
Cartridge, Drill, M12 107
Case, Canvas, Dispatch, M-1938 87, 131
Case, Canvas, Map, Roll Type 121
Case, Carrying, Carbine, Cal. 30, M1 92
Case, Cleaning, Rod, M1 95
Case, Magazine, 30-round, with shoulder strap 96
Case, Water-repellent, Bag, Sleeping 111, 157
Chair, Folding 121
Chaplains 235
Chest, Record, Fiber 120
Chest Set, TD-1 and Head Set, HS-30 200
Chest Set, TD-3 200
Cigarettes 182, 183
Climbers, Ski, Mohair 155
Clinometer 185
Club, Policeman, M-1944 168
Coat, Blue, Dress 26
Coat, Formal, White 27
Coat, Mackinaw 48
Coat, Pajama, Winter, Hospital 230
Coat, Parachute, Jumper 138
Coat, Service, Officer's, od, Dark Elastique 30, 32
Coat, Wool, Serge, od, 18 oz. 28, 35
Code, Training Set, AN/GSC-T1 200

Collar Discs 14, 15, 16
Comb 116
Combination, Tester, Triplett, Model 1183 C 213
Comics 249
Compass, Lensatic 86
Compass, Prismatic, M-1938 86
Compass, Universal, Sun 185
Compass, Wrist 142
Complete Round, 37-mm, Gun 107
Complete Round, 105-mm, Howitzer 107
Condoms 233
Container, Aerial Delivery, Para Crate M1 148
Container, Aerial Delivery, Type A-4 148
Container, Aerial Delivery, Type A-5 148
Container, PG-51 194
Container, PG-102/CB 194
Container, PG-107/PB 194
Container, Round, Insulated, M-1941 174
Converter, M-209 211
Converter, M-222 199
Cookset, Mountain 156
Cot, Folding, Canvas 110
Cover, Bag, Sleeping, M-1940 111
Cover, Canteen, Dismounted, M-1910 78
Cover, Canteen, Mounted, M-1910 (British made) 79
Cover, Canteen, Mounted 79
Cover, Protective, Individual 221
Cover, Waterproof, Pistol or Personal Effects 91
Cover, Waterproof, Rifle or Carbine 95
Crampons, Mountain 154
Creepers, Ice 154
Cup, M-1910 77
Cup, M-1942 77
Cup, Stainless Steel 77

D

Decorations 17, 18, 19
Desk, Field, Fiber 120
Detector, Set, AN/PRS-1 187
Detector, Set, SCR-625 186
Detonating clip, M1 191
Discharge insignia 243
Distinctive Insignia 12
Dog blanket 114
Drawers, Cotton, White, Special 57
Drawers, Cotton, Shorts 56
Drawers, Wool, od 57
Dress, off-duty, nurse's 159
Driver's permit 135
Dust, Respirator, M1 131

E

Entertainment 252, 253
Envelopes 122
Exploder 188
Explosives 189
Eyeshield, M1 67, 220

F

Firing device, M1 Delay Type 191
Firing device, M1 Pull Type 102
Firing device, M1 Release Type 102
Firing device, M1A1, Pressure Type 102
Firing device, M3, Pull Release Type 102
Firing device, M5, Release Type 102
Firing device, Pull Type, Weapons 102
First Aid kit, Gas Casualty 132
First Aid kit, Vehicle 132
First Aid Packet 80
First Aid Packet, Parachute 142

Flag, national colors	113
Flag armband	140
Flag Set, M-238	133
Flare pistols	88
Flashlight, TL-122	86
Foot powder	119
Frequency Meter BC-221	212

G

Gaiter, Ski	152, 153
Gas Mask, Assault	218
Gas Mask, Diaphragm	217
Gas Mask, Lightweight	218
Gas Mask, Optical	218
Gas Mask, Service	217
Gas Mask, Training	217
Gauntlets, Barbed Wire	54
Generator, GN-45A	208
Gloves, Cotton, Protective, od	221
Gloves, LC-10	196
Gloves, Leather, Heavy	54
Gloves, Wool, od, Leather Palm	54
Goggles, M-1943	67
Goggles, M-1944	67
Goggles, Polaroid, All Purpose, Type 1021	67
Goggles, Resistal, M-1938	131
Goggles, Ski, Mountain	153
Goggles, Variable Density	67
Grenades, Hand, Fragmentation, MK II A1	100
Grenade, Hand, Offensive, MK III A1	100
Grenade, Hand, Smoke, Colored, M18	100
Grenade, Hand, Smoke, WP, M15	100
Grenade Launcher, M7	95
Grenade, Projection, Adapter M1	95
Grenade, Rifle, AT, M9 A1	95
Guides	242-243

H

Hammer, Piton, Mountain	155
Handguns	88-91
Harness, Man, Two Trace, Apron Type	157
Hat, Fatigue, Blue Denim	62
Hat, Field, Cotton, Khaki	62
Hat, HBT	62
Hat, Rain	63
Haversack, M-1928	69
Helmet, Combat, Winter	129
Helmet, steel, M-1917 A1	64
Helmet, Steel, M1	64
Helmet, Steel, Parachutist's, M1C	140
Helmet, Steel, Parachutist's, M2	139
Helmet, Tank	130
Herringbone twill clothing	40, 41, 128
Holder, M-167 A	211
Holder, Message, PG-67	195
Holster, Assembly, Parachutist's, Rifle	143
Holster, Pistol, Cal .45, M-1916	90
Holster, Pistol, M3	91
Holster, Pistol, M7	131
Holster, Revolver, Cal .45, M-1909	89
Hood, Cloth	47
Hood, Jacket, Field, M-1943	63
Hood, Jacket, Field, M-1943, Women's	164
Hood, Wool, od, Protective	221

I

Impregnite, Shoe, M1	221
Inkwell	124
Insignia, collar	14-16
Insignia, rank	13

Insignia, distinctive, unit	12
Insignia, shoulder sleeve	7-11
Insignia, armored troops	126
insignia, airborne troops	137
Insignia, mountain troops	150
Insulator, IN-15	203

J

Jacket, Combat, Winter	129
Jacket, Dog, Water Repellent	114
Jacket, Field, Arctic	46
Jacket, Field, Lined, ETO	37
Jacket, Field, M-1943	38, 39, 141
Jacket, Field, M-1943, Women's	164
Jacket, Field, od	36
Jacket, Field, Pile	39
Jacket, Field, Wool, M-1944	28
Jacket, Field, Wool, Officer's	32
Jacket, Flying, A2	50
Jacket, HBT	40, 41
Jacket, HBT, Camouflage	44
Jacket, Mountain	151
Jacket, WAAC, Officer's, Winter	163
Jacket, WAAC, Winter, Member's	162
Jacket, Wool, od, Women's, Officer's	163
Jerrycan, Gasoline	134
Jerrycan, Water	112

K

Key, J-38	200
Kit, Demolition	190
Kit, Detector, Chemical Agent, M9	220
Kit, Homing, Modification, MC-619	205
Kit, Prophylactic	233
Kit, Sewing	163
Knife, Bolo, M-1917	84
Knife, Commando, Cattaraugus 225Q	84
Knife, Fighting, EGW	84
Knife, Fighting, PAL RH 36	84
Knife, Mountain	156
Knife, Pocket, M2	142
Knife, Trench, M-1918, MkI	84
Knife, Trench, M3	85

L

Label (contractor's)	24
Lamp, Signal, Equipment, EE-84	193
Lamp, Signal, Equipment, SE-11	147
Lantern, gasoline	112
Lanyard	90, 91
Launcher, antitank M1A1	104
Launcher, antitank M9 A1	104
Leaflets	250
Leggings, Canvas, M-1938, Dismounted	59
Life, Preserver, Belt	43
Lighter, Fuze, Weatherproof, M-2	191
Lighters	182, 183
Lineman's Equipment, TE-21	196
Liner, Bag, Sleeping	111
Liner, Helmet, M1	65
Liner, Jacket, Field, M-1943, Women's	164
Litter, Folding, Aluminum	229
Litter, Straight, Steel	229
Locator's, Level	185
Loudspeaker, LS-3	210
Loudspeaker, LS-6	192
Loudspeaker, LS-7	210
Louse powder	115

M

Machete, 18" Blade, M-1942	83
Magazines	245-248
Maintenance Equipment, ME-30	202
Manuals	236-240
Map cover	121
Marking Outfit, Stamping, Metal	114
Mask, Face, Launcher, Rocket	104
Mask, Face, Wool, Felt	47
Medical Department	222-233
Medic	223-225
Megaphone, M-64	192
Message Book, M-210	211
Message Envelope, M-40	211
Metascope	184
Microphone, T-17	210
Microphone, T-30	130
Microphone, T-45	210
Military Police	166-171
Mine, Antipersonnel, M-2 A1	103
Mine, Antipersonnel, M3	103
Mine, Antitank, HE, M1	103
Mine, Antitank, HE, M6 A1	103
Mine-lifting	186, 187
Mittens, Asbestos, M-1942	54
Mittens, Insert, Trigger Finger	55
Mittens, Over, White	55
Mittens, Shell, Trigger Finger	55
Mittens, Shell, Trigger Finger, Type 1	55
Mortar, 60-mm, M2	105
Mortar, 81-mm, M1	106
Mountain troops	150-157
Combat uniforms	151-153
Mufflers	52

N

Necktie, Black	27
Necktie, Cotton, Mohair, Khaki	28
Net, Helmet	66

O

Organ, Folding, Chaplain's	234
Outfit, Officer's, Mess, M-1941	174
Overcoat, Officer's	50, 51
Overcoat, Parka Type, Reversible	47
Overcoat, Wool, Melton, od, Roll Collar	35, 46
Overshoes, Arctic	60
Overshoes, Arctic, All Rubber	60
Overshoes, Arctic, Women's, M-1944	165

P

Pack, Field, Cargo	73
Pack, Field, Combat	73
Pack, Jungle	72
Pack, Medical	225
Packboards	75
Paint, Liquid, Vesicant Detector, M5	220
Panel, Signal, AL-140	147
Paperbacks	249
Paper clips	122
Papers, Personal	256-263
Parachute, Type T-5	145
Parka, Reversible, Ski	152
Parka, Wet Weather	45
Phone, P-18	210
Phonograph	253
Pigeon equipment	194-195
Pick-Mattock, Intrenching, M-1910	83
Pins, tent	110

Pistol, Cal. 45, Automatic, M-1911	90
Pistol, Cal. 45, Automatic, M-1911 A1	91
Pitons, climbing	155
Player, field, transcription	253
Pocket, Cartridge, Cal. 30, M1, Carbine or Rifle	92
Pocket, Magazine, Double, Leather	168
Pocket, Magazine, Carbine, Cal. 30, M1	92
Pocket, Magazine, Double Web, M-1923	91
Poles, tent	110
Poncho, Synthetic Resin	45
Pouch, First Aid Packet, Leather	168
Pouch, First Aid Packet, M-1910	81
Pouch, First Aid Packet, M-1924	81
Pouch, First Aid Packet, M-1942	81
Pouch, Medical	224
Power Supply, PE-204	199
Priming, Adaptors M1A3	191
Prisoners of war (POWs)	170, 171
Projector, PH-222 A	252
Propaganda	250, 251
Protective ointment, M4	220

Q

Quadrant, Gunner's, M1	109

R

Raincoat, Synthetic Resin	45
Raincoat, officer's	50
Range, field, M-1937	172
Range finder, M-1916	108
Rank, Insignia	13
Rations	176-179
Razors	116, 117, 118
Reel Equipment, CE-11	197
Reel, Unit, RL-31	197
Remote Control Equipment, RC-47	209
Remote Control Unit, RM-29	209
Respirator, dust M1	131
Revolver, Cal .45 M-1917	89
Rifle, Cal .30, M1	94
Rifle, Cal .30, M-1903	93
Rifle, US, M-1917	93
Rifle, Dummy, Training	93
Rifle, recoilless 57-mm	106
Roll, Bedding, M-1935	111
Roll, Commissary	173
Rope, Drag, with shoulder strap	157
Rope, Parachutist's	157
Rucksack	

S

Sam Browne Belt	30
Scabbard, Carbine, Cal 30, M1A1	143
Scabbard, Rifle, M-1938	94
Scarf	52
SCR-284 radio	208
SCR-300	206
SCR-511	204
SCR-528	133
SCR-536	205
SCR-593	207
SCR-609	207
SCR-610	133
SCR-694	208
Sandbag	112
Serial number (marking)	25
Shell, HE, M49 A2, 60-mm, Mortar	105
Shell, HE, M56, 81-mm, Mortar	106
Shirt, Cotton, Khaki	34
Shirt, Cotton, Seersucker, Nurse's	160

Shirt, Flannel, od, Coat Style	35, 36
Shirt, Flannel, od, Officer's	50
Shirt, knit	150
Shirt, HBT, Women's	161
Shirt, Officer's, Wool, Dark Chocolate Brown	33
Shirt, Wool, Elastique drab, Officer's (Pink)	31
Shoe Pac, 12-inch, M-1944	61
Shoe Pac, High	60
Shoes, Field, Women's	161
Shoes, Low Quarter, Russet Leather, Officer's	31, 33
Shoes, Service	58
Shoes, Service, Women's, Low	162
Shoe polish, brush	115
Shoulder Sleeve Insignia	7-11,137
Shovel, Intrenching, M-1910	82, 142
Shovel, Intrenching, M-1943	82
Signal, Ground, Amber Star, Parachute M21 A1	95
Size markings	23
Ski, Wax	154
Skirt, WAAC, Winter, Member's	162
Skirt, Wool, od, Dark, Women's, Officer's	163
Skis	154
Slacks, Cotton, Seersucker, Nurse's	160
Sleeve, Gas, Detector	220
Sling, Color, Web	113
Snowshoes, Bearpaw	155
Snowshoes, Emergency	155
Snowshoes, Trail	155
Soap	116
Socks, Wool	59
Songbooks	241
Souvenirs	264-265
Staple, IW-6	203
Stars and Stripes	240
Stationery	124, 125
Strap, Carrying, General Purpose	71
Strap, Carrying, od, Bag, Canvas, Field	71
Strap, Litter	224
Strap, Shoulder, Military, Police	168
Submachine, Gun, Cal 45, M3	97
Submachine, Gun, Cal 45, Thompson	96
Sunglasses clip on	254
Suit, HBT, One-Piece	128
Suit, Snow, Smock	49
Suit, Snow, Trousers	49
Sunglasses, clip-on	141
Suspender, Medical	224
Suspenders, Belt, M-1936	68
Suspenders, Pack, Field and Combat	73
Suspenders, Trousers	53
Sweater, Highneck	52
Sweater, Sleeveless	52
Switchboard, BD-57	200
Switchboard, BD-71	198
Switchboard, BD-72	198

T

Tacks	123
Tag, Emergency, Medical	225
Tags, identification	255
Tape, TL-92	203
Tape, Special, Friction,	188
Telegraph Set, TG-5	201
Telephone, Central, Office, Set, TC-12	199
Telephone, EE-8	201
Telephone, Repeater, EE-99 A	199
Telephone, Repeater, Set TC-29 A	199
Telephone, TP-6	201
Telephone, TP-9	201
Telescope, M-1915 A1	109

Telescope, M65	109
Telescope, M70	134
Tent, Mountain, 2-Man	156
Tent, Shelter half	110
Test Sets, Signal corps	202, 203
Test, Unit, I-76	212
Tobacco	182, 183
Toilet paper	119
Tools, carpenter's	114
Tool, Equipment, TE-5	189
Tool, Equipment, TE-33	193
Tooth powder, toothbrush	118
Toque, Wool Knit	47
Towels	116
Trousers, Blue, Dress	26
Trousers, Combat, Winter	129
Trousers, Cotton, Khaki	34
Trousers, Enlisted Men, ETO	37
Trousers, Field, Cotton, od	141
Trousers, Field, Over, White	49
Trousers, Formal, White	27
Trousers, HBT	40, 41
Trousers, HBT, Camouflage	44
Trousers, HBT, Women's	161
Trousers, Kersey Lined	46
Trousers, Mountain	151
Trousers, Pajama, Winter, Hospital	230
Trousers, Parachute, Jumper	138
Trouser's, Service, Officer's, od	31
Trousers, Ski, White	153
Trousers, Suit, Convalescent	231
Trousers, Wet Weather	45
Trousers, Women's, Outer-Cover	165
Trousers, Women's, Wool, Liner	165
Trousers, Wool, Elastique drab, Officer's (Pink)	33
Trousers, Wool, Serge,	35-38
Trousers, Wool, Ski	153
Trumpets	113
Tubes, radio	213
Typewriter	123

U

Underwear	56, 57
Uniform, Cotton, Seersucker, Nurse's	160

V

V-Discs	253
Vest, assault	42
V-Mail	125

W

Waders, over-the-shoe	43
Waist, Wool, Women's	161
Wash gear	116-119
Watch, wrist	254
Wire-Cutters, M-1938	83
Whistles	172
Wings, airborne troops insignia	137

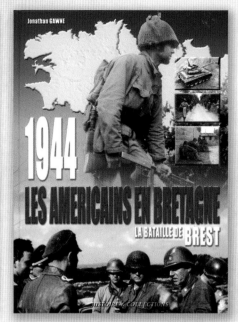

ENGLISH VERSION ALSO AVAILABLE

ENGLISH VERSION ALSO AVAILABLE

BIBLIOGRAPHY

● *American Militaria* series, privately published by Pierre Meunier in Belgium:
  – n° 1, *Quelques coiffures de l'US Army*, 1983
  – n° 2, *Military Police 1941-1945*, 1983
  – n° 3, *Les brassards de l'US Army*, 1983
  – n° 4, *Canteens, Cups and Covers et Field Ration Type D*, 1984
  – n° 5, *Les calots de l'US Army*, 1984
  – n° 6, *Les grenades à main américaines*, 1984
  – n° 7, *Dog Tags, US identification tag, Necklace*, 1984
  – n° 8, *First Aid Packet & First Aid Case*, 1985
  – n° 9, *Combat and Expert Infantryman Badges*, 1985
  – n° 10, *La ration K*, 1986
  – n° 11, *Sizes, Le Blue Dress Cap de 1938*, 1986
  – n° 12, *War Dogs, Bugle Calls*, 1987
  – n° 13, *Medical Department*, 1988
  – n° 14 et 15, *Le détachement médical du régiment d'infanterie*, 1988 et 1990.

● George A Petersen reprints (NCHS Inc, PO Box 605, Springfield, VA, 22150-0605, USA:
  – QMC Historical Studies No 5, *Quartermaster equipment for special forces*, Thomas M Pitkin, 1944
  – QMC Historical Studies N° 6, *The development of special rations for the Army*, Harold W Thatcher, 1944
  – QMC Historical Studies N° 16, *Clothing the soldier of World War II*, Erna Risch and Thomas M Pitkin, 1946
  – Quartermaster Supply Catalog QM 1, Enlisted Men's clothing and equipment, 1943
  – Quartermaster Supply Catalog QM 3-1, Enlisted Men's clothing and equipment, 1946
  – Quartermaster Supply Catalog QM 3-3, List of items for issue to posts, camps and stations, 1944
  – Quartermaster Supply Catalog QM 3-4, List of items for issue to troops, miscellaneous organizational equipment, 1945
  – Quartermaster Supply Catalog QM 6, Chests, kits, outfits and sets, 1944
  – War Department QM 6 supplement, 1947
  – Medical Supply Catalog MED 3, List of items for troops, posts, camps and stations, 1944

– World War Two US Army Regulations for the service and field uniforms, AR 600-35, 1941, AR 600-36, 1944; AR 600-37, 1945; AR 600-40, 1944; AR 600-90, 1945; AR 615-40, 1945
  – *The World War II Soldier's guide*, 1943
  – *American Women at War in World War II* Vol. I; QM 3-2, WAC's and Nurse's clothing and equipment, 1943; QM 3-2, 1946; American women in uniform by Mary Steele Ross, 1943.

● Army Manuals
  – FM 5-31, Land mines and booby traps, 1943
  – FM 21-11, First aid for soldiers, 1943
  – FM 21-30, Conventional signs, military symbols and abbreviations, 1941
  – FM 21-100, Soldier's handbook, 1941
  – FM 23-30, Hand and rifle grenades, rocket, AT, HE, 2.36-inch, 1944
  – TM 9-1904, Ammunition inspection guide, 1944.

● Miscellaneous American and French publications:
  – *American medals and decorations*, Evans Kerrigan, Mallard Press, 1990
  – *Notice sommaire sur les matériels de transmissions de l'armée américaine*, 1945
  – *Order of battle US Army World War II*, Shelby L Stanton, Presidio Press, 1984
  – *Organisation et équipement de l'armée des Etats-Unis d'Amérique*, 1943
  – *US Army uniforms of World War II*, Shelby L. Stanton, Greenhill Books, 1991
  – *US military knives, bayonets & machetes*, Book III, M H Cole, 1979
  – *The Officer's guide*, The Military Service Publishing Co, 1943
  – Notice sur l'armée américaine, ministère de la Guerre, Etat-major 2ᵉ bureau, juillet 1945
  – Misc. articles in *Militaria Magazine*.

● For further reading:
  – *Spearheading D-Day, American special units in Normandy*, by Jonathan Gawne, Histoire & Collections 1998
  – *Americans in Brittany 1944, the Battle for Brest*, by Jonathan Gawne, Histoire & Collections 2002.

A patriotic banner that was once hung in railway stations as a welcome sign for repatriated soldiers.

Acknowledgments

I would like to thank in the first place Philippe Charbonnier, my editor, for helping me turn this project into reality, and advising me all along its development.
Also thanks are in order for all the editorial staff at Histoire & Collections in Paris for their dedicated work in designing this book.

I also owe sincere thanks to Jean-Pierre Martin for his unstinting collaboration, thus bolstering a 20-year long friendship.

Thank you also to Georges Bailly for finding and selling me over the years the choice pieces of my collection, and who became a true friend.

I also wish to commend all the collector friends who have welcomed me in their homes and have let me take pictures of rare items in their collection, they are: Jean-Yves Capron, Jean-Claude Debout, Claude Foisnet and his daughter Annabelle, Frédéric Gratient, Lionel Paganet, Olivier Poirier, Jacques Ransac and Jean-Michel Selles.

I should also mention the militaria dealers who have helped with my collecting:
– Armies Of The Past Ltd, PO Box 3311, Trenton, New Jersey 08619, USA
– D-Day, 103-105 rue Marcelis, B-1970 Wezembeek-Oppem Belgium
– QM Depot, 38 avenue Prekelinden, B-1200 Bruxelles, Belgium
– Le Poilu, 18 rue Emile Duclaux, 75015 Paris, France
– Overlord, 96, rue de la Folie-Méricourt, 75011 Paris, France
– Quinéville Militaria Collectable, 9 av. de la plage, 50310 Quinéville, France
– Static Line, 16 rue du général de Gaulle, 50480 Sainte-Mère Eglise, France.

And special thanks to my parents for their dedication, and to my sister Liliane for her precious assistance.

And last but not least, I would like to thank the numerous friends who have supported my endeavor, especially Marie, Jean-Marie and Yacinthe.

Henri-Paul Enjames

The author and editor would also like to thank Pierre Besnard, Martin Brayley, Paul Gaujac, Jonathan Gawne, Yves Sacleux and Phil Coleman, as well as Yann-Erwin Robert, Nathalie Sanchez and Aurélie Saintecroix at Histoire & Collections.

NEW !
Volume II now available in English

Design and lay-out by Philippe Charbonnier, Yann-Erwin Robert and Jean-Marie Mongin © *Histoire & Collections 2008*.

a book from
HISTOIRE & COLLECTIONS
SA au capital de 182 938, 82 €

5, avenue de la République
F-75541 Paris Cedex 11 France
Telephone: (33-1) 40 21 18 20
Fax: (33-1) 47 00 51 11
www.histoireetcollections.fr

This book has been designed, typed, laid-out and processed by
'Le studio graphique Armes & Collections' on fully integrated computer equipment.

Printed by Elkar
Spain, European Union
November 2008